COMEDY DAVE'S BOOK

COMEDY DAVE'S BOOK

DAVE VITTY

Copyright © Dave Vitty 2011

The right of Dave Vitty to be identified as the author
of this work has been asserted by him in accordance with
the Copyright, Designs and Patents Act 1988.

This edition first published in Great Britain in 2011 by
Orion Books
an imprint of the Orion Publishing Group Ltd
Orion House, 5 Upper St Martin's Lane,
London WC2H 9EA
An Hachette Livre UK Company

3 5 7 9 10 8 6 4 2

A CIP catalogue record for this book is
available from the British Library.

Photographs © Nick Dawkes 32, 53, 68 (top), 69 (bottom),
71, 72, 73

Illustrations by Brian Roberts

ISBN: 9781409142331

Printed and bound by CPI Group (UK) Ltd, Croydon CRO 4YY

The Orion Publishing Group's policy is to use papers
that are natural, renewable and recyclable and made
from wood grown in sustainable forests. The logging and
manufacturing processes are expected to conform to the
environmental regulations of the country of origin.

Every effort has been made to fulfil requirements with regard
to reproducing copyright material. The author and publisher
will be glad to rectify any omissions at the earliest opportunity.

www.orionbooks.co.uk

For Nicole

The best thing to ever
happen to me

Me and my girl

ACKNOWLEDGEMENTS

There are many people who never thought I'd ever get this book finished, myself included, so to everyone who's made it possible, thank you so much.

In particular Grant Michaels, Sarah Jane Cass and Rich Howells at Somethin' Else who work so hard on my behalf and continue to believe in me.

Thanks also to Guy Robinson, Rachel Carlier and all at Hyper Agency who still manage to get me work as a DJ.

Amanda Harris my publisher and good friend, thank you for making me finish this bloody thing, even when I wanted to give up several times, and thank you to Guyan Mitra who's put in many, many tedious hours with me to make this book a reality. Big thanks also to the Orion team: Nicola Crossley, Helen Ewing, Georgie Widdrington, Brian Roberts, Julyan Bayes, Louise Edwards and Jessica Gulliver.

To everyone at Radio 1 who've become family to me over the last 15 years, especially Chris, Dom, Tina, Aled, Matt, Freya, Rhys, Andy, Ben, Sam, Rachel, Piers, Carrie, Uncle Ferg, Juliette, Will, Jocelin, Natasha, Joe, Lizzie, Mick and Melinda. Special thanks to Ben Cooper and Tarrant Steele for all your support and help in getting this book finished in the nick of time.

Chappers, Stuey, Neil and Big Steve, thank you for so many laughs on the road. You're all nob'eads but very funny.

Thank you to all my close friends who I love dearly, and in particular Jamesy and Al who've always been there through all the good, and more importantly, all the bad and difficult times.

Thank you to Jayne for being the best mummy Nicole could ever wish for, and thank you to her parents John and Kath for all their support.

Lots of love to my sister Ali, brother-in-law Mike and my two beautiful nieces Talia and Mia.

Thank you to my mum Brenda for everything she's done for me over the years and for everything she continues to do.

One of the reasons I wanted to do this book was for my dad Keith, who's sadly no longer with us. He was not only my father, but my best friend as well, who I miss every single day. Thank you for everything.

And finally, thank you to my beautiful daughter Nicole for making me smile every single day. You're the most important person in my world, and I love you so much.

For anyone else I've missed off . . . soz!

xxx

We came, we saw,
we folked around a bit

FOREWORD

HELLO

Hello, my name is Dave and welcome to my book. If you've actually spent money purchasing it either in traditional paper form or the new modern electronic variety, then I'd like to say thank you very much. If you've just found it or borrowed it off a friend, then that too is fine, as long as you tell everybody that it's great and that you enjoyed it enormously.

I always wondered how people had time to write a book, or what on earth they would write about. I still don't really know the answer to either of these questions but I thought it might be quite fun to find out. I'm regarding this whole 'book thing' as a learning curve, in the hope that it will teach me what is involved in becoming an author or novelist. I don't actually know what the difference is between the two, but I think it sounds quite impressive to say that you're an author. It implies a level of grand intelligence coupled with a masterful command of language that would make people think that I was possibly more interesting than I am.

The reality is that the publishing company approached me and asked if I'd be interested in writing a book that was full of light-hearted wittiness, obscure thoughts and comedic asides. That bit I thought I could manage; it's just the fact that it's got to be about 70,000 words long, which for me is like being asked to write *Lord of the Rings* or the Bible in a few weeks, and I would imagine that neither J.R.R. Tolkien nor God tackled their first book without a proper plan. So, I've gone for 'Lord of the Things' instead ...

I WONDER

I wonder whether there's an equation relating to the minimum number of books that you need to have read before you're qualified to write your own first work of literature. If there is, then my concern is that I won't have reached that figure, as my current ratio of books read to books written is four to one (and that includes this one). I don't know what the reading stats are for most writers, but I suspect that anything below seven or eight would be towards the lower end of the scale in terms of total books read for a man aged 37 and a bit years old.

The problem with me is that I've never really enjoyed reading. It's always seemed like a bit of a chore or something that I only do while on holiday; and even then I'd probably be happier floating on a lilo in the pool or seeing how long I can hold my breath under water. That said, once I actually got into them I thoroughly enjoyed all four of the books which make up my slight but significant literary awakening. As with cars and sex partners, I think you always remember your first, and for me that was *The Secret Diary of Adrian Mole aged 13¾* by Sue Townsend.

Reading it, enjoying it and, most importantly, finishing it all by myself is something that gave me great pleasure when I was a young lad. In fact, I think I was about the same age as Adrian

Mole at the time, so I felt that we had much in common and the book talked to me and my awkward ways – both Adrian and I embarked on a journey of acne and masturbation as we stumbled through puberty together. The rest of my reading consists (in no particular order) of a book all about the Stereophonics written by my good friend Danny O'Connor, the Billy Connolly biography entitled *Billy* by his wife Pamela Stephenson and Chris Moyles' first book. I think Chris thinks I've read both of his books, but the truth is I still haven't started his second offering even though it was published almost three years ago.

HOW

How on earth, then, did I end up writing a book? Well in all honesty it wasn't my idea. I was approached by Orion Publishing and asked whether I would consider it. I was unsure at first as to whether it was a good idea or not, and my opinion hasn't really changed. The main reason for my uncertainty was that I had no idea what to write about. I suppose the easiest subject for self-obsessives is themselves, but I just had no interest in writing some kind of autobiography. Sure, there are parts of this book that will be semi-autobiographical, but only for a bit of background, to explain or to put into context whatever it is I'm wittering on about.

Let's be honest: why on earth would anyone be interested in my frankly average and unremarkable upbringing? It's not like I battled against the odds to get where I am, or was orphaned at a young age and raised by wolves or otters.

I was born in 1974 in Hong Kong. Mum and Dad got married in 1969, and moved abroad six months later when Dad decided to take up the offer of a job with the Hong Kong Telephone Company. It was a two-year contract, which they extended somewhat, staying for a total of 25 years, by which time I and my sister Ali were born. Being brought up in Hong Kong meant that we led a good life and were financially comfortable and got to go on nice holidays and stuff, so it's something I'm very grateful for, and something that has moulded me into the well-rounded, albeit slightly cynical person I am today.

So anyway, back to the book. I said that I didn't want to do an autobiography like every other 30-something self-important bore, and was more interested instead in getting into the world of children's books. As the father of a four-year-old girl, I've spent many hours at bedtime reacquainting myself with the world of contemporary children's literature, and thought that this would be a less obvious, but still rewarding and financially lucrative route to take. Basically I'd like to invent the next Peppa Pig and have an annual turnover equivalent to that of Bill Gates or Tesco.

Alternatively, I could happily become the next J.K. Rowling and stumble upon a book and film empire that will make gazillions and afford me an early retirement aged 40. I could spend my time racing luxury sports cars and making my own marmalades, jams and chutney. I suppose I would be a bit like a cross between Jay Kay from Jamiroquai and Alex James from Blur, but more likeable and contemporary, and less likely to wear a Barbour jacket, which I always think makes you look like a bit of a tit.

Noticing the success of pig-based characters in children's books, my idea was to develop a character called Cheese Pig, who would essentially be a pig made of Swiss cheese, with holes in his body and hailing from a galaxy far, far away.

His superhero sidekick would be Mooncat, whom he met in space and who would help him in his adventures on Earth. It's no more random and silly than any of the other stuff that floods the current children's market. In fact, when you compare it to Iggle Piggle and the Ninky Nonk of *In the Night Garden*, which must surely be the result of long-term recreational drug abuse by those responsible, it seems quite normal and entirely feasible. So what I might do is use this book as an opportunity to try and launch Cheese Pig on an unsuspecting public. There's no reason why it wouldn't work, as my brief for this modern-day classic is that it should just be a random collection of thoughts that should be easily put-downable. I think so far it's incredibly put-downable and in that respect it's all going very much to plan!

This is my one and only embarrassing school
photo. Don't bother looking for any others,
as there aren't any

HOW TO GET THE BEST JOB IN THE WORLD

There are many things that you could describe as the best job in the world. Being a *Top Gear* presenter is normally pretty high on most lists, along with being Gavin Henson on *The Bachelor*, being head of quality control for Boddingtons or Megan Fox's personal masseur in Malibu. Actually, it wouldn't have to be Malibu. Being Megan's personal masseur in Mansfield or Moss Side would still be pretty good, and I bet everyone would want to talk to you if they spotted you in Asda. I am fully aware, though, that in many ways I have the best job in the world. The hours may be tricky but I love what I do and feel very, very lucky to do it. One thing I'm constantly asked is how did I land this perfect job, which basically involves titting around with my mates all day? Well, here's the tale ...

STEP ONE – Scrape through your education

You might be surprised to hear that I'm not as dumb as I often come across on the show. Sure, 'Comedy Dave' has been known to have trouble with numbers and is prone to the occasional blunder and bout of tomfoolery, but I like to think I'm smarter than my on-air character would suggest. Although, at school I was never one for studying or concentration and I was a lazy bugger to boot, so I coasted through my education, doing the absolute minimum to get by – which requires a degree of smarts in itself. 'Able but idle' was the standard cliché to be found on my end-of-term reports.

I'm the king of doing things at the last minute – always have been and suspect always will be. Whether it's writing for the show, essays for college ... this book even! I guess I've always bumbled along before scrabbling something passable together at the eleventh hour.

So I scraped through university with a very average Desmond (2:2) in Media Studies – after repeating quite a few exams, I might add. I even ended up getting a degree from the prestigious Manchester University, a proper red-brick uni that I only attended for my graduation ceremony. It turns out that my poly, North Chester College, was an affiliate of Manchester Uni and they kindly issued my degree, much to my sister's annoyance. She actually attended Manchester, studying Pure Maths! To look at the graduation photos on my Mum's mantlepiece you'd never guess there was any difference in intellect between me and my very brainy little sister. The few times I actually made it to Manchester were to watch Everton away at Old Trafford or Maine Road, and for the occasional night out, which would then result in us getting the last train back to Warrington on a Friday or Saturday night – the 'vomit comet', as we used to call it.

So, clutching my degree proudly under my arm, I headed down south to find fame and fortune, and along the way discovered the inevitable truth awaiting all graduates – that the only person who would want or care to see my freshly printed degree parchment was my mother. And as for what grade I got, forget it! Nobody has ever asked me what class of degree I had – I don't think it matters unless you're doing something proper like medicine or dentistry. As it turns out, it would have made no odds had I worked my arse off and got a first as it's never been a factor in my employment. So, the way I see it, it's a good job I spent the majority of my time messing about and watching football. It prepared me for a life of arsing around in a professional capacity. Something I'm proud to say I've made a fairly viable career out of.

STEP TWO – Take any job

My journey south took me all the way to the bright lights of Maidenhead, where the streets are paved with gold. Or, to the spare room at my parents', who'd since moved back to England from Hong Kong.

Broke and staring down the barrel of a hefty student loan, I took a job working behind the bar at Bray Cricket Club, of which Michael Parkinson is chairman, incidentally. My Dad's jazz band would play there once a week and there was a laid-back, familiar atmosphere. I also did some office temping for my cousin Colette, so I was making a little money, living cheaply at home and everything was going okay, to be honest.

It was while I was doing this office temping for Colette that Chris Evans was subconsciously becoming a major influence on things to come, as the highlight of my day was the drive to work in the mornings. It's 1995 and you can't switch on the telly or radio without seeing or hearing the flame-haired one. His brash, in-your-face style was a one-man media revolution and, like the rest of the country, I would listen to his Breakfast

Show every day, laughing along while stuck in traffic. I loved the all-inclusive banter he had with his team: Dan the producer, Holly Hot Lips, Justin and Jamie. People would then be talking about what we'd all heard in the car on the way to the office and retelling gags, in what I suppose we now call a 'water cooler moment' in the days before any of us had ever heard of a water cooler moment. It's weird now that I'm one of those people whose job it is to banter and hopefully give you a laugh to break up the tedium of the daily commute or the aggro of the school run. I used to think that everybody who worked on Chris Evans' Radio 1 Breakfast Show in 1995 had the best job in the world, and then for me . . . the dream became a reality.

STEP THREE –
Use any contacts (or in my case the trombone player's wife)

Here's a Tedious Link for you. What does a trombone player's missus have to do with me becoming Comedy Dave? Well, if it wasn't for Jan Burton I probably wouldn't be here today writing this book. I wouldn't have got a job at the Beeb, I wouldn't have met Chris Moyles, wouldn't have got my break, met either of my ex-wives or had my beautiful little daughter Nicole. Safe to say, my life would be considerably different were it not for the wife of the trombone player in my Dad's jazz band. You see, knowing that I had an interest in radio and media, she told me about a job posting she'd seen in Reading's local paper. The advert claimed it was looking for people interested in radio. It asked whether people knew their Ginger Loans from their Honk Your Horns (both Chris Evans features). More importantly, it was for a job in radio working for the BBC in Reading. As a result, I'm very grateful to Jan Burton and her tromboning husband Clive, as they both played a huge part in the destiny of my life.

The job posting was at the BBC Monitoring Centre in Caversham. The centre monitors and reports on worldwide mass media. It's been going since the Second World War and is a major source of geo-political information for the government. This job was slightly less important, however. They were looking for a two-man team to listen to Radio 1 output for musical copyright purposes.

Basically, the BBC has to pay a band or musician whenever it plays their song. This was done by some very clever automated system. However, what hadn't been accounted for was every time a song was played as part of a mishmash of different songs, such as in a specific trailer for Glastonbury or the Chart Show, for example. This job was to listen to endless hours of Radio 1 audio, deciphering and logging these songs. Very technical, menial and boring. But it was for the Beeb so I applied immediately and somehow landed the job.

I was officially an employee of the BBC! Sure, the job couldn't have been more tedious but it was a foot in the door and I was to be paid the princely sum of £9,000 a year, which was fine by me. I was living at home and my only significant outgoings were on fags and petrol, so everything worked and the job at Caversham was to be a crucial break.

STEP FOUR –
Stick out the menial crap and grab the first opportunity

My first days at the Beeb were spent cooped up in a cupboard of a room with my colleague, Zoe. We rarely spoke, our headphones were on nine-to-five logging song data. It was beyond dull and even though we were doing work for Radio 1, we were miles away and out of sight, in suburban Reading.

After a few months I began crawling up the walls with boredom. I made it my goal to push on and establish some contacts at Radio 1's base in London's Great Portland Street. I found out who was receiving all my reports – a guy called Stephen Mulholland – and decided to introduce myself. I went up to London a couple of times to try and get on his radar for any job opportunities going in head office.

After almost a year of listening to trailers at the BBC Monitoring Centre, I applied for the post of schedules assistant, working at the studios in London. I went through the whole interview process, got down to the final two but didn't land it. A few weeks later, another job came up with Radio 1. They were looking for a technical operative. Somehow, on the merits of my previous interview, I got the job automatically. Fine by me, I remember thinking at the time, even if I didn't quite understand the job I'd been employed to do.

My new job involved manning the studios at Radio 1's Yalding House during any pre-recorded shows or live radio shows coming from outside the London studios. I had some basic knowledge from my media studies degree but I learned, largely, on the job. To be fair, it wasn't exactly rocket science, but

I was delighted. My pay was now £16,000 a year and with my bumper salary I moved into a poky bedsit in Hampstead.

It was during this time that I learned the nuts and bolts of national radio. One of my main roles was manning the studio when the weeknight Mark and Lard show was being beamed into London from Manchester. Or if there were any outside broadcasts, I would make sure they were all going out properly and would fade in the news and things like that. At the time Chris Evans was still king of Radio 1, but it was all to end very quickly, when the show came to a close in January 1997. It was an event which was to have quite an impact on my journey, as the resulting on-air shuffle would involve my working day changing as well.

Once Evans and his team left, Kevin Greening was drafted in at the last minute as emergency cover; but who was to replace Chris long-term was the source of much speculation. Eventually, Mark and Lard were persuaded to do the Breakfast Show, which they began in February 1997. As they were staying in Manchester, I moved my time schedule from evenings to mornings with them and it was this that resulted in me meeting Chris Moyles for the first time.

STEP FIVE –
Meet the right people

I first met Chris Moyles when I was doing some work on an overnight show hosted by Jayne Middlemiss. She didn't do the show regularly, and was just covering for someone, as I recall; the producer Chris Whatmough had asked if I'd be around to provide some technical assistance that evening, as in those days I was considered to be quite useful when it came to knobs and buttons! I had very little to do that night, but was there nonetheless, just in case I was called upon to solve what could only have been a very, very minor problem. This show of Jayne's happened to be on just before the first ever show on Radio 1 by a young man who had arrived from Capital Radio called Chris Moyles. Chris had been signed up to present the Early Breakfast Show, which was on-air between 4 and 6.30 a.m. and I think he ducked his head into our studio to say 'Hi' before his first show.

I'd like to regale the story of our first encounter and how it was a magical meeting of minds but, if I'm honest, I can't fully remember it. It must have been about 3 a.m. and while Chris was raring to go and do his first ever show on Radio 1, I was gearing up to getting myself home to my little bedsit in Hampstead and go to bed, as my day was ending as Chris's was just beginning.

It wasn't until I was working as a tech op on Mark and Lard's Breakfast Show that I really started to get to know Chris, whose Early Breakfast Show preceded theirs. I'd stick my head into his studio for a chat and a cuppa as he was winding up his show, and we just got to know each other through that, I guess.

Such is his style, Chris would then give me a little mention on-air when I'd popped in. Before I knew it we were having these little chats, all on-air. So in many ways our friendship has been broadcast to the nation since the off.

I liked Chris's friendly Northern manner, and slowly I got to know him as a colleague and we just sort of clicked. I don't know which one of us first suggested it, but one day after he'd finished his show we were having a natter in the studio while I kept an eye on Mark and Lard's show, and we talked about going for a pint. Both of us were the same age, both fairly new to London, and didn't really know anybody outside work. The few people I did know in London were all doing a nine-to-five and were on a completely different time zone to me, and I think Chris was exactly the same at the time, so we were both looking for something to do. We went for a pint at lunchtime that day, and it was then that I first had a chance to get to know Chris and he in turn me.

Since joining the Beeb, I'd spent a fair bit of time scribbling down ideas for radio, so I decided to bring along my funny (I hoped) little list of very raw ideas to see what Chris thought over a couple of pints in the pub next to work.

At the time I was massively influenced by Vic Reeves and Bob Mortimer's cult TV show *Shooting Stars*, which was in its prime in the late 1990s, so my ideas were of that off-the-wall ilk that people either love or hate. At the time I didn't know Chris well enough to gauge his sense of humour, but I hoped that he was on the same sort of wavelength as me.

That lunchtime in the pub there was an awkward moment as I shoved this piece of paper in front of him and waited like an expectant child for his opinion. Silence followed as he read my ideas.

More silence, but then I saw him smile at a couple of them, and I felt relieved that I wasn't just some idiot with an entirely unique sense of humour. When I say entirely unique, I mean unique in the sense that only I found it funny; but his smile and his laugh reassured me that I perhaps wasn't alone and did in fact have a kindred spirit in the humour department. The idea that I remember made him chuckle was called The Candy Flip Moment. Basically, there was a one-hit wonder band from a few years earlier who'd had a big success with a dreadful cover of the Beatles classic 'Strawberry Fields Forever'. It was a shocking record which had quite rightly catapulted them straight back to musical obscurity as a band at the first opportunity, but what I wanted to do was an ironic tribute to the aforementioned producers of what could only be regarded as future landfill. The Candy Flip Moment would see us celebrate their 'great' work by playing their finest moment (i.e. the same song) every day at the same time in an attempt to create nausea amongst the listening public, in a way that Celebrity Raspberry has never quite achieved. Chris fortunately laughed at my half-baked musings, and from then onwards I felt that we were on a very similar page when it came to radio and comedy. But more than anything, over the course of a few pints, we just got on.

I think Chris felt that I would be an asset to his show. But things were quite tricky for me at the BBC as I was employed by a completely different department. I was a button-pushing technical operative and had no reason to be involved in production, so it wasn't as simple as going to work with Chris just because he liked my ideas.

It was clear from the start that Chris was envisioned by the powers that be as a DJ with bags of potential and that he was being groomed for big things. I'd imagine he was seen by the bosses as having the creativity and energy of Chris Evans without the headache. I think sticking him on the Early Breakfast Show (the harshest slot on radio) was a way of shaping him and giving him the kind of low-profile platform from which to develop.

It has to be said, some of the other DJs at Radio 1 weren't quite as enthusiastic about the new prodigy. As ever in the ego-driven media industry, there was a degree of resentment from the established old order who possibly felt threatened by this new and exciting talent, and Chris certainly wasn't going to keep himself to himself and come in quietly. I think he was seen as a bit of young upstart by the rest of the station's DJs, which he revelled in. It helped to foster the buzz and sense of excitement around him, even if it did piss a few people off at the time.

Chris's on-air style has always been to take the mickey and he didn't hold back when it came to his fellow DJs, resulting in a few noses being put out of joint at the time. However, once people actually met Chris and got talking to him over a beer or a cup of tea in the office, they soon discovered that behind the sometimes brash and abrasive on-air persona was a young man who was genuine and hugely excited to be given the opportunity he'd always dreamed of: working for Radio 1. The perception of him by those who had spent time in his company changed from moderate irritation to more of a fondness and certainly a sense of respect for this lovable cheeky chappy who was merely trying to have a laugh.

I think, in truth, that most broadcasters – especially those in radio – are quite different in real life from the image they broadcast to millions. They tend to adopt a personality that's sometimes an exaggeration of the real them in order to mask their own natural shyness and insecurity, which isn't any bad thing. I reckon there's a degree of that in all the great broadcasters, and you'd be surprised by how shy certain big names are despite their outwardly confident on-air personae.

Radio 1 was a very different place when Chris and I first started there back in 1996 and 1997 respectively. As far as I was aware, the DJs didn't really socialise with each other and there was nothing like the family feeling which exists today. Things actually didn't change until quite a few years later when Andy Parfitt, the recently departed Radio 1 Controller, introduced 'DJ dinners'. Essentially these were organised evenings for all the DJs, part management meeting and part social occasion, which forced everybody to bond with each other. It was a masterstroke that, in my opinion, nurtured the green shoots of camaraderie that we have at Radio 1 today. Up until that point, DJs very much kept themselves to themselves; but since these dinners we have all got to know each other – barriers are broken down and people from different shows genuinely get on and have a laugh, and I think that's been evident on-air for a number of years now, which can only be a good thing.

WORKING WITH CHRIS

Chris and I became very good mates, largely through the fact that we had our days free and liked spending them in the pub together. The other thing we had in common, though, was that I wanted to work on his show, and Chris wanted me to work on his show. So he set to trying to convince the powers that be that this would be a good idea.

It wasn't that easy. Despite having Chris on my side, I was still working in a completely separate department. I had to reapply to join the production department as a broadcast assistant. But even if I got that job, there was still no guarantee that I would be able to work on Chris's show. It was all very bureaucratic, but eventually Chris got his way and in 1998 I landed the gig as broadcast assistant on Chris's newly launched Saturday morning show – although I didn't sail into the job by any stretch. The senior people at the Beeb were still unhappy at having to give in to Chris's demand of having me work on the show, in particular the head of production at the time – who had already clashed with Chris a few times. She wanted to make a point of telling me that I'd only just scraped through the interview process. Chris and I felt a bit like the naughty boys at school who'd been split up for causing trouble.

So all was great, I'd moved to the production department and was now working with Chris as a broadcasting assistant on his Saturday morning show. Sure I was at the very bottom of the ladder, making tea and all that, but I was chuffed to bits to be not just pushing buttons but creating. Within months I soon moved to the weekday show. I started writing the odd segment and I've been part of the furniture on the Chris Moyles Show ever since ...

The Wyclefs of Dover
TUESDAY FROM 9pm ON

 **BILGE**

He's one of the biggest recording artists in the world, having worked with Tom Jones and Mick Hucknall.

He's also an accomplished actor, having starred in several adverts on the Telly.

And now he's going in search of asylum seekers who share the same name as himself.

Join WYCLEF JEAN as he journeys to Dover in search of his cross-channel namesakes to see who they are, what they're like, and whether they share more in common than just their names.

That's…**The Wyclefs of Dover**…

Tuesday from 9pm

ONLY ON UK BILGE

EVERTON

From Hong Kong to leafy Buckinghamshire, via Bedford, Warrington and north London, I've always been one of life's journeymen, but one of the few constants in my life has always been Goodison Park and my beloved Everton.

Everton certainly wasn't the glory choice, especially when you look at some of the crap I've had to sit through over the years. In true traditional manner, my footballing passion was passed down to me from my father Keith, who sadly passed away in 2002. He was not only my Dad but my best mate as well, and hailing from Eastham on the Wirral as the son of a shipwelder at Cammell Laird's in Birkenhead, he was a big Evertonian. Technically, coming from that side of the Mersey, Tranmere Rovers should have been his team, and he used to look out for their results, as do I to this day; but my Dad was a great influence on my life and his passion for Everton Football Club is something that he handed down to me, and it's something I'm very proud to continue as I know it's what he would have wanted!

Geographically, I was somewhat distanced from my family roots and Everton throughout my youth. It wasn't really until I went to college in Warrington that my current affinity with the club was truly ignited. Being only half an hour away from Goodison meant I could go regularly. It was a wonderful time during which I got reintroduced to a lot of my family, whom I'd hardly known until that point. Going to Goodison was a great way of bridging the gap with my heritage that had been missing for much of my transient early life.

Goodison is always somewhere that I feel I should be. I love everything about it: the atmosphere, camaraderie and excitement. Essentially, football is tribal and has that sense of belonging – win, lose or draw. For me what goes on on the pitch isn't half as important as the deep sense of historic ritual and tradition I get from going to the games.

Ever since those days in Warrington, attending the games has become a big part of my life. My Dad moved back to England with Mum in 1994, just in time to be there when we overcame Manchester United in the FA Cup final the following year. Together we'd travel all over the country watching Everton play. It was a very special time.

I still hold a season ticket, and try to go to every match that I can, home and away. My cousin Paul and I have our ritual of going for a pint in The Spellow like we've always done, and sometimes run into my cousin Alison on the corner by the church, as she's often in the church before the match having a cup of tea and a slice of cake. It's a very honest part of the world and somewhere I'll forever have great affinity for. I always look forward to going to the match, and I miss the fact that I don't get to go as often as I'd like these days.

In an obscure way, it was through Everton that my love affair with the media began. And it was in The Spellow that I had one of the proudest creative moments of my life.

All clubs have fanzines, and Everton are no different. There have been a few over the years but *When Skies Are Grey*, or *WSAG* for short, is the one that my Dad and I used to buy.

We'd leaf through the pages over a few pints every match day and deliberate the topics at hand – usually the woes of Everton's persistent mediocrity. We even started subscribing to it, so that we wouldn't miss out on edition if we turned up late to the match or missed a game.

In an effort to feel involved in it all I would send in articles, in the vain hope of them getting printed. I was desperate to be part of this club of hardcore fans that seemed to get regularly published, but, still wet behind the ears and doubtful of my own credentials, I'd use pen names such as Philip O'Fish and Roger Andowtt to maintain my anonymity!

Like an excited adolescent on Valentine's Day, I'd rummage through the post on the days my subscription would arrive. It took a while but sure enough persistence paid off and I got published more than once! I still feel very proud when I recall, one match day, spotting a burly, skin-headed Scouser, bitter in one hand and my first published article – in which he was duly engrossed – in the other. That was a seminal moment of acceptance for me. I guess it was my first dalliance with the world of media and as proud a professional achievement as any other in my career to date. In addition to a couple of pieces in *WSAG*, I also decided to write an article for the official EFC publication, *The Evertonian*, in about 2003. They hadn't asked for an article, but I decided to spout something anyway, just on the off chance that it might get printed, and sure enough it did! Once again I was very proud that my opinions were deemed worthy of publication, and somewhere in my Mum's loft I would imagine she's kept the article.

DAVE VITTY
Safe Hands

The weeks of isolation and loneliness are starting to take their toll. So much so that my behaviour has become more and more desperate as I search for some kind of solace and gratification. I've even taken to dressing up and watching certain videos when my girlfriend's out at the shops, and it's only a matter of time before she catches me. The other day I heard her coming up the path and in a moment of panic, quickly ejected the video out of the machine, got changed out of all the gear and put my jeans and T-shirt back on. It was a close one. Had she got home two minutes earlier she would have caught me right in the middle of it. Dressed in the new home kit (socks and all), halfway through the Cup Winners' Cup, semi-final, second leg against Bayern Munich.

She thinks I'm odd. She thinks that my behaviour borders on the obsessive, and continually bemoans the fact that I must love Everton more than her, despite my seemingly endless reassurances that I love them both equally. The problem is, of course, that I'm frustrated. I hate the close season, and I know that it's nearly over, but I can't wait. I'm bored of reading about the Russian Revolution at Chelski and how much Harry Kewell's agent made this summer. I just want to get on with it. I've already worked out which fixtures clash with dates of important family significance, and I know I'm certainly going to miss the Fulham game on the 23rd of August as I've got a wedding to go to that day (mine), but I'm all set for the 16th. I'm excited, and to a certain extent slightly apprehensive about what this season has in store. The reason being that I don't want people to be disappointed if we fail to better our seventh place finish of last season. At the time of writing we still haven't brought in any fresh faces to bolster our squad, despite numerous press reports linking us with all sorts of players. Personally, I think we desperately need some craft in midfield and an additional striker to take the pressure off Campbell and Radzinski. An injury to either of them, with doubts over Rooney's current fitness could really stretch our squad to its limits. David Moyes obviously knows this based upon his summer targets, and I assume is frustrated that deals involving certain players simply haven't materialised for one reason or another.

We'll be fine, of course. I do genuinely believe that the days of looking over our shoulder and getting caught up in the annual relegation dogfight are over. The new-found confidence, tactical awareness and improved fitness of the squad has been a revelation, and the reason David Moyes deservedly won manager of the season. It is no exaggeration to say that I wouldn't swap him for anybody in the world at the moment. I believe we have the finest young British manager around, and only hope that as a club we can provide him with the support, infrastructure and finances to enable him to fulfil his sizeable ambitions. Like all of us, I desperately want to see us challenging for honours, and with some shrewd financial investments and the continued ability to get the very best out of our players, I think that it could be achievable within three years. It simply can't be done overnight and patience is therefore paramount. Top six is once again our target for this season, nothing more nothing less. I think we're at least three quality players short of competing for a Champions League spot, and even further away from actually winning the league, but we're moving in the right direction.

I don't think that any of us really expected us to finish where we did last season, and while missing out on a UEFA Cup place was a bitter disappointment after a hard-fought campaign, it was probably for the best in the long run. There's a new level of optimism and a genuine excitement about the future. We don't have the finances of a Russian billionaire, or a squad the size of some of our peers, but we do have a hunger for success, and provided we give David and some of our young starlets the support they're going to need, the future looks very bright indeed. We've proved we can compete once again with the best of them, people are starting to take us seriously and for the first time in ages we're not being tipped to struggle before a ball has been kicked. We are well and truly back on track with the stability upon which to build a future, and the reassurance that after so many years of struggle, we are at long last in safe hands.

It was around the same sort of time that I decided to be witty and pen a parody all about Sky's domination of British football coverage. In order for this to work, you need to be familiar with the modern-day musical masterpiece that is 'Castles in the Sky' by Ian Van Dahl!

```
Do you ever question yourself?
Do you ever wonder why?
The Beeb's lost all its football highlights,
Snapped up by ITV and Sky

Oh tell me why
Is all the football just on Sky
It can't be true
They're charging more with pay-per-view
I want to see
Match of the Day on BBC
It's got to be better than Des on ITV
```

FOLKFACE

'Folkface are one of the most inspiring bands I've
heard since the seventies' – Dalai Lama

I'd like to tell you the story of the music phenomenon that is
Folkface. Now, I'd love to recall a romantic tale of two men who
shared a passion for rekindling the extinct art of British folk,
and how their lives collided in a cosmic clash not seen since
Lennon and McCartney. But I can't.

The truth behind the birth of Folkface is somewhat different.
We were away in Northern Ireland back in 2004 for Radio 1's
Big Weekend and on one of our days off we all took a trip to see
the world-famous Giant's Causeway. Doing the touristy thing,
Dom and I had our photo taken, looking out over the coastal
clifftops onto the magnificent rock formations.

Now, maybe it was the mystical Irish air – or the Murphy's
we'd been drinking the night before – but something beautiful
was born in that picture. Juliette Ferrington (our old sports
reporter) was the one to spot it first: 'There's something about
your slightly thoughtful poses and the craggy rural scenery
that makes this picture look like the cover of a folk album.' A
phenomenon was born.

At this stage I knew that Dom could play the guitar – he
was in the massively successful band Gutter Star – and I knew

I was about as musical as one of those hexagonal rocks on the Causeway, so the natural thing to do was form a band. Well, we already had the album cover, so it all made perfect sense. Another example of one of my many ideas without any substance – much like this book. Yet Dom still wasn't convinced:

'I don't know, I'm not sure I want to go through the ego battles we had to deal with in Gutter Star. It's opening up old emotional wounds. I'm not sure I can go there again.'

'It won't be like that, I promise. What happened with Gutter Star, anyway?'

'Our lead guitarist left to become a postman.'

'I promise I won't leave to become a postman.'

'OK, but only if you give me your word.'

And here we are, still going strong and topping the charts seven years later. Some say we have Rolling Stones-esque longevity. Or maybe we just won't go away; you decide.

The 'Hedge'

Obviously we needed a name, so I came up with Folkface –
a childish single entendre – Folk Off might have been a bit too
obvious. Unfortunately, Dom turned out to be pretty good on
the guitar, so we didn't really feel as if we had any excuse not
to forge ahead with this half-baked idea. It wasn't long before
we were performing these disappointing little ditties on-air
– with extremely limited success, I might add. The listeners
gave us a very lukewarm reception. Quite right too: there
wasn't much sense to why, mid-show, Dom, the newsreader,
and myself, the . . . um . . . I dunno, started breaking out into
song – with our bongos, guitar and nose flutes. It's a wonder
we kept our jobs.

The Folkface phenomenon really began to snowball in 2005
when somehow we managed to get our first booking for an
actual gig. Our humble journey would begin at Glastonbury! Ha!

'Um, shouldn't we start off with some small pub gigs first?'
Dom sensibly suggested at the time.

'Probably, but I'm not sure any pubs would have us.'

Talk about diving in at the deep end! While we weren't
quite playing the headline slot on the Pyramid Stage, our
show producer at the time, Rachel Jones, had managed to get
Folkface a slot in the Jazz World Café. Some genuinely amazing
musicians will go all their lives without playing Glastonbury –
Mick Jagger, Fleetwood Mac, the Cheeky Girls – and here we
were with a booked slot. Result!

So off we drove to Glastonbury like a couple of excited
kids, to live out our boyhood rock star fantasies. This was in
the days before the great marketing tool that is Twitter, so
we got some business cards printed at Chieveley Services on
the M4.

'Right, so that's the promotional side of things taken care of,' said Dom as he jumped back in the car with a fistful of our hot-off-the-press business cards. 'Now all we need to do is write some songs.'

Arriving at a flooded Glastonbury on the Friday, you might think we'd take the time before our gig on Sunday to write some songs and prepare our set. Well, we kind of got sidetracked by Glastonbury and its many temptations.

I was beginning to feel
at home at Glastonbury

Deep into the second day of the festival, with around 24 hours to go before Folkface would announce itself to the world, Dom and I planned on taking it easy. 'Just a couple of ciders and we'll head back to the hotel to work on our set,' we both sagely agreed.

In the midst of the merriment we befriended a couple of local lads from nearby Wells.

'Want some of our homebrew cider?' they politely asked in their amiable West Country drawl.

'When in Rome,' I nodded at Dom before glugging out of this petrol canister of scrumpy.

Before I knew it, our evening morphed into a blur of hysterical giggles. Dom and I spent the rest of the night staggering around the site, bent over double, screeching with laughter and howling at the moon like a pair of crazed banshees. In hindsight, I'm not entirely sure of the full contents breakdown of that cider. My last memory of the evening was watching Coldplay from the top of a transit van. Suffice to say, Folkface was still a blank-page project by the morning of our gig.

I woke up with a hangover worthy of Keith Richards or Denise Welch. I paced around my room until Dom arrived with his guitar and we ordered a couple of bacon sandwiches and two large full-fat cokes to replenish lost sugars and water from the night before. Our first gig was just a few hours away. So we sat on the end of my bed, in our underpants, and laid down the first chords of the now legendary Folkface repertoire. A historic moment in the annals of rock'n'roll, without a doubt.

We managed to cobble together three very, very poor songs, which were based on pretty weak parody covers. Kool and the Gang's 'Celebration' became 'Celebrate Glastonbury, Come On!' We threw 'Kumbaya' in there because at least we'd get some kind of singalong going that would mask us and my bongo-playing. Fortunately the masking of the bongo-playing was done expertly by the sound man who hadn't mic'd up the drums properly, or failed to turn them up. Either way, all you could hear was a dull thudding as we desperately tried to muddle along through a set of about 15 minutes.

We knew it was important to go down the route of style over content. It was a creative decision born out of necessity – largely because we didn't have any content. So we ended up spending more time arranging our look than rehearsing our act: 20 minutes trawling through the many ridiculous clothes stalls of Glastonbury en route to our debut gig. We purchased some luminous tie-dyed throws, in which we cut holes to make ponchos. We also purchased some Orbital-influenced headgear; only as opposed to the state-of-the-art torch-glasses the two DJs wear, we had these clunky, elasticated head torches.

Looking, and feeling, like psychedelic miners, we made our way to Glastonbury's Jazz World. On arrival we discovered a fairly sizeable stage and field with at least a few thousand punters dancing to SkaCubano.

'This is a pretty major stage, mate, are you sure this is us?' Dom mumbled into my ear.

'Yeah, I'm sure it's the Jazz World or something like that,' I repeated as I squelched my way through mud to the stage.

Nerves jangled as we digested the enormity of the task ahead and how poorly prepared we were. We rocked up to the side of this stage, only to see a sign for the more familiarly named – and considerably smaller – Jazz World Tent pointing off to the right.

'Ah, that looks more like us,' Dom sighed with relief as he turned towards this poky marquee.

The two of us lumbered onto the small stage to muted applause from a 200-strong audience. Clearly our business card marketing strategy had paid off – nothing at all to do with the shameless plug Chris had given us the week before on the radio show, you understand.

As I stood there on the stage I looked at Dom, who raised his eyebrows at me in bewilderment. His expression mirrored my feelings perfectly. 'What the fuck are we doing?' was all I could think. I then peered out at the audience, who were all giving me the same puzzled look of uncertainty. And then there was Chris, standing with a Cheshire Cat-sized grin, giving us the thumbs-up. Oh – and as if to add even more absurdity to the whole affair, he was stood next to *Dr Who* star David Tennant, whom he'd dragged through the mud to see us, for reasons which still aren't exactly clear!

Dom tapped the microphone.

'Um, hello, we're Folkface and ... um ... we'd like to play you some of our biggest hits.'

'Which we wrote this morning at the hotel in our underpants,' I added.

All things considered, the gig wasn't too bad. Well, it could have been worse. We managed to flesh out our somewhat flimsy playlist with some lengthy bongo solos from myself. Looking out at the audience at the end of the gig, there appeared to be about the same number of people as at the start. A success I'd say.

Afterwards, Dom and I high-fived each other – we'd played Glastonbury! Something many a more illustrious musician couldn't claim. It couldn't get much better ... could it?

THE CROWD CALLED OUT FOR MORE

Due to underwhelming demand Folkface appeared very occasionally over the following years. After the dizzy heights of the 2005 Glastonbury gig, the band essentially became a very infrequent feature on the show for our own amusement.

Folkface had begun to fizzle out when we were asked to play a slot in the unsigned tent at Radio 1's Big Weekend in Maidstone in 2008. The line-up included a few acts who have since gone on to major success, such as White Lies and Chipmunk. Leading up to the weekend, we plugged the hell out of the gig on the show in order to cram the tent with a sea of people who could all share the disappointment that we inevitably provide.

By this stage we'd increased our repertoire a fair bit from the 2005 Glastonbury fiasco, when you could have scribbled the entire lyrical content of our back catalogue on the back of a pack of fags. The now legendary 'We Will Folk You' – based on the obvious Queen classic – was our biggest crowd-pleaser.

So, we came out onto the stage at the Big Weekend to play the unsigned tent and unintentionally gave the audience – of a few hundred-plus – a very pure radio experience ... in that nobody could see us.

As we walked out onto the stage Dom whispered into my ear: 'I've forgotten my bloody guitar strap. I'm going to have to sit on a stool.'

'Quick, can we get a couple of stools?' I frantically asked the people running the unsigned tent.

The stage was pretty low and the entire audience were on their feet, so in typically farcical Folkface fashion we had to do the gig on a pair of plastic chairs. Such was the low height of the stage, nobody could see us except for a (not so) lucky few in the front row.

Somehow, we were invited back the following year to play again at the Big Weekend in Swindon, so someone must have seen enough to book us again – or more likely there was a lengthy set change between acts that needed filling, and we were regarded as being marginally more interesting to watch than a load of hairy-arse roadies de-rigging the stage.

'LAMB BHUNA'

Say what you will about Simon Cowell, but the ritual of weekends in front of the telly, watching *X Factor* and stuffing yourself with curry, is a gift to the nation for which I'm very grateful. It was on one such weekend that I had a moment of divine inspiration to pen what has become Folkface's ubiquitous anthem.

I'll have to bring you back to the *X Factor* final of 2008. Alexandra Burke and JLS were the two finalists battling it out to become that year's champion.

Jayne – my ex – was opening a bottle of wine, when our curry arrived. As I was plating up our food, JLS and Alexandra Burke both sang a cover of Leonard Cohen's 'Hallelujah'. I decided to join in.

'Hallelujah, my lamb bhuna, my lamb bhuna, my lamb bhuuuuuuuuuna.'

It was a light-bulb-flashing-above-your-head moment. Jayne, who loves that song, glowered me an evil, as if to say: 'No, no, no, don't even think about it.' But, of course, the lyrical wheels of parody were already turning in my head.

'I'm sorry, love, I've got to.'

In moments of inspiration, you've got to strike while the iron (or the curry in my case) is hot. So I skipped upstairs to my computer with a plate full of curry and poppadoms and penned the words to 'Lamb Bhuna'. I knew I had to get the song done for the following day's show, as I felt I needed to play it within the 24 hours that people can still remember the ever-disposable *X Factor* finalists and their songs:

Oh Saturday was a special night
The X Factor final was so tight
We ordered take-away from the 'Prince of
    India'
We had onion bhajis for the wife
And chicken korma with pilau rice
But when the food came they'd forgotten my
    Lamb Bhuna

My Lamb Bhuna
My Lamb Bhuna
My Lamb Bhuna
My Lamb Bhuna

I looked in the bag again in case
It was there all along and I needn't have
    chased
The man on the phone about my missing dinner
He offered a heartfelt apology
And 10 per cent off my next delivery
But it meant I never got to eat my Lamb Bhuna

My Lamb Bhuna
My Lamb Bhuna
My Lamb Bhuna
My Lamb Bhuna

The rest of the food was very nice
I had some of the korma and half of the rice
We voted about thirty times for Alexandra

```
JLS will do okay and Eoghan Quigg will no
    doubt say
That when he grows up he'll become a famous
    crooner


My Lamb Bhuna
My Lamb Bhuna
Should've come sooner
My Lamb Bhuna
My Lamb Bhuna
My Lamb Bhuna
My Lamb Bhuna
```

'Hallelujah' has been covered by musical greats such as Jeff Buckley, John Cale (of The Velvet Underground), Rufus Wainwright, K.D. Lang, Bon Jovi, Bob Dylan, Bono ... and Folkface. Although we never released the song, of course – we're not in the music business for the money, you see.

Now with a signature anthem to our name, Folkface were booked to play a cameo slot on the main stage of Radio 1's Big Weekend in Swindon the following year, 2009. Chris was performing a load of our song parodies from the show with our jingle band on the main stage, so Dom and I were then scheduled to come on at the end of Chris's set and do a little 'turn'.

Somehow, as well, it transpires that JLS have been lined up to join us on stage to do the chorus of 'Lamb Bhuna'! It's all very surreal and a bit mad and before I know it I'm in a trailer with Dom – who's inexplicably wearing a snakeskin cowboy hat – and JLS explaining: 'So it goes: "My lamb bhuna, my lamb bhuna, my lamb bhuna."'

And they start harmonising with each other, practising the chorus as if they're about to go out to sing in front of Simon Cowell.

We walked out onto the stage and I gave it a big 'Hello Swindon!' I had to grab hold of the microphone stand to stop my hands from shaking as I looked out over the crowd of about 10,000 people. It was spine-tingling stuff when everyone started swaying their hands in the air and singing the chorus back at us. JLS coming out and singing the chorus was just the icing on what was a very, very surreal cake.

At the time JLS were only just beginning their journey – singing with Folkface was the biggest gig they'd done up to that point. I like to think that we were the making of them. And look how they've flourished. Just another gift from Folkface to the world – you're welcome.

Like many perma-adolescent men who are fast approaching middle age, Dom and I share a mutual desire to be rock stars one day. That 'Lamb Bhuna' moment in front of a festival-size crowd in Swindon was like our 'Live Aid' except without the increased awareness of global poverty and millions raised to help save Africa. If that had been the end of Folkface, I'd have died a happy man.

Nicole makes her first
appearance on stage
in front of 15,000
people at Radio 1's
Big Weekend in
Maidstone, May 2008

Not a bad place
to watch the
Foo Fighters.
Radio 1's Big
Weekend

This is
the moment
I actually
thought I
was Aston
from JLS

WHEN FOLKFACE MET ANDREW LLOYD WEBBER

Folkface is still occasionally resurrected if we feel we've got a decent angle for it. So what better opportunity for Britain's favourite band than Eurovision? The *Song For Europe* television programme was being made in late 2009, in which musical royalty such as Andrew Lloyd Webber would choose the UK's entry for the following year. Dom and I felt it was an ideal opportunity to represent our country through the medium of folk. In accordance with the Eurovision rules, we wrote an original song called 'The World is in our Hands' and, using the power of the BBC, we managed to blag our way into arranging a meeting with the great maestro.

Despite being dressed in our Folkface attire of tie-dye ponchos (which still hadn't been washed since the first Glastonbury performance five years previously) and rainbow hats, this was all done in absolute sincerity. So when we arrived at Lord Lloyd Webber's HQ in Covent Garden, we were actually very nervous. I mean, we were going to sing to one of the world's great modern-day composers!

We arrived in Covent Garden ready for our lunchtime appointment with the great man. Outside Andrew's offices our taxi driver managed to reverse into a row of parked motorcycles, which duly collapsed like dominoes. We grabbed our bongos and guitar and legged it from the scene of the crime as an angry mob of bikers circled on our cab. Dom and I then sat rather nervously in Andrew Lloyd Webber's waiting room. I'm not sure what I was more scared of, the angry scenes outside or waiting to play for Andrew Lloyd Webber.

As we walked into Andrew's office, he asked: 'So which one is Folk and which is Face?'

'No, no, *we* are Folkface.'

'Ah, I see.'

The audition went pretty well, I thought. Andrew actually dealt with and spoke to us like proper musicians, as opposed to the halfwits we really are. But unfortunately he had issues with some of the lyrical content.

'The World is in our Hands'

Language and clothes have made us different
War and religion as well
But underneath it all we're the same people
Trying our best to gel

Turkey and Greece may hate each other
But we'd like you all to know
That here in the UK we love everybody
And Eurovision is a great show

The world is in our hands
We embrace those from foreign lands
Like Latvia, Greece and France
Hello Helmut and Dimitri and Hans

If we could choose our favourite meal
We'd have tapas with some haggis and veal
We're from Europe and it's our decision
To make Folkface win this Eurovision

Israel find it a welcome diversion
From their normal everyday routine
And Albania are always massively delighted
If they finish in the top seventeen

The competition's rigged and everyone's
    scared
Of the Russians and their sinister past
And the Balkan states are heavily reliant
On Moscow for their oil and gas

The world is in our hands
We embrace those from foreign lands
Like Latvia, Greece and France
Hello Helmut and Dimitri and Hans

If we could choose our favourite meal
We'd have tapas with some haggis and eel
We're from Europe and it's our decision
To make Folkface win this Eurovision

[In the style of 'Lord of the Dance']

Choose us and you will cer-tain-ly
Be the lord of our destiny
We are Folkface and we'll do our best for you
We won't let you down, and our word is true!

After hearing our song, Andrew leaned back on his baby grand piano, hand on hip and pondered ...

'I'm just worried, you see, that we don't want to be too divisive and that might come out as being divisive.'

'Well, we don't have to use the oil and gas bit,' Dom compromised.

'Well, you see, that could be very dangerous for us. We could start a big European conflict again,' Lord Lloyd Webber countered, poker-faced.

Things got quite heated and artistic sparks flew as he dissected our lyrical content.

'You're talking about haggis and very specifically about Scotland. There are so many nations, I think all their food ought to be in there too ... really take this seriously. I want every nation and as many sorts of food. I want a good menu in there.'

I was nervous about the artistic cul-de-sac the lord was leading us down, but I tried to appease him, saying: 'We could base it on a European meal maybe, with different courses for different verses?'

'So we need a new title, verse and chorus,' summarised Dom.

'Exactly.'

Andrew Lloyd Webber clearly didn't get Folkface.

DILL DOUGH

For years the Italians have been making pizzas from a special type of secret dough.

They roll it, they load it, and then they bake it… in a custom-made pizza oven. But here at PIZZA PIECE we've improved the dough to make pizza even tastier.

We've added a touch of salt and pepper, and a generous portion of dill, to create new… DILL DOUGH.

That's right, DILL DOUGH will transform your favourite food into culinary masterpizzas.

SO IF YOU WANNA TAKE PIZZA TO THE NEXT LEVEL

YOU NEED NEW DILL DOUGH
'THE CHOICE OF CHAMPIONS'

PIZZA PIECE accepts no responsibility for any offence caused as a result of this smutty and juvenile ad

TOUR

For a while after the Lloyd Webber debacle, it seemed that Folkface had run its course and fizzled out – until May 2010, when Dom and I received a call from our gig agent, Guy Robinson.

'How do you feel about bringing Folkface on tour?'

'What? We've barely got enough material for a 15-minute gig, let alone a tour.'

'Well I've spoken to this promoter. He's done the maths on it, he's got good contacts with a few small venues around the country and is sure it would be a success given the following you've gathered to date.'

'OK, I guess . . .'

Again, another example of me doing things arse-over-tit. We had a tour booked but barely an act or any material.

Guy reckoned that we needed to piece together at least a 45-minute set. Even with our powers of bullshit, eking our few songs over that length of time seemed a mighty stretch. In truth we only really had three songs, of which only one was remotely good, 'Lamb Bhuna'. We agreed to the tour anyway, hoping the minor details (like not having any songs) would sort themselves out down the line.

The promoter got very excited that we were on board – he clearly knew something we didn't – and suddenly three gigs turned into nine. At first this seemed pretty daunting, but we figured if we could blag our way through one night, then it didn't matter if the tour was three, four or fifteen gigs!

The nights were booked, posters started going up and all of a sudden the Folkface train was hurtling ahead at full steam! It all seemed rather ridiculous. Dom and I were – through no design of our own – being thrust into the musical limelight once more.

We were suddenly entering into a world we really knew nothing about. While radio people and musicians lead somewhat symbiotic lives, there's still an immense gulf between the two professions. While we didn't consider ourselves anything like musicians, we were being paid to play music and were entering the world of touring. It all felt very real, as if, in a weird way, the joke was over and we had to give this thing a degree of serious attention.

From my point of view it was an interesting insight into the world of unsigned touring. We embarked on a fun adventure of small, local venues and unscrupulous promoters, and life on the road with nothing to live on but our talent and dreams, man!

Folkface had now become its own commercial entity, so we weren't really allowed to plug the tour on the radio show. That meant we couldn't even rely on our normal gravy train to drum up support. We had to gain notoriety on a local level as best we could – basically the promoter would stick a few posters up and hand out the odd flyer. All these things enhanced the reality that we were being regarded as a proper band, which was fun, if a little scary given the distinct lack of material we had.

So the gigs were all confirmed, opening night drew ever nearer, and about a month before, Dom and I agreed it was about time that we actually wrote a few songs! We sat down one afternoon and wrote some music to try and forge a kind of set. Our staple of old faves was there, of course: 'Lamb Bhuna', 'We Will Folk You' and 'Celebrate Manchester, Come On' formed the spine of our gig – three lyrically witty and complex songs. The latter was often a bit of a stumbling block in any town with more than two syllables; but, in true Folkface style, we made it work.

If you're ever thinking of playing music live and have a limited amount of talent, like us, a great mid-gig time-waster is a raffle. We'd give away things that we'd picked up in motorway service stations: disposable barbecues, fold-out fishing chairs, frisbees – anything that would buy us a few minutes of the set. We also had a Q&A session. Nobody asked any questions, so we'd make up impromptu ones like 'Do you have any merchandise?' To which we'd reply: 'Yes the Folkface T-shirts are available in all sizes and colours for a very reasonable £10 a pop.' Touring is all about marketing your brand and making every buck that you can.

We'd always finish our gigs with our Folkface encore song (to the tune of 'Hey Jude'), whether the crowd wanted one or not. Come to think of it, I'm not sure I remember there ever being any demand for us to continue playing; but who can't resist joining in to the 'na na na na na na naaaaaa' bit of 'Hey Jude' after a few beers? It was a winner.

'Sunday lunch' on the road

LIFE ON THE ROAD

'We Will Folk You'

We are in a band, in a folk band
Playing folk songs to lots of people almost
    every night
We don't care what they say
We do it our way
Folk you to all those people, who say that
    we're shite

Sing it

We Will, We Will, Folk You

We Will, We Will, Folk You

We know life is hard, life is tough
Are you tough enough, come on feel the folk
    cos it feels so strong
Put your fists in the air
Like you don't care
If people say you're stupid, then tell 'em
    they're wrong

Sing it

We Will, We Will, Folk You

We Will, We Will, Folk You

```
The planet is our friend, and we need to
Think the about long-term effects before it
    gets too late
The world listens to us
In us they trust
The global politicians all agree that we're
    great

Sing it

We Will, We Will, Folk You

We Will, We Will, Folk You

We Will, We Will, Folk You

We Will, We Will, Folk You
```

Even though our gigs seemed like a farce, ironically we actually put in some serious work to make it look that way. It was loosely structured chaos. So, we hired out Dom's local village hall (for the grand total of £4 an hour) and rehearsed our performance for a few weeks before the show. It provided us with a taster of what was to come: very small crowds and lots of empty space and that echoey feel that only an empty church hall can give you. We were acutely aware that, after a while, standing around watching someone forget the lyrics of their own crap song wasn't going to be hugely entertaining. Despite the perceived shambolic nature of it all, we felt we'd put together a tight and mildly entertaining little show in the end.

Twitter and Facebook were fully fledged social media tools at this stage, which we used to heavily publicise ourselves

Let's folk

Our first ever Folkface
photoshoot on a farm
somewhere

(join up on twitter.com/FolkFaceFans and www.facebook.com/
folkfaceontour). We arranged a proper photo shoot for our
website down on a farm in Kent (www.folkfacebook.com) to
provide an authentic folksy backdrop.

We even had a couple of support acts – who, in hindsight,
provided the main bulk of the entertainment! I mean, we were
charging about £15 a ticket, so we had to give some kind of
value. Amy Wyke, an angsty singer/songwriter who had far
greater claim to being a musician than either Dom or I, was our
fabulous opening act. She was lovely and a genuinely talented
girl. It was a bit weird because she wasn't a joke act. I think
she was quite happy to ride our Radio 1 publicity bandwagon
– for all the good it did us – but I'm sure she must have felt
that opening for two musical dickheads, Dom and I, was a tad

humiliating and very much beneath her. Either way, she was good fun and we had a laugh.

We also employed an MC/comedian to warm up the crowd for us – Dan Schreiber, another accomplished artist who has written for respected programmes like *QI*, *Flight of the Concords* and *The Museum of Curiosity*. He was very funny and a great giggle to have on tour, and clearly quite smart. Like me, he'd also been raised in Hong Kong, but, unlike me, he'd managed to pick up some Mandarin whilst out there and would regularly use it in his set for his exclusive amusement, which tickled me.

So off we tottered around the country with our instruments and a box of T-shirts. We played to largely disappointing (and disappointed, I imagine) crowd numbers. We opened to a hundred or so in Bristol, which wasn't bad, but had to cancel the odd show, such as Cardiff, due to a distinct lack of interest – such is life for budding rock stars. However, I have to say I was mighty proud to have played some pretty well-regarded venues. We played The Boardwalk in Sheffield, where The Clash performed their first ever gig – in a line-up that also included The Sex Pistols and The Buzzcocks. The 100 Club was another iconic punk venue that we played in. It was quite surreal walking in the footsteps of the likes of Johnny Rotten.

In truth the tour was a bit of flop. We didn't get any huge numbers to our gigs or make any real money. But we had a laugh and got to live like real musicians for a while, even if our seven-date global onslaught was met largely with a tidal wave of apathy.

Of course, the gigging wasn't without its rock'n'roll moments. We played a super-trendy club called Audio under the arches in Brighton. Dom and I arrived at this very dark, edgy, underground venue and immediately felt out of place.

'It's the kind of place you'd expect some kind of cool DJ, not us two idiots singing crap songs and doing a raffle,' Dom mumbled to me as we arrived.

High quality promotion
for a high quality act

Sure enough, our reservations proved correct as only about twelve people turned up, eight of whom were Dom's mates. The other four were random Brighton types. The gig went okay and the few people who were there that night walked away knowing that they'd seen our band in the most intimate of surroundings, and that there was no refund policy whatsoever from us, the promoter or the venue.

The after-show party dragged long into the night as Folkface and all twelve of our audience members hit the town. Naturally, Jägerbombs made an appearance as we revelled like rock stars in Brighton. The last thing I remember is talking to a man who claimed to be a wizard about the secrets of magic before retiring towards my luxurious seaview room to sleep outside the door in the hotel corridor. I'd clearly been having trouble getting in and decided to just have a little rest for a minute, which ended up being the rest of the night. As morning broke on the south coast, I let myself into my room, packed up my bag on my pristine and entirely unused bed and went downstairs for breakfast to meet Dom, who was chuckling into his morning croissant at the state of my dishevelled self.

'What happened to you?' Dom asked.

'What happened to me? I kind of didn't make it into my room.'

'Oh yeah, what have you been up to then, get lucky with that wizard?'

'No thankfully, I couldn't get into my room. Bloody key-card wouldn't work.'

'I had a similar problem. I got locked out of my room when trying to take out a tray of food when I got back last night. I had to walk into the reception in my pants to get a new key.'

'Our music may be folk but we're rock'n'roll,' we thought as we prepared to buy some Nurofen from Boots and get the train home.

'Folka Face'

We've never gigged in Germany or gigged in
    France
Or on the beach in Benidorm in just our
    swimming pants (nice Speedos)
One day we might play a concert somewhere on
    the moon
But, being realistic, it won't be any time
    soon

Oh, oh, oh
We'll get you hot
We do it a lot

Oh, oh, oh
We'll get you hot
We do it a lot

Thank your Mum
Thank your Dad
If they bought your tickets
For Folkface
You were lucky to get in

Thank your bird
Thank your bloke
If they bought your tickets
For Folkface
You were lucky to get in

We've never gigged in Russia or in Kazakhstan
Or in Jamaica, Tunbridge Wells or even
    Amsterdam (nice Speedos)
One day we might play at Wembley or maybe
    Stonehenge
And bring along some druids and pretend that
    they're our friends

Oh, oh, oh
We'll get you hot
We do it a lot

Oh, oh, oh
We'll get you hot
We do it a lot

Thank your Mum
Thank your Dad
If they bought your tickets
For Folkface
You were lucky to get in

Thank your bird
Thank your bloke
If they bought your tickets
For Folkface
You were lucky to get in

'We're on a Tour'

We're on a tour
Going to places we've never been to before
So open the door
Be yourself once more

God created the world in seven days
And on the eighth he made us
Said take your folk on the road in a big tour bus

We agreed and said hey we can do that
There wasn't much to discuss
We quickly packed up our bags
Amazed that he chose us

We're on a tour
Going to places we've never been to before
So open the door
Be yourself once more

Now we plan to go international
The biggest stars in the world
God said that we should be kings
To all the boys and girls

But take away our music and our gift
And we are just like you
Although we are God's favourites
And you know that's true

We're on a tour
Going to places we've never been to before
So open the door
Be yourself once more

[Nose flute solo]

'Little Cat'

Little cat, that is a little friend
Your furry coat, so soft and brown

Little cat, with a little nose
Little paws and little toes

Little whiskers, and little ears
Little eyes, full of little tears

Little cat, with a big ball of wool
Playing by the A38

You never saw, that articulated truck
Well not until it was too late

That was the last time, I saw you little cat
And now you're as flat, as a dinner plate

Flat cat

'My Lamb Bhuna reprise'

We only arrived in town tonight
We had a quick shower, a shave and a shite
And fancied a tasty Indian for our dinner
We went to some Balti place in town

And to be honest we felt a little let down
Cos when the food came they'd forgotten my
    Lamb Bhuna

My Lamb Bhuna

The waiter apologised to me
And asked if I'd like to try Lamb Jalfrezi
But I told him I'd prefer Tikka Masala
As a goodwill gesture they didn't charge me
For the six poppadoms and the mango chutney
But it meant I never got to eat . . . my Lamb
    Bhuna

My Lamb Bhuna

[Break and key change]

The rest of the food was very nice
I had Tikka Masala with chips and rice
We all had a couple of pints of draught
    Kingfisher
The only letdown . . . was my missing dish
And next time I just sorely wish
That the waiter hadn't forgotten my Lamb Bhuna

For many people, the nicest thing about going to an Indian restaurant is the smell that hits you as soon as you walk through the door. Well, now you can recreate that experience at home… with new **CHAPUTTY.**

CHAPUTTY fits into the gaps in your window sills, which means that as soon as the wind blows, you'll experience instant korma, as the baltiful aromas tikka hold of your senses. **CHAPUTTY** can fit into any gaps in your house, replacing window putty or polyfilla, and bringing the aromas of the East… to your hallway or lounge.

TIKKA HOME A NEW TRIAL SIZE CAN OF CHAPUTTY, AND EXPERIENCE THE SMELL… FOR YOURSELVES!

From the makers of Chappatio Furniture and Pilau Cases

'Folkface' (Na...na na, nana...na na)

Folkface, that is our name
You have loved us, and we've enjoyed it
Remember, to tell all of your friends
And then we can start
To get some more gigs

Folkface, we're here for you
We write music, for everybody
Remember, there are some T-shirts for sale
If your sex is male
Or if you're a female

And when you feel it's time to leave
If you're called Steve
Or you're called Deborah or Amanda
Or maybe you're called Paul or Claire
Be cool don't stare
Cos we're just two normal guys remember

Folkface would like to thank
You for all coming out to see us
Remember to please respect the neighbours
Cos this is a residential area

Folkface, what can we say
You have made us both so happy
Remember, this is our very last song
And we love you all

```
Oh yes we do
Oh yes we do
We love you yes we really do

Na...na na, nana...na na
nana...na na
Folkface
```

[Repeat to fade]

MAN OF MANY TALENTS

While Dom appears to be the main thrust of musical mojo in Folkface with his fancy guitar skills, I have in fact become a man of many musical instruments. I guess I picked up my bongo skills from my Dad, who was a serious drummer in lots of jazz bands throughout his life. But beyond providing the percussion for Folkface, I've branched out into other musical forms. One of my favourites is the nose flute, a quirky instrument I bought in Germany during the 2006 World Cup. I like to think I'm something of an expert at it now and it's a regular feature in any Folkface set. For those unfamiliar with the instrument, it's a musical treat. You've never really heard Debussy's 'Clair de Lune' (the song at the end of *Ocean's Eleven*) until you've heard it on the nose flute.

GLASTONBURY ENCORE

You might remember that in 2010, U2 pulled out of the Friday night headline slot at Glastonbury. We were clearly the people's choice to replace them. The bookies gave us 66:1 odds, the same as Jay-Z (seriously!), who had headlined the festival before. We were given shorter odds than the likes of the Beastie Boys and R.E.M. Despite my £10 bet on us, the call from Michael Eavis never came. He went with the Gorillaz, who are, in effect, a CGI version of Folkface, really. Michael realised the error of his ways and made up for it by booking us for two gigs at Glasto 2011. Initially we didn't want to do it after being snubbed for Damon Albarn and his cartoon. But we eventually agreed . . . for the fans.

There's some sort of poetry in the Folkface story coming full circle with us playing Glastonbury again. Six years after our debut performance and we were asked to play not one, but two gigs. There wasn't really any money in it but we got free tickets to the festival, which was enough for us. Given our now VIP status at Glastonbury we had a highly sought-after backstage parking space in the artists' area. All we needed was a luxury motorhome to put in it. Two weeks before Glastonbury this can prove quite tricky . . .

HOW TO BLAG FREE STUFF

Two weeks before Glastonbury there isn't an available campervan in the country. We both thought it would have been a bit ridiculous to have pitched a tent in our backstage artists' parking spot, so we embarked on the wonderful world of Twitter to see if any of our half-million followers could help.

Dom and I had a 'private' conversation on Twitter pondering the problems of our getting hold of a motorhome. It went something like:

domisatwit

Not long now to go now until Folkface play Glastonbury!! Still need to sort a campervan and write some songs!!! Other than - all set!

davidvitty

@domisatwit: Oh yeah accommodation folk friend. If only we knew of somebody or somewhere that would rent us a motor home at a decent price? Mmm...

davidvitty

@domisatwit: I don't want people to think we're a pair of cheeky folkers Dom. Just need to find a campervan to rent at a competitive price?

domisatwit

@davidvitty: I'm totally with you there great mate. We're all about the music! And getting a decent night's sleep of course! #glastoface

CharlotteEsland

@domisatwit @davidvitty: What will you be using the camper van for? There's a possibility that the company I work at could loan you one.

davidvitty

@CharlotteEsland: oh wow! We're playing Glastonbury and have backstage parking access. We'd promise to look after it, if we could rent it? x

CharlotteEsland

@davidvitty: We could loan you one of these which sleep two http://bit.ly/kpLR5O or one of these http://bit.ly/jscLJb which sleep more?

davidvitty

@CharlotteEsland: Charlotte, they look amazing! I'm following you now, so could you DM me your number so I can give you a call and chat? x

CharlotteEsland

9 hour drive today delivering #maxandpaddydoglastonbury - was well worth it mind!

davidvitty

I'd like to say a massive thank you to @CharlotteEsland and all at 'Elddis' for loaning us an amazing motor home for the weekend. Thank you! x

davidvitty

Fortunately, even heavy rain won't be able to penetrate our Folkface motor home, thanks to our good friends at 'Elddis' luxury motor homes!

davidvitty

@CharlotteEsland: We had the best time Charlotte, and loved the motor home. Got some great piccies for you as well. Thanks again x

davidvitty

@sarajcox: Likewise, me & @domisatwit would like to thank our good friends at Elddis for supplying our Glasto motor home! x #meetthefolkers!

Sure enough, I received a message from a lovely lady called Charlotte at Elddis stating that she could loan us a motorhome. So we had a chat, during which I explained that I couldn't plug her company on the radio (but I could on Twitter and in my book), which she was fine about. So our six-berth campervan was delivered from Durham to Dom's house in Harpenden, all free of charge! She was a beaut – a vision of mustard and grey interiors and a cosy fit with just three beds. As the 'artists' Dom

Thanks to our
friends at Elddis
who kindly leant us
an 'Autoquest' for
the weekend

Stuck in traffic
queuing to get
into Glastonbury

We devised our setlist
on the journey down
there

Glastonbury
essentials

En route to Glastonbury.
Dominic is very good at
writing up the setlist,
while I make sure the
cider doesn't spill when
we go round corners

Our recipe
for success

and I grabbed a bed each, the other two would have to share.

'Sharing a bed with another hairy-arsed bloke is better than camping in the mud,' I explained.

Sure enough, we shamelessly plastered pictures all over our Twitter account and everyone was happy. Result!

We were now getting very excited and, like all true rock legends, Dom and I rolled up to Costco in Watford to stock up on supplies the night before our departure.

We duly filled up our campervan with wet-wipes, crisps and plenty of cider, did our Friday morning show and all set off for Glastonbury in our Max and Paddy-style transport.

DAY 1

We set off from London at about noon – six and a half hours before our gig – plenty of time, we thought. A calamity of errors saw us getting stuck behind a rubbish truck in Ladbroke Grove and gridlocked on the M4 while we rehearsed our show in the back of the van with Guy, our agent, at the wheel. A quick stop at Chieveley Services – where we printed our Folkface business cards all those years ago – for an M&S sandwich, and a few hours and many miles later we're stuck in knee-deep mud.

Just an hour before our gig and we were half-buried in a field, or swamp, quite a way from our pitch, but at least we were on site at Glastonbury's Worthy Farm. We enlisted the help of a few friendly people to push our vehicle out of the swamp we'd got stuck in. It was getting so close to our gig that Dom and I had to leave our van – which was drowning in mud, weighed down with 100 bottles of cider – and trudge through the sludge to our gig. Eventually – after much radioing and phone calls for help – the motorhome made it to our pitch in the hospitality section of Glastonbury . . . long after we'd abandoned ship.

We made it to our dressing room portacabin behind the Spirit of 71 stage, which we were sharing with Howard Marks, who was performing before us. Dom and I made ourselves at home by tucking into his supply of 'munchies' while he wrapped up his show. Chris then ducked his head around the corner to give us a pat on the back and a bit of moral support.

Just as we thought our rock'n'roll moment couldn't have got any better, an important woman – well, she had a clipboard – peeped her head around the door and asked: 'Are you Folkface?' We proudly replied that we were, grateful for the recognition. 'You've got to vacate this dressing room, we've got a VIP on the way.' We skulked off to finish our stolen crisps outside in the mud and rain.

Our egos were somewhat soothed once on stage, where a scrum of two or three hundred people crammed in to see us. The gig went great. We had really good banter with the crowd – they actually *asked* for an encore! After the show, Dom and I high-fived each other and hastily got to work flogging the 'Folkface Say Relax' T-shirts we'd had printed for the big event.

'I can't believe how well that went!' I cheered at Dom, drunk on performance adrenalin.

'I know, we've even sold out of T-shirts!'

Dom's always been the corporate one.

DAY 2

After a busy night that saw Folkface and U2 both play to bumper crowds, we were aware that we still had another gig that evening. While our first gig had been talked about heavily in the week running up to Glastonbury, we weren't sure how many people would be at our second. We expected about half a dozen people sitting around having a cup of tea and a falafel. As it turned out,

Together we were
campaigning for an
end to war, nuclear
weapons and mud

Reservoir Nobs

Here's Dom filming his
'mudumentary' on his
phone, while I concen-
trate on not having my
wellies sucked off

It was at this moment we began to fully
appreciate how meganormous we were

Just put your hands
in the air, and
wave them like you
just don't care

It looks like an enchanted forest, but
it's actually Fleet Services on the M3.
We were trying to create an 'arty' shot
for the album we haven't made

Thanks to our good friend and ace photographer, Nick
Dawkes. He came, he saw, he took a load of photies

there were more than the first night, maybe over a thousand! There was a crush of people unable to get in! Everyone was up for it and it was one of those magical Glastonbury moments. We were so pleased with the Friday night in the Spirit of 71 Café that we never thought Saturday's gig in the Avalon Café could or would come close; but the atmosphere in the tent was amazing, and we were just really proud and pleased with how it had gone, and the fact that at long last we'd done two gigs that were everything we'd hoped the tour would be, but sadly never quite was.

The success of both the Glasto shows has rekindled our passion to get the Folkface bandwagon going again. We always knew we had a decent little product. We felt there was a place for our brand of comedy and music (without really achieving either) but we hadn't quite managed to get it right until Glasto 2011. So Dom and I have big plans for the future. Expect an album and Wembley in 2012 – failing that we'll be in a student union near you, SOON!

Folkface Glastonbury Shopping List

4 x family packs of toilet roll
1 x bumper pack of crisps
5 x wet wipes
10 x packs of paracetamol
100 bottles of cider

@toaster672 @mykek @BiloHobbit @sambroomfield @fayeve @yarner99 @nicguil @heavyhand85 @MarkJ348 @UpYerBumCharity @kaystewartphoto @MaffTee @JollyJenCJ @mattysadler11 @AdzyBeecroft @Babephoenix @brianyearling66 @JoshWadBolton @Brettski01206 @bumblelight @laurayoung26 @KATZ78 @Lethers14 @alisannebell @jamiemcnabb1 @LeighMcCormack @chrissheldon285 @Ctillbrook @SianBallance @kjtew @drivergary1971 @amandakerin @louiseamyellis @fivestarreds @nphow @FrankiiArcher @BenAlldridge @davidburstow @katiefmc87 @PaulaSmith79 @burkmar23 @mattyboyski @NicolejadeRees @Mattyc407 @s_annable @KerriGrice @IWannaHelpFolks @RichTyler7 @GemmaBell32 @KNnicky @loveblissrings @ElliottNHCam @jace_anderson @juliedlacey @SarahCoop11 @JoAnnJ72 @rlyon1986 @Emaleena @danih1991 @Eddibaby @leestevem @cat_holman @kyla_pyle @KellyShanahan14 @mandrossian @buzzrobb @Amy1997_ @morganocc @markc666 @alston_joe @KazParkinson75 @sexyronald89 @Hayley_Mace @simonedoc @Clare_Hunt @dazhawthorn @newmankate @uktrucker11 @MTL2081 @ljtink35 @baznewman @Eleanore_Glynn @ashg4884 @simons_nick @daveshowell69 @TomLEFC @crinio19 @SuperDuperCraig @Jacqui66 @wonder100277 @ArmstrongJake11 @LeahDoddPT @scoobieloo2 @crazeetanya @JamesHavill @natg37 @happytrucker1 @DebG76 @katie_leach @natmel @politepaula @pooley_505 @KillerGipsyFish @rebeccairons @craigl21 @lucy2011efc @yozzerlad @auramashiter @Chiquatitakelly @lisa3111 @BettyBeth_cymru @siftb @RyanChesters @kellymac13 @Kevmondo @rachellogue1 @bobkom @SimonTCRose @harleycrux @taylorrob30 @MarthaPointing @vikkigilson @hankanc @MeJuliee @miv1878 @laSmeg @uplands_blue @Chris_Padget23 @jonboy_t @richdeluchi31 @GeHarrison @ljsotis @nippa21 @matt_killick @ToniStein @SkyHomepage @LynRhiPea @Relic8 @Markpanter @aellis089 @K3rryGraham @Ms_linzi_D @originalVIX @BigBrewUp @ianemmens @Jonny_RD @SusansGosport @berternie104 @LianneTyers @stevemalloy1973 @GudtheGnome @paulantell @nathanmitch91 @TedTrippin @Amy_bennett1983 @Pickled_Onion_B @May_Macleod @razwot1985 @XxxxFlissxxxX @chesh81 @ispy_internet @Debs52 @WrightStuff @Hevstar @syjonesxxx @jdanswiggy1 @ralphster950 @Tweeting_Nic @VictoriaPavry @evans_ellie @leahreed1987 @haribo288 @stdthrash @cameronashaw @spanner3178 @W4nkyWanderer @hells83bells @FacesForXpress @kteft @iron_fist_1964 @Simon4United @StephanieSandal @dpowuk @gavqpr @KerriEvans2 @shereenCFC1888 @Craigiep88 @carlyozz @coombsyim @Mishmell01 @dinohay @MsLozzaloulilei @MariaMargetts @Benjojojam @Filthmeister @jkingy1984 @GherkinCircle @emilysevenoaks @RachelHoney92 @TUPodcast @shadowwolf422 @chiefflorence @Sabrina_Brie @MissNicsF @sgthorse @M71 @Ben_Shaw @MrNathanHarmon @akcooner @small1989 @mand7437 @TheLilCountry @joeyboybarker @davegaston1 @laurahunt26 @scottferguson74 @ClaireOttaway1 @Jack_Mayo @elllmooo @RFieldingMartin @Adam__wright @mltew @Karenwal1985 @s_winnie89 @1875BRFC2011 @bethg1976 @therealkp_83 @befster @paulbaggies71 @JosieeD @ElvisCastle @wightman22 @_HannahLouiseT_ @Swoody87 @Munnsey @Cheapy1 @XxX_jennie_XxX @Bevylar @Mattsenior999 @katy_jill123 @HMSmithie @HannahWh88 @stevec2406 @LouisaKing100 @garybennett118 @zoehannahben @katielaycock @jpats77 @jj_lewis20 @fiona_prince @nicholls_79_2 @PaulBrown15 @helz2727 @ElliotNicol @BMFAO @laurenjayparker @glentarps1310 @sharonmcmaster @mlmleightom @GemmaPhillida @AlanMeikle @TheLyng @iDev8 @kateh46 @robjpoole1984 @cathyellin @ChrisRollinsPip @Chelseajayne_x @onhardy59 @aidangcampbell @CharBrankin @JoshJenkins5 @realdealcraig @Clubpromoworld @joeallison3 @tomonewing @Alison_Hughes90 @NickiHoney @Lorbarca21 @DavidIble25 @RichyBoii @Laurennn_C @benshipp79 @tew190 @chazzymoo96 @J_Pocky @Stewbaca @Micmac1981 @leftfootwinger @luke_b_warm @whoop74 @iceskaterlauren @Random_Richard @xxxAlyshaxxx @TeaMCordeezy @Saffymeg @missalikey @djtwistedb @dantheboxingfan @leejackson @GoonerTom84 @dazsimmo26 @MariosbudLuigi @cubbyRAF @hunto442 @AmyOC1981 @sammylyfordx @williamson_x @Kateeb83 @JackieVerity @Lu29Lu @leechappy74 @kevin090909 @evabuts94 @yvonneherbert @CalunaLimited @Recru1tment @phill74d @davebradders7 @dinky65 @HelziiD @DarkeRob @chipperleah @MatthewHarman1 @grantmynott87 @EuanBazAndrew @TheFitnessMix @shazpots1 @anjhancock @Cbob74 @mmaconachie @bethpearce23 @davidmckee @jabrewer01 @_ski_ @Joshevans21 @IanTodd3 @brownpants2 @deluxe2103 @benslater91 @JamieFord77 @JD141180 @K_Smi12 @stevenagekarl @lewisbedgood @Emskibeat @enkinseb @linzbaggott43 @Greek583 @alisonmartin8 @Paul_Woodward @molly_dolly86 @jemcompton @EmmieBrown1 @sammybingman7 @leighanddean @jess_85 @PMimps83 @HippyDen @The_LongDong @Lauren_Findler @Laurawiggy @meglo90 @bigfish51lb @Dobbers81 @astevo99 @mattyboy000 @clrouise @scotkillieboy @moldybury @NuttyNatty3003 @keri_1 @jaimeiles @dannyjo2011 @Reggie_Fizzle @SophieER93 @BenGladman07 @lewington_peter @scattiehattie88 @DixieD44 @JayneRobinson3 @Toondogwdl @Andysmith1986 @EvoneCymru @azadoody @Rcrowe83 @Leeslade87 @CallMeKempy @Hello_Lori_Mack @emilyrosewaite @alleyne22 @bigbadvoice @greenybum88 @karrydotj @PaulineMarland @DanThomasUK @Tammydaniell @Rezzi79 @w888dyy @Gramboski @massbaileygates @sjmuttock @Cannings19xx @cunniffe1982 @Mattgivo @heathermay1805 @Towser023 @sam576 @DrGilesy @TeresaDodd2 @SquallyC @richo164 @amyjdearing @Brian1701 @Bradders31 @JadieMarie_x @6ftSarah @ChelseaKinsman @louisebarbour @Tressie_Kneip @kemp640 @newtsarella @frewby @CallumCatterall @pauljsheffield @kingroan76 @CGault83 @vousbingbing @S_Campbell7 @vincenunley @Charleodi @hazab11 @busymummichaela @barry3161 @Rachel_French @immytennis29 @davey_gibson @DarnoHannah @davecrowy @espa04 @wallacegrom @Lucyglad @SarahJaffe1 @J0_OConnor @paulmurph14 @meriamjippes @djdawes @mcfcste85 @davidblaikie @finfish79 @RICKYHULL27 @clairelj24 @iambigbarba @debs_weatherill @cutmycostspleas @emmastal @billy_sullivan @TheProofReadr @rekhahaughton @kellyh77 @Jo_Newby @mr_stuartkenney @chimptastick @stu8j @themoonpig @richyrichrx @Girpitt @Greavesie1977 @chalkum @LesleyJones13 @eubenmummy11 @dstuartdouglas @ChrisBranks20 @janeclare63 @justiceben619 @stevengraham82 @StuartRents @MollyBuszard @ArchieBoos @mark197 @reeves87 @lisaastevens86 @dazjamie @PettTv @FrankieCefai @Jamjim @biddy41 @cindersoots @Becwedfern @Smurray28 @Elly_Martyn @Sugarcube82 @JasonPye @RhiannonC1986 @mattyuk75 @harmitfc @webdawg76 @leeakasnappy @1marktyson @mrszoecourt @pbl87 @Ayeshazgj @ep1clm @obeyyourears @lucyperkins12 @KayleeBabe @nettienoo1702 @nicola_hampton @LornaB141 @nickjeffers_no1 @moranis10 @Wendywoowoo72 @montyperves @AlanaLCompton @Jemma_Gilb @skinnytrucker35 @Ja5onDougla5 @chaseoverton87 @nornmanwk @joslin21 @jacko15021976 @Dreena72 @jaylees289 @AbbieGowen @CarlyMomber83 @Bowdi1985 @hellybelly81 @jakecousins44 @Kelius1 @AdamJohnCullen @steveporter92 @ouisep2402 @ten_twinkletoes @MetalMidknight @ingo0412 @ClareD87 @woolie999 @amarandith @MeganAstall @grahamceast @kenneth_waters @Ash1285 @jo7319 @LiamAWalsh @BlackpoolNorth @MrsAkehurst @discodjsame @EDSPETROW @ezzamae1999 @ticmike3 @joelfishfry @SketchleyLane @Junobabii @Zo_Rose @DImaher @KieranBonner @kylefarrant @hofnar @adamjcollins @rolymay @Wedgie_1988 @Vic_Spencer @lil_nicnak @ListenToMeMoan @craigie89harris @sophie_green2 @shaun_zeebs @PinkFish_Lucy @LooNoo75 @RobertPilkingto @Jackson_Patrick @Darran_Yates @mikeyd333 @CHRISserious91 @pronaghKelly @kirstyloo @CeriSimmonds @Bigdave867 @AMPoade @jenmopsies @Acerxx @Gordonmcd46 @Izodynamic81 @mikeydonartin @missthompson77 @untied30 @ReeceCalderbank @seanio87 @glenneldridge1 @Kelsdg81 @allanb1903 @Sweet_SW13 @saunddog @alexishonfire @shelleywhite147 @CCJ310582 @Claterisimo @lauralizstubbs @PeachMelba84 @RosieEvill @AdventuresInRad @richbull76 @bozretro @richardgibney @godsofghana75 @Matt_Simmons33 @missk007 @sarahnewing73 @sarahgilliam1 @lynneroberts10 @CLeachyy @mr_jones2010 @pauljones270382 @Emmi_J_T @Buddwiser89 @johnducati @sophiejoypaul @rayraslnier @shanacollings @rayevans81 @ian_doc @Brown_Owl_4thCB @northerndelboy @JoshACowell @jamesrooke @Adam_J_Parsons @mrskbenney @dowle86 @MJTucks @AmbaaHendo @mikedorr1972 @sgrindlay @turripotter @therealjonnyx @robsalt1 @jdcs1981 @lucindadonnison @danspindle79 @maryfox13 @spunkiey_123 @PaulHewittKiwi @leigh_6899 @BJL_wa12 @Pittsthepixie @benbrown97 @MUFC_Redman @lwescott @lukebailey17 @albahoggy85 @WTMBF @feehaig @pajspencer @scott82mason @dibley1982 @str20081 @VKay77 @sarahbeggs123 @lee_chuckles @JAM_2605 @Swindon_ultras @CarolByrne6 @blongey @loti83 @Emast_boys @rhiannonjones2 @KTLousiee @lizbrooks80 @hayleyball42 @MrJohnBrooks @rickstar125 @lookingrough @timmyprompt @jbloc @Linnydot @spiv85 @Sally_Sunbeam @daisymay0768 @jan0512 @Lupips @andcah1966 @Heskeyisgod @suzierees @TiaraS85 @storadora @VictoriaPayne2 @AD__Cook @Adders79 @tinamchale1 @ChristelLuise @Dottydowdy @JWS_999 @kimmieeee @TheNath @GemmaHearnden @imsocool_28 @davidhoylecool @markrusher @rhonamcsherry @thecbear1985 @paulbutters11 @jamiedavies123 @_michelle_evans @searle_lee @mppayne76 @hulhul11 @mcoops73 @houseofdowler @Katiescott04 @noodle9252 @PaulGrant1977 @Mste89 @spooner91 @sophieglanfield @moggs350

@samanthahaggis / Will McKenzie
If you had to release an album of all your favourite songs,
what would you call the album?

Idiot Village. A nice name for an album or a book.

@wickers5 / Jennie W J
What's the furthest distance you think you could cover
#shufflingonyourbottom?

From here to Northampton.

@LizRoseKnight / Liz Rose Knight
Would you rather have lion's paws for hands and feet
or a giraffe's neck?

Lion's paws – having a giraffe's neck would make you far
more conspicuous when shopping.

@JayRG1990 / Jamie Gillmore
If you could be a type of sandwich with any type of filling...
which would you be?

I'd be an all day breakfast sandwich, always.

@nwiggins02 / Nicola Wiggins
Why do walk about with barbie's shoes in your pocket ;)
and how do you cope with early mornings?

It's a dad thing.

@TracyBideford / Tracy Green

My husband @iphonedevuk wants to know if you'd drop 'comedy' from your name if you were no longer funny?

I've never been funny.

@koisteeeee / Kirstie Eley

Out of all the guests you've had on the Chris Moyles Show, whom would you choose as an ice skating partner?

Kylie Minogue because she's small and easy to lift. AND she is shorter than me!

@pauldavis1976 / Paul Davis

Would you rather see Moyles lose 3 stone and achieve a ripped look or Everton win the carling cup?

Everton win the cup, every time.

@LesneyB / Lesney Billings

What's your TV guilty pleasure? And will you marry me?

Location Location Location, and you never know.

@according2dg / David Green

There was lots of money, now there is none. Does someone still have it, somewhere? Is it down the back of the sofa?

Probably.

@Real_RobDJ / Rob DJ
I have maths question for you 25 x 20 -163 + 50,000 = ?
Do this on a calculator and turn it upside down!

Ha.

@CDA92 / Chris Armstrong
Would you rather be attacked by one horse-sized duck or
a twelve duck-sized horses?

It's a good question. One horse sized duck 'cos being a
man I can't multitask.

@guriben / Ben Smith
Do you remember rehearsing with The Garden Party in
Martin Ross's mum's house in 1989 or thereabouts? You
played drums.

I think so. It's vaguely ringing a bell.

@simonmclaren / Simon McLaren
How did u and Chris first meet and then start working with
each other?

We met @ Radio 1.

@nmc216 / Natalie Cranny
Best ever Everton goal? Mine was @WayneRooney
against Arsenal to win 2-1! What a day!

Mine too!

@joemclay79 / Jow McClay
Hey Dave Joe from Glasgow here what's it like doing the voice over for coach trip?

Fun and an honour to do it. It's a top show and I'm proud to be a part of it.

@myates25 / Matthew Yates
You narrate coach trip (obviously). Would you take part yourself and who would be your partner in crime?

Good question. Yes I would and I'm not sure.

@captainhut / Robert Jennings
What's the difference between an ECG and an EKG in medicine?

N.F.C.

@Nic_Fletcher / Nicola Fletcher
Did you ever want to host your own radio show? Or do you enjoy being a 'sidekick' too much?

I enjoy being a sidekick, I love the banter and it's not my name above the door.

@charlienasher / Charlie Nash
What do you call cheese that's not yours?

Nacho cheese.

@Martharley41 @abipaige94 @shrinkmybills1 @lewace07 @stokieflo @lyndajm2964 @emma4lee @Gruff75 @Jedward_ftw1 spuddu69 @piersbrad @webb_simon @amy28craggs @74gaffer @Jadelee83 @natwalker1683 @mole6653 @flixelpix @kfb1979 stevesmith677 @Kobelcotom @nealherbert @laraegood @Sarahlouisereay @msbrightside81 @al__tee @sammfieuk @ScottThaxt @domtech90 @Sassieb @kewell883 @mike10cc @lewis_tanner1 @stc60 @Nikki_RCampbell @Nassauboard @craigmc1983 ThainMark @ryandunlop85 @NoOneFollower @ArtParky @srs1971s @MattG1981 @mike_rhodes007 @fisherman343 @florencebarr @Hel_Womo @nooobie @Beverrlina @suzeparke @Chalky_Whitey @AbbieTWSykes @Jamiec1986 @danielrainbird @popznbobz JohnMaddock1 @connorholmes4 @1987tinytony @RobertWeston1 @thebestfaru @adele322 @Reeveisatwit @FarhanShal @JoeKaniecki9 @mr_icklepickle @IsobelHayward @toppers1984 @RoadsBead @000BrownLyes @smroc @out8b1t @York_Festiva @c_medhurst @Sez0177 @rose_harri @JesikaTorossian @Kindereggs15 @rm_dawson @MichaelDraprr @Jezamiah @couchy86 Riley404 @x_Nicola_Cassix @shatters84 @Andyfnwck @stumpywar @trebon1 @lauramreid @ginagibbons8 @Luubyloo19 @gemsb84 @no8smash @scary1802 @B7OWN @GrahamGoodship @princesssarah60 @LookAtMyMotor @VB84254 bigbluenose1982 @DawnLBurrows @KJGrocott @foxTimfox @Roscopico @darnellmichael @Caleb_Not_Onlys @topman69 FlashForman @WampitWeb @CecBarber @stephb36 @jackg91 @TimCarhart7 @tig30 @debbietyas @talulatornado @kristianj @DocTCS @thealbanyclub @KatrinaLeffs @Becki_HL @PeekaBooFaces @dannystewart89 @jakepickford @timmo99 @david_obi @macca660 @SaharDanesh @HolForbes @ozzzy91 @carlyhesp @vodkasally @chickadeeee4 @inkedmarcus @pervster @jo parris85 @garethfindley @EmilyDThompson @jimfriend76 @AnnaFairnington @tom_causer @Fluffyhead @ladycharly1 @jeffers19 @RobGreenhalgh @1Asquith @Fat_Out @Aamir1Adam @emmaburton55 @lagertripagain @StarKidChloe @umammaguma philgasson @Burls1987 @IanClark75 @M1G9S88 @Turrasuz @dooseg32 @alexbrown1987 @tombruv @richmoody @ianpetergibs @Mazz89 @Hombre_no_hair @Mattyp282 @kleechambo @Tommylee5000 @Ni1786 @EDSengines @paulbretton @craigspudha @spookylaw @dignifiedkench @scottw8e @ErinGalway @MegsElliott @raindrop345 @FayGittins @juniorgiles @chris_gj @la Wedgbury @t_gillen @johno1975 @NatalieF86 @MicEngland @SJT25 @Vonsteve @NatashaStill @kanderson221 @ju_ferguson midgetjonesy81 @Discopc @WarrenFandango @Siriuskay @princesspea76 @Morris_Michaela @adie1976 @pcellblockhfan JosabelleT @vickieejones @jude_marshall @Bravelaney @mph256 @stephen33horn @fidyson @cp1974col @Daviebarr74 @i_hat you_ass @andreah99 @sarahjpickett @craigtbull @rogerwilliams01 @emz_moz @JWoll06 @ShelleyTaylor22 @AnnaCorbe @beddy1981 @Stevep_897 @kerryroxby @andyham11 @hwinters92 @JRG113 @leighsear @sazzlep2011 @claireclj @NicolaAshle @lynseytabbenor @loubylou46 @TheClivey @eggbilby @CShillingford @MaureenBoyle2 @Octoberbilly @Face1980 @AdMaine lisarickards @Lizforsyth @MatthewJ11 @ProFalconer @BrodieMarc @beelaw91 @SPanther9 @TheRobster86 @Libbyemilymae AndyHighton1 @BullensBantam @JudyL33 @lisa191221 @takkatakk @jennytelllya @clucka1409 @ThePeppermints1 @emmahen @jonnygetty1 @Stuey_gran @michellekieran @catfarrell83 @bottomburp2010 @emilyv25 @the_real_holls @Ellebess85 @sparkle_ @WelchSharon @3diana @jamesdurham71 @chrisrarger @Lauren91rbf @celestinewest @AnnaLouThomson @Mike7knight ClareMiller1 @debs_112 @katielaing17 @jasebee101 @Sarahlousl @traceytheringto @waynerh1973 @VacuousSponge @Walkir @SophieMG_1995 @LauraWilcoxson3 @paulreynolds84 @Steviefisher85 @steeley_b @beccae1986 @Loueze0112 @mattster155 EleanorusEliza @iancally @Karleen_x @darylblo @holface89 @skybluemick @LeighAnn1974 @Lady_bee_coops @BethMaguire1 sezzylu @bigandy4or5 @SingletonKatie @Kat_Sandford @hookedoncarp @williamhart4 @DREWSTAAR @strongarm @TibbsMonster @johill3 @ZielinskiJen @murph_cat @chrisramsey100 @RACH_HANNAH @LozaHB @annestfflur1 @Redmen05 woody9901 @stewartcott @SFletch8 @fozzyrozz @Ten_Bears @dcastle2 @Cormac79 @nathpoloedwards @Emily_Russell84 sammymarck @m_griffo @vectorboro @lsparkyl @PhilisRoss @LindsayPoole32 @rose_posey @hatwell88 @Clatlee @MissVixHardi @hellomrsh @jameseelliott @iwanttogotoOz @sazhman @revoltstyle @davidwar64 @kevede1980 @ratty_85 @sweeweed @TSVS1507 @cemetery_cherry @darrenvilla @TimGearey @00daz007 @andynye1983 @renaeoldham @lady_vince @clairelgreen TheJoshwink @RUBYSLIPPERS6 @Jonnymac_85 @elliebobster @abuey00 @paulbrown67 @WIZ_Messenger @LeighHoward88 MikeyGyppo @jamieolle1122 @Littlewoodc @ILostmypen @_BIG_LEE_ @sazzlej2011 @CrowleyAli @willywams @Martin_R_Fr @LeeRiches1 @KateelRQ @Mitchie_Moo_Moo @ClurSkip @higgznyx @newwwwj @beccy1888 @Ajyates75 @pastortomcc @Smithy_Thomas @amy10024 @shaunno30 @malcybaby @NeilDWheeler @dazwhitey70 @AmandaTomkins2 @PhoebeWildHair LeoandtheLion @joelfigueira @Paulalby @tommyk1 @Ffi_Davies @roz1203 @haydyson @futter21smiles @wannabejock @robbbbbinn @milesteve77 @mathewhamer @ozbum82 @kristababee @Laurakathryn7 @chris_k2011 @FORRESTERS4WALL Billmcghee @Kezzerlittle @famedapone @trishtrashtash @JoeFrecknall @Pumba133 @Elaine_Bahia @Sammieboots @mattallsop1 @toni_starling @laurarenniebds @mamajojo26 @stackerstu @tuccy29 @Caris_Iles @applesimon @Mollie_Green @tweetingstokie MagnusPersonnel @dactaz @DanGeyStrath @pltkrdnz @hehunts @nacht__ @katytann @Hollyander28 @morvydoc @LouiseNicols @turtle080310 @4444elaine @assemblydirect @lizzylou1280 @steveyeu @BrittasEmpire @catlewin @si_BeBen @MissAllen @sjcardiff @Andytay79 @Shepsygal1991 @elliepurnell @DelythEOwen26 @doodlepinki @huskins30 @1cinni @HayleyBarnes5 Mazda2309 @kittywalks1 @manney_b @markfletcher83 @Evie_K26 @heathermcneill1 @theno1gunit @waltdisley @jaye_pattis @tom_boxall @giant_hands @jpt1984 @Bladestotop2 @Laura_Crossan @want20 @RyanGIANT @unemployeddj @Ant_G_Gardir @MWardLFC @gareth_brooks @HaydnBBA @ineedelp14 @photogirlruns @caroline_barlow @craigbeauwater @rusty_mca @hgilks bleasek @mummy_Star__ @beastofingy @jessharve @donlourob @Vicks2 @McMockers @edwardburns99 @haltoi01 @Fifi_85 lindasparey @nicolaholman1 @MarcusSaunders @vip0194 @leasty @JamesBarnes1979 @masterw990 @Sarahp0404 @gavroberts @SeanMerson @gemwilks @thestav82 @MartinPBerry @lisadeeboo @paulparky @biddyrich @mummynash @nathnorm1 dawnosman @jonnylove25 @LauraJJames @courteney_jane @baby_essie @Modalmart @steeddyp @Jenny_BudgetB @RebecAR(@daddywaberto @cordantium @TERIMALLY @jackburrows_2 @jlllea @milliepeeches @PAULYIDO1 @JACLOU77 @kaz_gray DanielPiper_ @SpikeDarbyshire @helenlowe @TheMrEncore @goonerleestaps @ben_h99 @cupcakecoomber @krin_b Carl77James @ObeyMyHat @nade43 @AbbytheCat84 @ChloeLawie_x @AlanTervit @JamSam261 @shane1927 @tangoba @CazT1978 @craigwilko83 @YTJ05 @timbuckley23 @lyndaj181 @michyclairey @hewittdido @DoubleVisionBnd @danielduggan @smingey69 @kriswalt @BryonyDJones @jgillespie79 @sarahrose1234 @RachyBaby6969 @TheMatty_P_B @PaulNorton @casutton1989 @jumpafitness @thewantedlove1 @Beth_TW_GMD3_xx @ckirby38 @ellisisla11 @kraftykirsty @Big_Gay_Follc @angibabes @steveburgess83 @unigeek80 @farmboy1994 @CathySco_ @EmilySco @SRose1977 @byrne_neil @l_flesher leeallard @gerryconiff @AstonLivingston @lairdypop @porky32 @TheBeccaClarke @joby246 @inspiration_iis @DCFONTANA Davep06 @conorlaing @abargh @kieshaspence @colinsingleton @tattoo_jock @Maz294 @doddadinho @mrpalm3r @Jac Cheeseman @mistresshlc @dooseg1 @julia82 @alexjaynewoods @ams2220 @AndrewGallivan1 @Lucy_Isabella @goughatronic vickilewis33 @katmore32 @bryelly74 @Chapman9 @Robinson23Laura @MrsR_N @lcbt @HCDigitalPhoto @MASH4 @benjamesbason @ria1308 @linsb24 @mc_rosie @marklappin45 @kgall27 @MTSGames87 @Daisybrewster @Jo_1067 madmoolou123 @garrymunro1888 @pbdham @tiberiansun @Kirkyy97 @A_Grinham @DCtheG11 @LauraDorara @Richardmke @shanf1fan @BradBlackburn54 @5kyman @sammygads @chris_dobbie @juddyboy79 @LyndseyD88 @Scarybiscuits84 @Jodi Stafford @oggyswfc @PetalPells @mariahh_me @soul_man_boris @nomiedwards @ScarletAd @nickp450 @annmaried2002 GaryDLockett @CwmgwrachAdam @Rich_Wato @CSIPComputing @philclark76 @NicholasBall23 @louanastasia @Louisemarie @Sarahmerrien @JoeLMaybury @JasonAppleyard @SeanCurrie2 @EmmaGearing @steph_louise91 @Lauren_critoph @Becoa @shezzy1972 @leehorden @ellenandnick @lucylangridge @richie_edwards @gill3891 @Buzzmonkey90 @vtecmatt @LauAshley lazygiraffe @kawkawkaw_ @mandimaustin @ReillyLucy @timbo_g08 @annemariebell @MattLorimer @drunkjellyfish @trolleydolly @mark_874 @1983_jamesgreen @luciagiorno @LauraBADDAMS @lizirasket @crazyrawlings @vikki233 @Rbatters @pinkryan VinnyVinton @00nothing34 @kevineden1 @rjmol1988 @Sosmummy @rachybabes12 @HolThom @gilders1100 @gazzpjor. @BethMayCooper @xsam_jones85x @guessgirl6 @DarylHasellSims @hayleyamy87 @ishtah84 @adamwest85 @Tom_ellis_1 @donnacarne @m_j_proc @Thechrishartry @MarieHarrison78 @major_barry @SchofieldLizzie @walton84 @lhunter675 BMWscott21 @Adam__7 @We_talk_RNS @knoxie97 @scottrenwick8 @Abbie_Anderson_ @pmaduk @Animaledge @daveyra

A DAY IN THE LIFE OF DAVE . . .

Despite what many of you may think, my days are actually very busy. The common misconception is that we do our show and then piss around for the rest of the day; and while that may have been true at one time when we were all young and immature, these days we do genuinely fill our days and work proper hours. I tend to have a few jobs on the go at once outside Radio 1, whether it's ice skating, DJ-ing up and down the country, presenting on Radio 5 Live, doing voice-overs for *Coach Trip* or even writing a book. On the one hand I'm always just grateful for the work; it also comes as something of a necessity when you've got a hefty mortgage, plus rent, two divorces and a young daughter to pay for. It's an expensive business.

A BAD DAY

WEDNESDAY, 6 JULY

4.30 a.m. – Alarm goes off. I make that all-too-familiar mistake of pressing the 'off' button instead of 'snooze'. I don't wake up.

5.30 a.m. – I wake up. This is bad. I peer outside my window to see if my cab is still there. I can't see. I call the cab firm who, thank God, assure me it's waiting. After a quick trucker's wash (spray under the arms with Lynx Africa), I throw on a T-shirt, shorts and flip-flops (it's early July) and I'm out the door.

5.45 a.m. – My cab leaves for the studio. We're pushing it as we're on-air in 45 minutes and I live 25 miles outside London. I scribble down that morning's Tedious Link and Car Park Catchphrase on the notepad section of my iPhone (I don't have any paper).

6.29 a.m. – I crash into the studio as we're about to go live. Just as the news and sport jingle is finishing, Chris gives me a hug amd says good morning pal. I get a knowing nod from Dom and Tina as I quickly print off Tedious Link and Car Park Catchphrase. I'm in front of my mic, just in time, with a cup of tea in my hand and ready for the show – sort of.

6.30 a.m. – The show goes pretty seamlessly, Eddie Izzard comes in and is as charming as ever.

10 a.m. – We're handing over to Fearne Cotton, and I'm daydreaming away, pleased to have the show over with for another day. My mind is on the big celeb bash I'm going to that night at ITV boss Peter Fincham's house in Notting Hill. Everyone from ITV is going to be there: Ant and Dec, Jeremy Kyle, Holly Willoughby, the cast of *TOWIE*! I'd been invited on the back of my *Dancing on Ice* appearances – it was a real honour to have been asked.

During the handover to Fearne, we have the usual banter and Fearne starts harping on about this ITV party she went to last night. So I ask: 'Fearne, is there another one of those parties on tonight?'

Typically, I'd got my dates muddled, oops. Moron. Turns out I've missed the biggest work do I'd been invited to all year. At least it made for good radio as the rest of the gang and Fearne took the mickey. Hopefully I'll get an invite next year.

11 a.m. – I spend the morning doing office guff – emails and writing a little skit for the show. I get a phone call from my ex-wife, Jayne, saying that she's got to go to a gym class at two and asking if I can take my daughter Nicole swimming in the afternoon.

12 p.m. – I step outside my office into an out-of-the-blue summer monsoon – I'm wearing a lycra T-shirt, shorts and flip-flops. In my haste to get out of the door that morning I didn't bother checking on the weather.

12.30. – I go to pick up my car (which I'd left in town the night before) from Broadcasting House. I'm wet to my core from the thunderstorm that's drowning London outside.

1 p.m. – I sit in a puddle of rain in my car seat all the way up the A40 to pick up my daughter. En route I get pulled over for speeding – 60 in a 50 zone. Shit. After ten minutes of deliberating, mercifully, the policeman lets me off.

2 p.m. – Pick up Nicole – go swimming. Such is my luck today that I wouldn't be surprised if it was the one day that a rogue shark was loose in the Amersham swimming pool. Thankfully all went well. The only good part of my day.

4 p.m. – Back at my flat and I open a letter from North Wales Police: £60 and three points for doing 37 in a 30 zone last week, when I went to Anglesey for my Mum's birthday. THIS IS NOT MY DAY.

6 p.m. – I go to drop Nicole off with her mother. I drive very carefully.

7 p.m. – I get home, lock the doors and just hope that nothing else can go wrong.

This is the invite to one of the biggest showbiz gatherings in British telly. I got the date wrong and missed it. What a NOB!

DO YOU FIND IT IMPOSSIBLE TO GET UP IN THE MORNING?

DOES YOUR ALARM CLOCK NOT HAVE THE POWER TO WAKE YOU FROM YOUR DEEPEST SLUMBER?

Well if that's the case then you need new **ROBOCOCK**

ROBOCOCK is a lifesize aluminium cockerel that can emit a realistic 'Cock-a-Doodle–Do' at up to 8,000 decibels!

No more sleeping in, and no more rushing to work, if you've got new ROBOCOCK.

Just attach the cock extension lead to the mains, place ROBOCOCK in your garden or porch, and bingo… No more snoozing, and no more lazy neighbours too!

GET ROBOCOCK AND GET GOING IN THE MORNING

'COCK-A-DOODLE-DO' IT! …YOU FAT LAZY BASTARD!

Robocock can be heard within a range of 4 miles and may interfere with emergency sirens and air traffic control systems

A GOOD DAY

FRIDAY, 8 JULY

4.30 a.m. – Alarm goes off. I'm not that bad in the morning if I've had enough sleep (six hours), which is a good thing given my profession. I'm pleased I haven't slept through, which isn't that uncommon (see A Bad Day). I know that I've got one of those days where I don't have a spare five minutes from when the alarm goes off. I get up, shower and get dressed.

5.15 a.m. – Leave the house. It's an easy slip into work at that time, so I get into the office for 6 a.m., no problems.

6 a.m. – Say hello to everyone, have a cuppa and do that morning's Car Park Catchphrase and Tedious Link in our office above the studio.

6.30 a.m.–10 a.m. – I do the show. It's the British Grand Prix weekend, so there's lots of hype around that. From 9 a.m. we have our Golden Hour – always a nice weekly marker point.

10 a.m. – Office chores. Believe it or not we do have proper desks, just like all you office people. I have to send a few emails, post some mail and I'm supposed to write my material for the show now, but I always leave it until the following morning.

11 a.m. – I have to leg it off to Halo Post Production Studios – five minutes walk around the corner from Radio 1 – to do the scripted voiceover for *Coach Trip*. This week is a celebrity special with Michael Barrymore, Brian Belo (from *Big Brother*) and John McCririck. The coach is travelling from Nice to Monaco. Throughout the episode, a deluded Barrymore keeps trying to sign autographs for French people who have no idea who he is. I've got to do three episodes in a two-hour session. It basically involves me drinking tea and chatting over the rough edit.

1.30 p.m. – I'm running a little bit late and have to get up to Harlesden in north-west London to meet Guyan, who's helping me write this book.

1.50 p.m. – On my way to Harlesden I pull into a petrol station on the Harrow Road to grab a ham and cheese sandwich that I eat in the car.

4 p.m. – After my two-hour writing session, I head home to my flat in Beaconsfield. I get changed and sort out my music for a DJ gig tonight. Usually I play student unions or local pubs. Tonight I'm playing the A-list shindig that is Phillip Schofield's daughter's 18th birthday party. Oh yes, I'm big-time, baby!

6 p.m. – Pop over for tea with my Aunty Carol and to see some of my cousins who are usually spread around the globe but are all in the country at the moment.

7 p.m. – Head over to Phillip Schofield's house in Berkshire to DJ at his daughter's birthday. I'm certainly no DJ to the stars or their children, but I've been very kindly invited to DJ at Molly Schofield's 18th and it's a great do. It's a fun Moulin Rouge theme with a marquee and all that. After my set, I go to sit on the grown-ups' table with Phillip, his wife and some aunties and uncles for a few beers before getting a taxi home for the very respectable hour of midnight.

THE HORSE AND GROOM
YEARS

Behind every great male friendship – or 'bromance', as it's now called in Hollywood – there is a great pub. Back in those early days at Radio 1, Chris and I became afternoon drinking buddies very quickly. We were the only people we knew who were free and finished work by lunchtime so we'd go round the corner to the Horse and Groom, which soon became our local. It's a proper old-fashioned boozer that's the same today as it always has been – nicotine-stained walls, heavily patterned bench seats and pub stools, a dartboard, pinball machine, frosted windows and a good choice of crisps, nuts and even mini poppadoms.

At 11.30 a.m. most days we'd walk in as Ian, the Glaswegian landlord, had just unlocked the door. By the time we'd gone round the bar to the snug at the back he'd have our pints poured and waiting for us. It was a bit like the classic American sitcom *Cheers*, even though Ian didn't look anything like Ted Danson. It got to the point where we spent more time there than at home. In fact, it was like our living room, where we'd have little catnaps on the sofas in the snug at the back.

People would always know they could find us there – there was a steady stream of colleagues who'd always pop in for a pint. Still to this day I know every squeak of every door in that pub. We were both 23 when we started going to the Horse and Groom, so had no responsibilities except to play pinball and darts in our local. As different people we knew would come in and out of the pub throughout the day, it was a bit like our own chat show (this is probably a very grand way of looking at it!) where we'd have a little natter with them before they'd go back to work or home or whatever, and then somebody else would come in and sit in the hot seat! We got to meet loads of people, and soon we pretty much knew everything about who was doing what to whom and all the insider gossip!

If we'd been for a few beers in the Horse and Groom after work, Chris would go one way back to his flat above Baker Street tube, and I'd head in the opposite direction towards Tottenham Court Road and jump on the number 73 bus back to my flatshare in Highbury – only to wake up in Stoke Newington, or worse, Tottenham. I once even woke up in Victoria, where the route starts. It must have got to the end of the line in Tottenham and gone back. I'd been on the bus for three hours! Not big and not clever, but sometimes an occupational hazard of getting up at silly o'clock and then having a few jars. Lack of sleep and ale are not the best combination for keeping alert, which is why my dozing off is something that has been well documented over the years.

Lots of people presumed that because we were on the radio, we were living a celebrity lifestyle and going to media parties – which couldn't have been further from the truth. We lost days, weeks, months and years to that pub – it was a golden era of fags, beer, darts and fruit machines. Except we were both terminally single, which, in hindsight, was probably due to the fact that the Horse and Groom was the last pub in London where you would meet girls – which is probably why we didn't.

In fact, the only time I remember any woman of note being there was when we brought Kelly Brook in. A few years later, when we were doing the Saturday show, we'd often take our guests for a pint afterwards, if they were up for it. One week Kelly Brook came along with us – you should have seen the bleary-eyed gawps of disbelief from the old soaks as she strutted through the pub behind them all sat on bar stools. She was wearing tight jeans and an even tighter top, and her journey to the loo created a kind of Mexican wave that went from one end of the bar to the other, as the old boys craned their heads round and followed her path to the ladies. Some of them turned round so much that they had difficulty staying on their stools. It was very funny.

That pub will always hold a special place in my heart. It was where Chris and I really established our friendship and where many of the creative seeds for the show were first sown.

I'd like to say that the Horse and Groom era came to an end because we both grew up and moved on, but that wasn't quite the truth. It got to the point where the office would start calling us on the pub's phone with whatever work query there might be that day. We'd got way too predictable, so we thought we needed to become more elusive. We didn't move very fast and we certainly didn't move very far, so with that our tenure of the old sofas of the Horse and Groom slowly fizzled out. I still pop in every once in a blue moon and it's not changed one bit. It's somewhere I think I'll always love.

IBIZA

As Chris and I moved up in the world we never forgot our Horse and Groom roots, but our job provided us with the occasional opportunity to socialise in more exotic environments, such as Ibiza. The summer of 1998 saw what felt like the whole of

Radio 1 head out to the white isle to broadcast their shows. It made sense that all the people like Judge Jules and Pete Tong were out there, but I never quite got what the relevance was of our show to Ibiza. I wasn't complaining, however, and was very excited about our first trip abroad.

Suffice to say, we all had a right old laugh. It was the year that Zoë Ball and Fatboy Slim got together and there was a really fun party atmosphere among all the DJs. Chris and I flew out to do a couple of shows and stayed in a sort of chalet complex with a lovely pool just outside San Antonio. Our studio was set up in a villa about ten minutes' drive away – it was all very nice.

One of my very few responsibilities on this trip was to be in charge of what's known as a programme box – the container with all the music CDs, scripts and all the other essentials to do with the show.

On our first night we all went out in San Antonio before heading back to our poolside bar where we were staying. I had a few too many and got chatting to some girl at whose chalet I then ended up.

Night swiftly turned into morning and I woke up an hour late for the show! I'll never forget the cold sweat and churn of stomach adrenalin as I hopped out the door and off to the studio. People had been trying to find me – and the programme box – for hours. It wasn't a good look at all. I was given quite an icy reception as I bumbled into the studio, except from Chris, who thought it was hilarious, and was happy to be provided with such rich material to chat about. So my disappearance became the plot of that particular show. Of course, my Mum and Dad heard and were, naturally, very concerned. I managed to worm my way into the last bit of the show, where more ribbing took place. But while it was all laughs in the studio, I knew there'd be trouble brewing for me when I got back to London.

I got a fully deserved written warning when I got back, so was on my best behaviour for the following few months. And it was at least four years before we were invited back to Ibiza again.

Thankfully, things didn't get too serious and I never got fired. The lovely Lisa l'Anson – who was presenting her show at lunchtime that weekend from the same villa as us – stole most of the bosses' attention after she went completely AWOL for roughly 24 hours. Her disappearance far outweighed my little indiscretion. It was a brilliant smokescreen – so thank you, Lisa.

THE WORST SLOT ON RADIO

Here we go again – another rant about early mornings, but they're a dominant theme of my life, so a dominant theme of this book. It's a commonly held belief that I have some of the worst hours in broadcasting. Well, I don't. While the Breakfast Show hours are pretty anti-social, nothing quite competes with Early Breakfast Show's 4–6.30 a.m.

It's a completely odd and unnatural time to be working. These days I get up at about 4.30 – ridiculously early. But there was a time when Chris and I were getting up at 2.30. A lot of people do it as a late night and go to bed after the show. But in my experience you just can't do that, although everyone is different I guess. To really make it work, I suppose you should be going to bed at 6.30, but who wants to do that? So, I'd still go to bed at 10-ish and get up at 2.30. It's a horrible and bizarre twilight existence. The only people up working at that time were the pimps and hookers in King's Cross that I would drive past on my everyday commute.

The show is seen as a show for insomniacs, security guards and lorry drivers, which it basically is. But there's a golden 30 minutes between 6 and 6.30 when you're dipping a toe into primetime radio. The final half-hour is when Chris would bring out some of his best material. For the most part it was a time-filling slot, and we were certainly given a free rein by the BBC. So Chris and I got to experiment with our act quite drastically. We used to play an on-air game called throwing sugar lumps at the studio clock, which was pretty much as it sounds.

From those very early days, I think what made us click was that our sense of humour was very similar and we found each other funny, which was the most important thing in setting a solid foundation on which to build the show.

GETTING ONE OVER CHRIS

Chris will be the first to admit that he's the ultimate radio anorak. All he's wanted in his life is to be a DJ, ever since he was a little boy. It's what makes him so good at what he does. Unlike some of us, he's someone who really served his apprenticeship in the industry. Coming through local radio he's learned every trick in the book and written a few himself. We all know he's extremely quick-witted, but what's not quite as well known is his technical in-studio ability. His skills way pre-date the digital revolution that's taken over the media world. He's from the school of splicing and sticking reels of tape together. His technical radio production skills are impeccable – the best, I'd say.

I guess that's why he's the top dog in British radio, and has been for some time. Such are his technical skills and know-how that getting an on-air surprise in is next to impossible. Except for this one, very sweet, time on his birthday.

Every year on Chris's birthday we plan a surprise show for him. We've done all sorts of things. We've done the show from his house, from bars, the BT Tower, we have had Abi Titmuss jump out of a cardboard box, all of that stuff. So, around the time that Will Kinder was our producer, a few years ago, we decided to get in some very, very special guests. It would top everything we'd done before!

So on the big day, the studio is abuzz with birthday cheer. Chris has got a big party planned in a central London bar later and we're all off on holiday for two weeks afterwards. Midway through the show, Will Kinder – aka 'Grey'ead' – says to Chris: 'Just push that fader up.' As he fades up you hear guitars tuning and drumsticks banging together and then –

'One, two, one, two, three, four . . .'

Chris's jaw dropped to the ground. He couldn't believe that U2 were playing live on his show for his birthday. Unfortunately the satellite link broke down at the end of the track and we got cut off so Chris didn't get to speak to Bono and the boys. He was cock-a-hoop with his birthday surprise nonetheless. Who wouldn't be? He'd had U2 play live on his show, and by anybody's standards that's meganormous.

For the rest of the day Chris was like a kid at Christmas, delighted that the biggest band in the world would play for him on his show for his birthday! He told everyone at the party that night. We all went off on our holiday very happy, none more so than Chris. Even our big boss, Andy Parfitt – 'Parf Daddy' – was delighted, saying: 'This is a coup for Chris, isn't it?' Even the *Daily Star* ran a piece on it the following day.

However, there were a few rumblings in senior circles, with Jo Whiley apparently not happy that we'd managed to get U2 on our show when she and her producers had been told that they weren't available at the moment and were away recording their new album.

Fast-forward two weeks, to the live show after we've returned from our holiday:

Dave: 'We have a game, Chris, called "Guess What?"'

Chris: 'Is this similar to "Guess Who?" by any chance?'

Dave: 'It is; it requires some of the similar elements.'

Chris: 'Does the game require some music?'

Dave and Will: 'No, I wouldn't build it up.'

Chris plays generic game-show backing music anyway.

Dave: 'Basically myself, Will and Lizzy have done something really bad – a really bad thing.'

Chris (*still playing game-show music in the background*): 'Have you stolen something from me?'

Dave: 'No.'

Chris: 'You slept with my ex?'

Will: 'No, it's not that bad.'

Dave: 'Just start with some "yes"/"no" questions.'

Chris (*getting a little irate now*): 'Is this something to do with me?'

Dave: 'Yes.'

Chris: 'Is this something that I'll be embarrassed about?'

Lizzy: 'No.'

Chris: 'Was this done deliberately?'

Dave: 'Kind of.'

Chris: 'Is this something that has gone wrong?'

Will: 'No, it went very well actually.'

Dave: 'Yeah, quite the opposite.'

Chris: 'Is it something to do with my phone?'

Dave: 'No.'

Chris: 'Have you told somebody something?'

Dave: 'No.'

Lizzy: 'We told you something.'

Chris: 'I don't understand.'

Dave: 'It's to do with an event.'

Will: 'You might have to cast your mind back a couple of weeks.'

Chris: 'I still don't get it.'

Dave: 'We've done something really bad, the last time we were sat here, which was your birthday show on Friday, 22 February.'

Chris: 'You've done something really bad, regarding one of our guests?'

Dave and Will: 'Yes.'

Chris: 'One of our guests that was in.'

Dave and Will: 'No.'

Chris: 'Have you lied to me?'

Dave and Will: 'Yes.'

Chris (*getting very angry now*): 'Did you lie about a feature on the birthday show?'

Dave: 'Maybe.'

Chris: 'Did I get very excited about said feature?'

Dave, Will and Lizzy: 'Yes.'

Chris: 'Is this something to do with U2 on the show?'

Dave and Will: 'Yes.'

Chris: 'OK, I heard U2 on the phone and they were "live" from Dublin. Would the problem be in what I just said?'

Dave: 'You're in the right region definitely.'

Chris: 'Right, so U2 weren't live on the show.'

Dave: 'They were live, but on tape.'

Will: 'Two years ago.'

Chris: 'Two years ago! Are you joking? So that world exclusive from U2 playing live, for *me*, on my birthday, was from two years ago!'

Dave and Will: 'Yeah, it was from Simon Mayo's show.'

Will: 'You know when there was interference at the end?'

Chris: 'Is that because it had Simon Mayo at the end?'

Will: 'Yeah, and we didn't want you talking to them afterwards because you couldn't as they weren't there.'

Chris: 'When were you going to tell me that it wasn't U2? Do you know how many people I've told this to?'

Dave: 'We had actually tried to get U2 to come on the show but they were "too busy". So Will and I managed to get hold of an old session they'd played on the Simon Mayo show a few years ago. We re-edited it to make it sound like it was coming live from their studio in Dublin.'

Now Chris is so technically aware that the slightest clue would be all that he'd need to guess something was up. We never thought Chris would fall for it the way that he did – the whole thing was done too well. I presumed that he'd cut into the U2 set or say afterwards: 'Good one guys!' And that would be it. But the situation completely snowballed out of control. I recall sitting next to Will at the party – as Chris glided around on a U2 high – saying to each other: 'What the hell do we do now? We're in big shit.'

I remember, in the back of a cab that night, Chris turned to me and beamed: 'I thought for a second that Bono was going to swear like he did on the Simon Mayo show a couple of years ago.' I had to turn my face away, thinking 'That's because it was the same fucking show, mate.' It was a rare and isolated coup to get one over someone who usually does that kind of stuff to us. He's still bitter about it to this day.

VIADUCT

This was one of our first games, and was basically a rip-off of an old *Two Ronnies* sketch. It became one of our most popular early games, yet I always found it funny how nobody seemed to want to know why it was called 'Viaduct'. To be honest, there isn't any logical reason really. We needed a name and I quite like the sound of the word viaduct and nobody seemed to ask any questions.

RULES
You ask each contestant a question, but they always answer the question before, if that makes sense. For example:

Question to Player 1 – How do you pronounce c – o – u – g – h?

Question to Player 2 – What is the opposite of 'Yes please'?

Player 2 answer – Cough

Question to Player 1 – What do you get if you put together the word 'sweaty' and 'Betty'?

Player 1 answer – No thanks

Question to Player 2 – What is the name of the Hollywood hooker who shot to fame after getting caught servicing Hugh Grant?

Player 2 answer – Sweaty Betty

Question to Player 1 – Larger-than-life female comedienne whose name rhymes with Blo Grand?

Player 1 answer – Divine Brown

Question to Player 2 – Name the female British sailor who broke the world record for the fastest solo circumnavigation of the globe.

Player 2 answer – Jo Brand

Question to Player 1 – Complete the film name starring Eric Idle and Robbie Coltrane, something *on the Run*.

Player 1 Answer – Ellen MacArthur

Question to Player 2 – This is the opposite of drunk

Player 2 Answer – *Nuns on the Run*

The game goes on until someone gets an answer wrong . . .

BANTER

I guess one of the hallmarks of Chris's show is the banter we have. Somehow, over the course of time in those early years, I gained more of a speaking role on the show. At the start I was just scuttling around in the background making tea and taking calls. But such is Chris's style, he would involve me and Ben, the producer, quite heavily in the programme. You see it's not at all normal for the DJ to involve the other members of the team in the show. Steve Wright has done it, Chris Evans has done it, and to a lesser extent Simon Mayo did it when he did the Breakfast Show, but it's certainly not the normal format for a Radio 1 show in any slot.

As time has gone on I've developed into a fully fledged voice on the show. If I'm honest, there was no one real moment or decision made that I would have an active speaking role. I just sort of started being involved more as the show evolved.

I'd say that Chris and I have a good on-air relationship because we've grown to know each other's speech inside out. Another important factor is eye contact, which is crucial in the style of radio that we make. You always need to be looking when the other person is going to come in and talk, otherwise you end up talking over each other and it just sounds clumsy.

VIDEO KILLED THE RADIO STAR ... ALMOST

There was a time when I was a fully functioning, useful member of the radio show team, as opposed to the on-air gobshite that I am today. My first role on Chris's show involved assisting the producer, writing script notes, researching guests, making tea – all the stuff that keeps a radio show ticking over. I was where I wanted to be and in a place and hierarchy where I could contribute in a creative fashion. Such was the increasing value of Chris's stock, he was soon offered a television show on UK Play, which was an early forerunner to BBC Choice I think, which then in turn became BBC Three.

Chris asked me if I wanted to do it with him. It was technically a music show but we were given free rein to do as we pleased.

I remember being really excited about the prospect of working on television, but there was a catch. The difference between Chris and me was that I was a BBC employee while Chris – like all presenters – was on a freelance contract. If I wanted to do the show I had to ruffle a few feathers again by asking to be a freelancer. This was a big risk: holding a staff job at the Beeb brings with it all sorts of measures of security and I was looking to jump ship again by going freelance. I mean, I'd only just got my foot in the door of the studio and I was now asking to change things again. I remember being really confused as to what to do. This was a big gamble and I've always been one to play things safe. On the one hand, I was embarking on this fledgling career at the BBC with all the perks and benefits that accompany it, while on the other hand there was this fresh and exciting opportunity to work with Chris on his new telly project.

Before I even asked my superiors about changing things, I'd have to get an agent. So Chris introduced me to his agent, Bruno Brooks. Now Bruno's a nice bloke, but he certainly put the cat among the pigeons when he went straight to my bosses before I gave him the go-ahead, and told them that he was looking after me as well. My boss at the time quite rightly called me into her office and gave me a bollocking. I'd intended politely to request the chance of going freelance in order to take up this role on the telly show with Chris, but unfortunately Bruno beat me to the announcement – which made things awkward, to say the least.

After some apologising, I was able to go freelance and work on both the radio show and the telly show. My first foray into the televisual world was a real eye-opener and a lot of fun. The channel's idea was to have Chris chatting in front of green screen while introducing music videos; but Chris, being Chris, wanted to do more with it. So we did.

WELCOME A 'LITTLE FLUFFY FRIEND' INTO YOUR LIFE

The long winter nights can be very lonely when your husband is away working on an oil rig… or in a 24-hour petrol station...

Independent ladies need some independent companionship. And the best friend a girl can have is... a **Rabbit**. Oh yeah, soft and silky to the touch, the **Rabbit** is great company for a lady who has to spend her nights alone.

It doesn't eat much, it doesn't say much, and it doesn't need to go walkies in the middle of the night.

So, if you're feeling a little lonely and are in need of a soft little something to put inside your hutch...

Get yourself a **Rabbit** AND WELCOME A 'LITTLE FLUFFY FRIEND' INTO YOUR LIFE.

Rabbits need to be fed and watered on a daily basis, and failure to keep their living area clean can result in your whole house stinking of shit

Looking back, that show on UK Play provided a great opportunity to get paid to learn a bit about how television works. The shows were repeated at all hours of the day and night, and in a completely random fashion, which made the New Year countdown show or the Christmas special, for example, an interesting watch in February. Fortunately for us, the viewing figures were so low that we had real room to experiment without there being any pressure. It was very much a television version of our radio show, except nowhere near as good! I dressed up in silly costumes, such as a matador or a jockey, for no apparent reason, and we got to chat with A-listers like Limahl from Kajagoogoo and Lionel Blair. As I said, nobody watched it, so it was a perfect opportunity for us to experiment, learn about telly and tit around while nobody was watching.

The biggest lesson I learned from that time is that television takes so much longer, and involves so much more mindless hanging around than radio – agonisingly so. I mean, in a radio studio, especially in a live environment, there's no room for retakes. You don't have to worry about light, camera angles or anything like that. Most of our radio show is impromptu and flying by the seat of our pants. But it's very difficult to do that with telly as there are so many more factors that have to be just right.

I guess someone must have been happy with what we did, as over the course of two or three years we did about 150 shows for them. It was a fun time. It was a new channel with a young vibe. Looking back, a lot of people did their first television work at UK Play – Scott Mills, Vernon Kay, Josie Darby, Joe Mace and Jayne Middlemiss – so it was all new and exciting.

BEING A LONG-DISTANCE LORRY DRIVER CAN BE REALLY HARD WORK...

BOLLER CUTOR

Driving long hours, on long roads can make you feel really sleepy...

And research proves that nodding off at the wheel can increase your chances of having an accident by up to 93 per cent.

THAT'S WHY WE'VE INVENTED THE NEW **BOLLER CUTOR**.

BOLLER CUTOR plugs into any standard cigarette lighter and delivers 12 volts straight to your gonads every two minutes – and that's enough to stop anybody dropping off!

SO IF YOU WANT TO STAY AWAKE ON THOSE LONG, BORING JOURNEYS, GET BOLLER CUTOR ... AND MAKE NODDING OFF A THING OF THE PAST

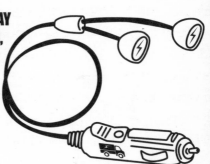

From the makers of Hot Rocks, Power Plums and Electric Testicle Jumpleads

WHAT'S IN A NAME?

I have to say I do love nicknames. If used in the right way, they're absolutely brilliant. When I was a kid of about eight or nine years old in Hong Kong, I had a good mate who was half Chinese, half English. He was called Jonathan Fung, so we used to call him 'Fungus'. I thought this was the funniest nickname in the world. As you can imagine, the hilarious moniker for the poor kid really caught on. Everyone, and I mean *everyone*, called him 'Fungus'. Our parents, even the odd school teacher would refer to him by that name – it became his identity and nobody called him Jonathan, not even his Mum and Dad! Of course, I was a major perpetuator of this name, so it's mildly ironic that I should now be on the receiving end of an all-dominating nickname – granted, 'Comedy Dave' is nowhere near as bad as 'Fungus'.

As a kid I was never cool enough to get as witty a name as 'Fungus'. Sadly my little-known surname, Vitty, rhymes with quite a few things – none of them good, though. So I was called things like 'Shitty', 'Titty', 'Nitty', 'Zitty' etc. The latter was particularly fun during my adolescent acne-ridden years. Thankfully none of them lasted any longer than a school term.

In my teens I was often called 'Vito', which always puzzled me because it sounded like an abbreviation but wasn't. Years later, when I was at uni, I did a work placement at the famous

DJ company DMC (Disco Mix Club) – best known for being the parent company of the dance music magazine *Mixmag*. I used to work in the post room sorting out the mailouts that we'd send to various DJs and members. Because I was pretty crap and slow at doing this – and just my generally gormless self – I used to be called 'Flash' by this lad called Colin who ran the mailout department and post room. Ha! It was very apt.

Over the years, some of the best nicknames have always been football-related. One of my favourites is Gilles De Bilde, the Sheffield Wednesday player from the late nineties, who was christened Bob de Bilde by the Wednesday faithful. But the all-time greatest has to be the QPR defender Fitz Hall, whose nickname is 'One Size' – One Size Fitz Hall . . . genius!

'SUPER DAVE'

Back in the early days at BBC Radio, when I used to work on the Sunday morning Clive Warren Show, Clive used to call me 'Super Dave'. Much like 'Flash', it was steeped in irony. I was still new to the production side of radio and I wasn't the sharpest, quickest or most efficient broadcast assistant. Things would happen but always at my own pace, which isn't great in a live radio environment. I like to think that I've got better over the years. Well, a bit at least.

So Clive would holler out to me in the studio things like 'Oh brilliant, here comes bloody Super Dave! What have you bodged up this time?' It was all piss-taking banter that was part of Clive's humour.

'COMEDY DAVE'

I guess many of you reading this don't even know, or care, what my surname is. 'Comedy Dave' has taken over my life, something I'm very thankful for. But it's a bit of a mixed blessing.

The name originates from my very early days at the Beeb, about a year or so after I started working with Chris.

We had the comedian Lee Hurst in that week, and a long-forgotten, throwaway comment changed my name forever. I was still a broadcast assistant and I was giving Lee his cup of tea in the studio during the interview when I think I piped up with some cheeky comment. Lee asked Chris who I was, to which he replied: 'That's Super Dave.' Lee sharply retorted: 'Comedy Dave, more like!' And I've been Comedy Dave ever since. Thanks, Lee. To be honest it's been a wonderful thing: it's created this persona through which I've had a very fruitful and rewarding career.

WHAT COULD HAVE BEEN

I've never felt truly comfortable with the name Comedy Dave. Let's be honest, it's not the best of nicknames, is it? I mean what kind of a tool would go around shouting from the rooftops (or national radio) 'Wha-hey, I'm Comedy Dave!', which is why I've always shied away from calling myself it by that name.

At the risk of sounding self-obsessed, I have often thought about what would have transpired had Super Dave stuck, which could so easily have happened if it weren't for Lee Hurst. In many ways, I do think I would have preferred it as it doesn't carry any social expectations.

I'd never refer to myself as Comedy Dave. And I find it slightly awkward when I'm introduced as such – I feel as if people are expecting to meet some gregarious comic, and instead they get boring old me. As Comedy Dave, people – especially those who don't listen to the show – expect me to be some form of comedian or funny man, which I'm not. There's also definitely a degree of fear at being unmasked as a fraud. I suppose I'm worried that people are going to have me on the Trade Descriptions Act!

But please don't get me wrong. In the grand scheme of the things the identity has been amazing for me, and the social expectation and awkwardness is a very, very small price to pay.

REMEMBER MELINDA?

I've certainly given as good as I've got in the nickname stakes at Radio 1. Another favourite nickname of mine was attributed to an old colleague and pal, Simon Hollis – some of you long-term listeners will remember him as 'Melinda'. A broadcast assistant on our afternoon show for a couple of years, he started out working in the mail room, I think. I began calling him Melinda because he was a messenger and it just sort of stuck. He was a big strapping lad, a former Royal Marine even, whom everybody called Melinda, even 'Mel' sometimes. It became so well used that many people had no clue what his real name actually was. Poor old Mel, I always loved his version of Eminem's 'My Name Is (Melinda)'. We tormented him so much that he ran away to the other side of the world – Australia – where I still haunted him, giving him a ring sting, of course. Last I heard, he was working as an estate agent in Kent and doesn't go by the name of Melinda any more.

THE REAL DAVE

To be honest, all of us involved in broadcasting export the most marketable parts of our personalities. It's the best way of engaging and enthralling the audience. I mean, I've already chatted about how, in real life, Chris isn't the same bolshy character he sometimes portrays on-air. I'm very much the same. Don't get me wrong; I *am* still pretty dippy at times. I wasn't lying on-air a while back when I said that I thought leap years were a random, infrequent occurrence – I have only recently learned that they happen every four years, and are, in fact, as frequent and timetabled as the World Cup or the Olympics, and aren't in any way a random phenomenon of nature that just happens sometimes like an eclipse or Halley's Comet.

'ROSS GELLER'

As my friends and I fast approach middle age, it would appear that I'm still unable to grow out of nicknames. My latest one has been 'Ross Geller' – a poke at my ever-changing marital status. You see, aged just 37, I've been married and divorced twice – well almost, my second divorce is yet to go through.

I guess this is as good a stage of the book as any to discuss my apparent inability to maintain a marriage, or a relationship for that matter.

Relationships were never my strong point. I was for many of my early years at the BBC miserably and involuntarily celibate – largely due to spending every waking moment either in the studio or in the Horse and Groom with Chris.

Although, to be fair, he did hook me up with my first wife, Emma. We were doing a DJ gig in Birmingham years ago when Chris hollered out to the audience: 'Who wants to snog Comedy Dave?' I was shunted to the front of the stage as Chris picked out three girls – one of whom had caught my eye earlier. The crowd had to cheer for the one they wanted me to kiss. They picked out this pretty girl, Emma, who gave me a little peck. At the end of the night she wrote her number down in eyeliner pen on a napkin, which I lost, of course.

Weeks later I was randomly going through our post – something I've never done before or since – when I found a letter from Emma with her number. I gave her a call and four years later, in 2003, we got married.

Of course the whole affair was heavily documented on-air – including plenty of ribbing about my lame proposal, which was so rubbish that Emma made me do it twice! The first time was a bit of a disaster. I'd planned on asking her in this fancy restaurant while we were away on holiday in Greece, but I left the ring in my washbag back at the hotel. I ended up proposing after we'd got back from dinner on the balcony of our not-so-brilliant hotel, overlooking a half-built swimming pool and cement mixer. It was a beautiful moment.

The show encompassed all the pre- and post-wedding hype. Chris came up with a silly game called 'Aisle Be There For You', in which we got listeners to call in with their wedding horror stories – thanks, Chris.

Obviously, there was a tongue-in-cheek, on-air bidding war for the wedding photos. Yet somehow, completely to my surprise, *Heat* magazine came in with a generous offer of making a £3,000 donation to Cancer Research – a charity very close to my heart, given that my father had recently passed away after a long fight against bowel cancer.

On the last show before my wedding Chris serenaded me with a brilliant version of Bryan Adams' '(Everything I Do) I Do It For You' – he even offered to sing it at the wedding. I politely declined. (Have a listen on www.chrismoyles.net on the sound vault and you'll understand.) Of course, Aled had a bit of the pre-wedding jitters himself. When discussing what to wear, I told him: 'An injection of colour wouldn't be a bad idea.' I hadn't planned on the factor – well, not much – that Aled might go out immediately and buy a very striking shiny red suit. Of course, Aled had some doubts after his impulse purchase, but not because he thought his suit might be a bit brash. No, he asked me: 'Dave, what are the bridesmaids wearing? See, I'm going in a red suit and don't want to clash!' In the end we were all relieved that he never upstaged or clashed with the bridesmaids and came to the wedding in a black suit. Part of me would have been intrigued to have seen him wear the red suit, though. He'd have looked like a smaller, pastier, more Welsh version of Lenny Henry on Comic Relief!

The whole gang from the show came along to the big day. One of them nearly got ejected by the venue staff for trying to smuggle in his own bottles of spirit in a rucksack and someone else had to be taken home early; and Chris made a lovely speech in which he showed me up by mentioning how lovely the bride looked – something I'd forgotten to say. Making special mention of how lovely one's bride looks on the big day is something that should never be omitted from a groom's speech. I, more than anyone, should know this – not that it changes the eventual outcome, in my experience.

When it came to announcing divorce number one on-air, Chris, once again, was there to put a comedic shine on the event. Ever the cupid, he asked any listeners who fancied me to text the show. After all of about two people texted in, Chris alluded to the fact that there had been some hot gossip about me online.

On the show's fansite, www.chrismoyles.net, a thread entitled 'The truth about Dave's marriage' gained over 3,500 hits, speculating about my marriage/divorce with bizarre comments such as: 'I've heard this from quite a few people now and done a little digging and probing and private investigation myself ... If you study recent photos of the [Breakfast Show] team in Germany, you'll see that Dave's not wearing a wedding ring ... Dave has been talking about cooking a lot recently and about going out.'

It seems my private life had been seeping out into the public domain through little telltale actions. Fans had deduced that I was now single. The forum thread went on and on, with all sorts of rumours and bizarre discussions. Well, they were right about my divorce and the online speculation prompted me to announce it. It's quite a weird thing to broadcast something so personal to the nation; but there you have it, it's all part of living in the public eye, or ear, as the case may be. I have to admit, I do find it quite fascinating that people are that bothered or interested in my private life. It's all a bit odd, but, doing what we do, I guess people are intrigued to find out what's going on behind the scenes. In my case, currently, not a lot.

I actually met my second wife, Jayne, before my first, Emma. Of course, it was through Chris once more. Given the regretful termination of both relationships, I can't work out if he's a lucky charm or a curse. So, as funny as it now seems, Jayne did some work experience on *The Chris Moyles Show*, the TV show which Chris did on UK Play back in 1999.

Jayne would run around doing odd-jobs for us like making tea and photocopying; I seem to remember we made her dress up as a turkey for some silly skit, for reasons that are still not fully clear. In fact, when I look back on first getting to know Jayne, the enduring image in my mind is of her in a ridiculous turkey costume. Whenever things get too heavy and trying between us, all I have to do is resurrect that picture.

While Jayne and I vaguely knew each other through mutual friends, we didn't hook up until many years later, about six months after my split from Emma. We started dating after bumping into each other on the set of *All Star Family Fortunes*, when the Chris Moyles and Fearne Cotton families went head-to-head.

We were in the green room before the show when I met Jayne again. She'd come because she was friendly with Chris's brother, Kieron. As fate would have it, we'd both recently come out of a marriage break-up. Things progressed pretty quickly, with our moving in together and Jayne falling pregnant within months – neither of us were even divorced yet!

We'd both had enough of London, so we set up nest in leafy Buckinghamshire – a little cul-de-sac in Chalfont St Peter, which was very *Brookside*, to be honest. We did laugh about the fact that we were the youngest people on the street by a few decades. We could just imagine the curtain-twitching neighbours gossiping about the unwed, pregnant couple, both of whom were still married to other people! Thankfully, that latter information wasn't public knowledge. Whichever way you want to spin it, though, we were very much in Jeremy Kyle territory, and both of us felt a certain sense of legitimacy and suburban respectability when our decree absolutes came through – meaning we were then merely an unmarried couple expecting a baby. It signified that we were now a substantial step closer to fitting into life in the Chalfonts!

Throughout all my ups and downs, the show has been one of the few consistencies of my life. The show has always been a bit of real-life soap opera, in which my trials and tribulations have been a major plot line. Almost every incident of my life, since the age of 23, has been discussed live on-air. I can tell you there have been some dark days when the last thing I've wanted to do is put on the Comedy Dave mask – and be full of 'show-banter' – and broadcast the show. But in its consistency, I'd say it has been more of a help than a hindrance.

It's always a weird one when it comes to announcing any major life changes live on-air. I always feel quite awkward about it. But I have to accept that, as far as the show is concerned, I'm a character with a plot line that listeners want to follow – which is actually a massive privilege for which I'm always grateful, if I'm honest. But I never enjoyed announcing my divorce or break-ups. I certainly felt a bit awkward mentioning that I had a new girlfriend – I mean, it's embarrassing enough saying that to each other. This time round I haven't made any on-air announcements about my second divorce. It's pretty tough as my daughter, Nicole, listens to the show every morning and that's not a nice thing for her to hear being discussed aloud to the nation. So, now there are factors such as children in my life, I guess I have to be a little more guarded about how my on-air persona divulges personal information – which might not be too bad a thing.

I have to say, it was fun going through the birth of Nicole with the radio show. I loved the wealth of support that came flooding in from all the listeners when I announced that Jayne and I were going to have a baby. Instead of taking paternity leave, we set up a mic at home so I did my part of the show and could be with Nicole. Of course, my little girl was gurgling on-air within her first few days. It was a magical time that I got

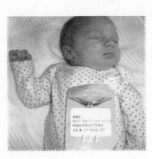

'I'm with the band!'
Two-week-old Nicole
Katherine Vitty gets
her first AAA pass
for the Foo Fighters
in Brighton!

Daddy's girl

to share with the nation. From a broadcasting point of view it made for some quality radio, even if I was sometimes making up bottles or clearing up poo when the lads were trying to talk to me on-air, or hopping up and down to answer the door in the middle of Tedious Links. It just gave our show that warts-and-all feel that we've always gone for.

I guess our show is a real-life soap, or a radio version of *The Truman Show*, in that we've broadcasted all the highs and lows of our lives to the nation. There's very little about my life that hasn't been discussed, celebrated or ridiculed on-air. And the same goes for the others as well. It's only really in writing this now that I realise how public our lives have been. And, just in case you've missed anything, here I am dishing it all out in book format.

Despite there being sadness for me of late with my divorce, the show must go on; and if nothing else, it encourages you to laugh at yourself. Doesn't Ross Geller get lucky eventually with his third marriage to Rachel?

HI, MY NAME'S JOHN COUGAR MELLENCAMP

You probably remember me from my Hits like 'Jack and Diane' and 'R.O.C.K. in the U.S.A.'

Well, now I've given up on music and moved to Shropshire to set up the UK's first female-only nudist camp.

That's right, **John Cougar's Melon Camp** is the only place where ladies can let it all hang out surrounded only by other ladies... and me.

So, if you're a lady and you want to get away from it all, call for a free brochure or visit my website at www.melon.camp.shrophire/jubbly

GET JIGGLY WITH IT AND PUT A BIT OF BOUNCE INTO YOUR LIFE

AT JOHN COUGAR'S MELON CAMP IN SHROPSHIRE

John Cougar's Melon Camp is a subsidiary of Bush Gardens

@dunloprebecca @Rebecca_Brown11 @Lisa_of_course @Rich_100 @tompett26 @pierremontroose @cassielockett @jessicatwanny @MUFC_Hess @KevinOxland @Hubbs74 @Nobweld @super_stuff @emmzie31 @Stanfordcalling @mrsluco @catwells1 @khoady @CatK16 @deebs73 @crowdfiction @LukeGriffiths21 @angharadhafsh @louluscott @GeorgieP83 @woobaer @xraychiepiex @ WXIN @Wirralbird @Martynsnowball @StaceyL1986 @KatMcNie @toria123 @kayzcorraz @crazy_haigh @tisjcar @Infidel83 greig_b1 @c9mmy @quiggin @agudle @bramatlotvin @Kellylouise84 @NickyJAllen1172 @SaraAnnTurner @Lazyluccaandcat @ igecurtissss @minxholt @MonstersMayhem @thefawks @kirkbydave @colliwoggle @AnGeLXxXx @ClaireWynarczyk @tora_gill CharlotteLou9 @becky23a @markstumpy @tmc41 @SEREN_DDISGLAIR @jodee_reynolds @HannahCameron5 @cloakey @ rrikezza @vicky_taylor27 @kimbers28 @dowlerdl @ritchiewals @charlieoxf @Kherbie82 @66plenty @rufusfleck @Milsey @clare_ enham22 @JoPrice5 @stephTT4eva @lisakirkby @jojo58dixon @VIEkatefreeman @Clharris8 @Princess1977 @OceanRedBand @ nmdavidson @Natty_1079 @katiesturgess @PaulGregory31 @chrisglenton1 @chris_blossom @bigpat_2011 @Jeni_Wink @ eorgie0099 @MissKateyWilkes @blicklingben @gibgod @Paulfp1967 @ExquisiteGH @madbotes @BigBenBogo @alanhunter1967 chuggyswife @Nifster82 @Rossoefc @Samantha_Dodd @jeremybtaylor @moobsmoore23 @SusiePots @beckiblueeyes @ wnwoof @drew79uk @CJR9587 @greciancms @collettefdohert @nicolleabbott93 @Lady_Grey14 @froggyjr257 @mitchellturner9 MrsALHuggins @craneylis @munton86 @Possum1977 @iamchristucker @KatyBlois @StephenLeonard5 @SassyBrew1 @bransaun ZooeW @treeseebee @saalex11 @nadiastones @The_Skills @acmilano5 @martynp39 @lmnotdonkey @Cloughy7 @Fillifjonk nicxrobbrown @leewbacowell @mrslisajanewebb @northernmonkie @Fezza_9 @mushroommagee @Anna__Tucker @onegaz @ 3nuttess @AbigailJudd @adambowkett @An_walk @terribletowel85 @mondeoman155 @Joe_Billster @jake_bridge @chrisbricks1 NEILRJONES @dazzlemx @RichieJ_101 @hollyy_j @Sarahkatehughes @curlywurly45 @kestral_matt @Kevplumb @pmjones23 andytheangler @LPatterson41 @JonnyEBet @Lulabelle1989 @ZonkeyD @Ashley85cf @louisemcuk @AliBobJ @ParkyDav @ wnroe @Alice_Bryan @HBUX @PeaOfThePod @JenniLambo @jenniferhampso1 @tonytheprince @browny_74 @OllieMoo1998 matt_satchell @Allic9 @Teresa_Holland @katwait @jcakesgould78 @Lulupads @Sweensc @Philly_G84 @DTowls @littlemisems shazmiller @HWU_Secretary @AdamDarke1 @northernmonkeyc @jesstaylor2 @Siany_Pie @sandraallen74 @dawnbould @ ackHeelBlog @natalielynn_ @CharHuntley @AJB_KRO @danleee @JoJoClarkey76 @Phoenix_kiddd @111aimee111 @JulieThornett White_Pedro @jimbobrighton @Peavis293 @daviemac77 @yuley66 @junaidahmed01 @chelleokane @LilMacca81 @deejbee @ andvik @Clarepear7 @lauren_cutts @petters77 @real_ego @dobson101 @Geaney31 @Kathryneire @EmehLynn @guntm8 @ ejayBBT @NurseSoucy @Emily_Smiths @bjv1982 @jamesfutcher @HerbyTheGnome @killie_andy @Monkeymazza CharlotteCarlis @hrdandrew @alanwells31 @twinklestar49 @sarahgrahno @fingertash @fRoGG83 @angekeys1302 @Hayley_ wers @CelebritySatNav @Scaz50 @queeniebee2304 @MarkeyMark051 @Taffie2 @curlylisa30 @Goldilocks1976 @zcakx70 @ ulie130184 @SJSparkle66 @JonnyStrudwick @MAGIC72 @darnallowl @ChrisDavies30 @clareasmith @staceyc69 @AlexGrew ruthglabs @HannahThompso19 @jacqui257 @katewinning @MarkMcJimpsey @kevcowl @Sloany_rfc @lukehutchings1 @creedmc NatalieLloyd2 @KevP_79 @Phatduck @richyward @Howellsy @Skitz2bitz @Jonie_bear @jonnyd_83 @baker_b2 @richmarshall120 mmmandib @pip_says @mike_c_lewis @dewirhysowen @sje23_ @JudeGoodrich @Kennyboy6000 @PestKontroller @clairesname Fay_Michelle @ashersabertawe @lrowey @debbierolinson1 @Molly_Panter @SASBAHOFFICE @AndyHopkinson @gcollier1987 lone___gunmen @Gillsaino @elieilal669 @Elaine_reeves07 @D4NCL4RKE @chille39 @pilsoriginal @SteveMatsell @jsnj122 @ oysei @deeley78 @jesswaring @jamcowen8 @Speirs09 @gratbags @bethyboop2009 @MissEmCookie @chippiecarroll cakeybaby01 @shesballasofia @sezj @Smurfje71 @GillHenney @philipmercer1 @JAGedman @goonyladdy @Quecumba @ anjfriend84 @joe892 @Samh68Hill @trivianni1 @matt_hayes @Carlybear83 @DmFry89 @NickBrewer91 @FAColeman arsenalsmith @meeeshell30 @idodclare83 @IanNapier29 @xbeccipowellx @guesty86 @neilshenton @louymac @deanmontano @ oodiec @J_Cuthbert @MiniPete26 @Sam_Baker86 @LloydLydia @emmaberry26 @ManicCafc @Wonky_Wilbo @matt10hirst @ KrisW @Amberydwi @Onelly_90 @pjrmcilwaine @helengs @Davierich76 @Simon_Clifford @mark64hughes @misskrking @ elouies @OceanBayBaby @surferharrylee @K8ie1987 @Freddie1808 @dannybowmer @G_Robinson95 @ambeeerx3 @ppjhbcfc radio1sima @DomLancers @Jennybenno @bexsd1974 @sunny_purewal @staggieman @tobzgh @maisiemoose @Stedale23 charmarten1 @doggboy_nffc @Pikachu74 @GeorgeFRichards @MrWilkinson1986 @munchrao @Wayne_Murdo @LauraHalliday @ az_finch100 @RJW_87 @PaddyStephenson @13mikev @sezzie69 @BeanieStudios @studson14 @emilaaymaay @ohmygoodgrace CurlyH @richb1990 @wendydines @fairfootellie @Emstertron @HolleySinclair @beckyjs2008 @nball7 @SuzieEAndrew @sirkarlos get_funkd_up @deanbichener @tjdayz @Rowgriff @mikeyhenrys @LisaPocko @LauraLouO @ClaireBollans @SteveKitchen @ key9495 @Roggiew @mellejaneC @HannahLaight @Lorenzo2004 @stevestfc @shanus81 @sassysez74 @sarahx1727 @ ondeteacher @Danchez69 @ShellHak @stanmond @Saragowan @LaolaLimeng @mattlocke84 @mark_childs @21stCenturyCat adam_feather09 @shonaamurphy23 @oneijim @Swissdibble @afrench88 @estelle_hemming @Dave85Penney @richie2622 @ fsriffs @CrissleyJ @tamsinlowe @MrsTynedale9 @IJRussell43 @ShelterForXmas @dylangillooly @beboadz @emmamarshall1 rachelbailey87 @JamesDMurray @Michael1emms @hannahpudner @damienhopkins @Dylanthebunny13 @sheikra7 @morgmun @ ylaCaffrey @LauraAB33 @chamus35 @Wendall77 @Jess5rose @wdavies10 @carlin91188 @susanjoshua @SimeonGibbons @ ougjohnfrench @Peapod1981 @Paulsowman @Annaluvstorun @Cheebyee @j4z @deanireid @loladiva92 @mpoly74 @gooddolly Fee_Edinburgh @sarah3300 @Pea10pea @JaniceGleeson @pitty78 @justfortoday12 @Belinio @theboysovs @Michael__Jasper beth_hampton @CancerCanKMA @matt83evans @dairymoorbee @davies1587 @Spamamfa @leemurphy79 @sdannell10 @ ang2011 @JohnStimpson72 @Holly_dalee @samuel14rea @JAY_NORN_IRON @eriktorresx @mwhelan69 @Anyag24 @soph_ own @LiamKirkham27 @Richywiecko @Cjbunnie @mikelightwood @stewbevin @DarrenB74 @SamPullen1 @JJEvsy10 @ Mcleavy @saltwood15 @Sionzee @racheljacko @timbohendon @SticksterMoore @ukgunboat @Sheepbandit @braddersley gavjones77 @Evaduck @oo_Deano_oo @briancolton1 @HazelHammond @Lionpjones @xXdaniellej87Xx @macs_3 @mezza9999 imclare84 @M1k3Perry @scottydav3 @ToxicDeath @lexloofa @milkyf3 @Matthew_Yeoman @JustListens @mdoa515 @ walkerster @dave4jaz @HWUnion @LauraJennings @NaomiDaniel1 @QPRbennyboy @Gem_5x @stegjack @AngelaHatten jpthreelions @alibubba40 @ganglion25 @Henjo73 @Miss_Bell85 @mattyroberts81 @MistaDriscoll @Pierre_DeadCat @ChrisHurst2 Triitra @MckittrickHelen @bonus8zero @jbutler122kuk @kijosan @snufes @Kensa2010 @kellymp79 @Gary_McKeating @ arkhensley @heiniej12 @Daly01 @tandy347 @MichPreston @iainjamber @carolinestokes1 @ShaunS91 @LewisBrigden @ mcardus @DJTSDave @peterstellaboy @Swindonlad @chrisg_unit @bigdaddyglewis @lindak85 @MichaelDawson18 @FloDix stucker73 @greenexile77 @WeGeorgiaKings @heather_j_sloan @SimmaSim @fatboytanner @stevejshaw @macatnewacres @ mucker @conny_dodger @hilsbills38 @amy_e_mason @DominicHadfield @simonb77 @fellacios @bigjohndicko @matteo3618 bobber61 @Ezylpha @MattingleyGrab @m11chell_hall @GORDONatClyde @danmarchant @theformermsdean @missharri2 @ 00tap @KeifferM @daaaaaan1 @Slimadey78 @therobprosser @joworky04 @Allyi87 @PettitHannah @SamRuddick @whibbler @ nileyy789 @WowWowWubzy @Aliceeeeee12 @danwiss18 @susieleggate @bradsbabe82 @pubehead8 @Samw37 @svernond1 jameshyde30 @ClaireHammond2 @Brooke99999999 @gapgob1974 @jamckenna @missperrie @1Garyd @chris_brookes @ obHerrick22 @andygregory79 @errrrrm @anniehill28 @dodboy00 @lee_rat91 @86sepho86 @BurmanDonna @rednwhitepc @ ariuszgregory @picutech @rwb221 @Lighting_M @ashleydonnison @Jax_Lloyd_Jones @tomattwit @Emmamoo @potatopilot ali_8 @sweetFA_ste @bobbyssnacks @LizSaich @miamaytwiter @feefi_c @EllieHenderson @GMF79 @justmozza @adamskeys65 Taylor1389 @lozwhite83 @jessefluff84 @Perryjulier @empiregasman @Lauren2304 @davec01745 @loynsey @Awesomby @ anjackJohnson @BellendBoys @PaulPoppyJaffa @methatch @emmajamieson83 @shambles_online @kimblethimble @rksfc superanimalman @_oreet @LeePearson29 @leannes274 @rhyshymas @gingerlau83 @swall_al @martinspeed3 @andypayney BigDomSpong @Booga_FKFF @Bluemoonlass @philgthethird @madmana @Lynnehollier @PaulLloyd3 @RaRa_starz @JessAldisx MarkoHam @kimgoy1983 @cojoboy @mrsk0412 @KatyVN @LiamFleming2781 @the___monk @Rob_Jamo @manthy1 @ apysuperstar @sofa_713 @mortsie16 @CllrIenJunier @aerron_marie @VikkiH @shaggawanks @Arctic_Tern9 @nickmathieson mrpmac75 @louby_do @daveelvin89 @Carlloulou @Steve70882 @_maz15 @JoCleggie @JoanneBrown1981 @jamiemayers

@Doogal / Doogal
What's the greatest song ever written?

Easy. Elbow's 'One Day Like This'. Perfect in every way. Can't top it.

@scoeylad / Jon Scoffield
Do you miss the uk play days when you used to dress up in that matador outfit?

I do a little bit. Those were the crazy days.

@rodneysykes / Rodney Sykes
Why are you so bad at maths?

'Cos I is, innit.

@jimmytwoshoes / James Hendley
Would you go on a coach trip or a ski trip?

Coach trip with Brendan.

@CraigTheAwesome / Craig Brown
Can you scratch the sole of your foot without laughing?

Yes.

@churchym / Marc Church
Why are you called Comedy Dave?

I don't know.

@matt_r_smith / Matt Smith
Is battle nips the greatest game you've invented?

Quite possibly. Nip nip hooray.

@darrenpstone / Darren Stone
Who is your favourite king: Andy king (ex Evertonian),
Mark King (level 42) or king of tickets?

King of tickets.

@Ezzzzymay / Erica McCarthy
What is the question you get asked the most?

What time do you get up and go to bed? The answers to
which are '4.30 a.m.' and 'it depends'.

@PBav / Peter Bavin
White lightning or 20/20?

Neither, thank you please.

@duckydarren / Darren Gray
What is the most star struck you've ever been?

Madonna @ Brit awards a few years ago.

@Laurindaisla / Laurinda
Do you like marmite?

Yes I do. But not too much of it.

@AdamPudDavis / Adam Davis
Have you ever imagined a world without hypothetical situations?

No.

@TRUPLAYERS / corpseclothing.com
What was the first band t-shirt you brought?

A t-shirt with the WonderStuff on.

@damiansullan66 / Damian Sullan
Why Everton???????

'Cos of my dad and family.

@MissMynett / Helen Louise Mynett
Other than the time you made Radio 1 'accidently' go off air, what's the biggest slip up you've made?

Too many to mention.

@Yiddo1975 / Tim Stevens
What REALLY happened in Hunstanton?

Everybody had a great time in Sunny Hunny.

@gemmaaustin / Gemma Austin
Would you rather have no right hand or no left foot?

No left foot.

@Bigshermi / Matthew Sherwin

If you could be any animal, what would you be and why?

Killer whale 'cos people like you and will come and see you but never take the piss.

@mo0ncat / Ian

Have you managed to convert any celebs into Evertonians or taken them to see the Blues in action?

No.

@Pcengine007 / Kevin Scripps

Has it been hard writing this book?

Yes, it has been hard because I never realised how much work went into writing a book.

@ kac118 / Karen Cooke

If you weren't on the radio what would you have done for a job?

I'd be a bounty hunter.

@PAPACALLSOP / Callum Allsop

if you could have any job in the world, other than yours, and if the pay did not matter what would it be?

Top Gear presenter/ International Playboy writer/ Megan Fox's masseur.

@BeccaVaudin @verygoodfriday @JonReynolds4 @LisaAshelford @stocksy13 @amybelle91 @NatJChild @Branden398 @kstock
@frogg64 @louthepoo @mac_mcconnell @olliewatts1 @Richardgilbert5 @PeteMartin2 @lills111 @Paul_Dustan @Danb20ltfc
Mikekennylfc @LemonBarley22 @MichaelSpooner8 @Morten_Evans @lukegiles @tompriz @Wayasboy @AndyBaldwin1984
BigJack1873 @marcushogan86 @ryanmulvey81 @chadspeeps @M_Planty @SamTFriskney @Richiepajfc @AidanStoker @ricepa
@thomaswwebb @bigbellymum @amydowner1 @jodybotting @racert7 @jamesholmes19 @MikeAlexLee @l_bowyer @irons87
stoner_uk_80 @Kanz666 @Fingerswalsh @KatyKatiaaaaaaa @amywalberton @the3browns @NatashaFirth @scottcorriga
@Lewie13289 @benmickers @neilreid1972 @Deanowill @SophieeeeeLouu @ausum031267 @Team_Shireen @NeilPanayi
jonnyborders @Sarah1979lewis @1clairejames @MarkReynoldsUK @debb13h @HarryWorth442 @boardman90 @claireypick
markdbolton @JulieGelder @andy_sh1ft @Louiseramsay @pedmanning @TheFilmNinja @JayDavies84 @wedding_dan
@tommydunits @KATHERINENICEBE @Cdjmg42 @bhyett1 @kingy_king @BigEasty @iain_baj @benstanc @Jeds80 @TaxmanB
@phil_busby @Glesni @leegane75 @jynsayhay @Lronjen @mechamperz @cjbyrne87 @kchadwick007 @ChimpPingPo
@0xYg3n72 @chimpola72 @AdamButler04 @Lynzf010 @Sj_BooMchugh @vicoharabelfast @lovelacewalne @MezzaMary
Barmster @louansell @ChrisCowhead @mickyclay @fatned001 @AmyBillett @elly41D @Cain_11 @catslater107 @sdwilliams96
DizzieLizzie88 @IsThatCameron @moleymblaze @darenpearce @brionywalton @perfectBOB1 @Gillycov @chriscarey
@TheCarbonero @stu_hill1982 @NickyJF24 @Dave_Pr1tchard @IParry_MuFc @Lamy_G @iammaxwell88 @LeBeauJeuBlog
mosley24 @LuLuHUB @JackTheNinjaDon @Storminhorman @AndyJamesdeBoer @SnathP @Ben_Milner @AnnieAitken
cococoles84 @MeowSaidSam @Pete_the_meat1 @LiamHocking @gj1979 @ellbohtr @lozmgcol @JumboGoulsbra @tom_hewitt
@brentsmiffy @luapjones @Seguindovoc @littletwonk @Yunni90 @MikeAllen35 @richardmizuro @joeissofine @moules1
engmedge @jennybails @misswiggy @colinb1980 @ryanthomas9 @sammld @ScottShaqNelson @katy_creswell @KV_
@katyrperry83 @pompeyqueen @watsrob @eireds @crystall94 @Gabi_B25 @Foz6657 @MyNameIsFrazer @ColetteParsons
ITRDC2 @Theuns990 @johnbrimblecomb @LukeFatherley @KathrynBoydell1 @rroosssss2008 @m4ttbaker @Jlavery5
@F1mad12 @tl78ftd83 @markberry11 @stevenduffin64 @ChrisGardner73 @Dawn13131313 @frig_off @AaronSuperG @gemmi
em_30 @faustinoasp @clairebear2788 @thomas10285 @LeeCarey1977 @VictoriMidd @mchad86 @Reid79 @copey5068
Eddo81 @jon_shan @SazzAld @TimmehWimmy @rhall82 @woods_rachael @Ginawaite @Danieljcharman @DiscoStubert85
JessicaT_01 @JeliDeli88 @Lunny2522 @MaryAnnPayne @MattSkinz10 @Steve9791 @Tinkster85 @foxfowler @mattclarke
@MotownJunkie83 @Robbo1446 @Consigliari_UK @perswah @shonzieface @summits_up @triciamcfadden @Adam_carter01
DeezLloyd87 @CarlieNowell @baldiedaz @julie2710_ @pups78 @Jimbo_Crook89 @CrystalHigginbo @SMcCrae77 @crutcher19
@Danielle86Hall @kasoid @CallumBriggs46 @Cleggy32 @hanntawe2 @reefus2 @hazeladamson @gchristieson @shoogs4
nathan78833 @Lornington_Baby @ab1lynch @thunderingfoals @pallescere @davesmed65 @barrystonehouse @gcross
@jimmybigfish @frosty925 @mikewmarley @kerrywoo1 @NandiePandie @eamonn_kingwick @gillianm @tommbaker1991
juliankey @PhysioStu @L_Gaunt @TimSanders88 @ncmncm @katej1977 @Ronniegan @johnglass82 @buddah74gsm
NancyJayneLaws @Adam20Saunders @gooseybadger @Jawa1975 @hayleybishop15 @sammiefielding @utvhitman @JakEvan
@SavannaLana @R0ssC00ke @Lisa2621 @nicolesedgmanx @MLGriffo @blaggy86 @leighwills @rickdooley @proconnor86
stopm3ss1ng @robertclegg85 @gracehodgetts @jonpanderson @bigwadge @Horselegshedley @mbelectrics @trickydicky304
Bombom6969 @little_ciara1 @CSWPorter @xanderstevens35 @justjude80 @mimi8811 @tacwilson @DaveMCoggin @keiraatkins
@statsportssean @Mandymoo197 @Andrew_L_D @T_ina_82 @Kingfosters @Music_Angel612 @scotty_a_s @AndyGomarsall
Hayleybella1 @Wilde_Dave @amiephillips85 @stomp84 @Amanda_Gilbride @Amilcarhoef @miguelmerry @MrsBTOI @sar
steve20 @JustineAston1 @cataaron24 @darrenf76 @jimmya123 @LauraMeadows88 @vfmoore @Meliss3317 @liam_tweddle
stu_chef @Miri_Kirby @RockAsylum @27RomanBear @retro_rachey @stoneleighwhu @richardhorton84 @mummaevans @esmic
@bruciemufc @keithygdotcom @laura1982mcnair @love_my_life1 @Freaky4McFly @cardicoke @79wolfie @Student_Bargain
flynnyboby @danmac151 @JJharris90 @DaveWilson112 @LiamJM10 @leckers78 @jameswalton85 @GingeElise @happycamper
@tic40 @3joel33 @chimpquin @jacqssewell @FaultlineShaun @doig86 @AKittridge @cmcchoppie @lewins19 @christyema
@nzabbar @Danjwatt @thereverend316 @castleman8 @dangardner6 @alberry70 @bethosdad @cullumrussell @nettameadows
ChloeRW @Stag1979 @jocav1 @nobbie1969 @fleischman1977 @rianna_ @lynshill @alicelouisehowe @PiNkFalrY24 @dazwil
@PhilGriffith1 @grantyplanty @Jon7896 @Fitzd1987 @spc1989 @richsmithson @abbielady @garyjagr1 @JackLiffen @LeeWardle
@AdeBroadway @tuckerphil @JeffMWilliams1 @Sam_Stephenson_ @cne_77 @davepetherick @ShowTempoLivre @dezzydu
@daykind19 @clairespearing @KTAppleyard @Bowbankers @ItsaMeMilo @CharlScully @Jonny__Howard @kscully66 @Doodleo
@Allisonmw80 @Joeywatson @RozanneBanks @aimeevandenhrik @PetervanderLugt @DJTIBNFIB @Kez0827 @kaka_malaka
c0sm0123 @samconnolly1231 @liam_4_mufc @SmithBoy1988 @shabbading @chrisjameshall @stuartmorgan1 @auntiek
@bertrude89 @emmilybridges @HelenaMelons @DavidRowe9 @Bartsfamquotes @rhysharris1988 @S_Carts @djallamdavlar43
evaaverill @radiocode43ep @danw83 @chrisefc09 @Rugchard @bikerbarryswife @rainbowmrs @carolquinn27 @shapland
gravelpants77 @carlfoster01 @charlotteA95 @AliceJones06 @DougieHealion @mr_geem @tonyWalsh64 @Stevepittaway
MckieLaura @rikmason @SimonPRhodes @LauraJBould @tolly321 @jgibbons88 @kayjiee @rgummer @MikeRichards440
dakes101 @niuswim @ClaireLouiseRiz @daviddownie17 @LindsayShaerf @AMBarwell @jordankenefick @Hope1967 @Lucia
@willisjackson69 @MartinGreenhill @MattJagucki @HelenBWatts @gilyle123 @SamClarke20 @AmyBinding1 @MichaelaD
@LAJones_xx @kateconnole @stephenlaity @LucyEdney86 @TonyLord74 @Katecollins86 @IamGaryBTR @torturequeen1
titchyange @m1ke_potter @bcfc_jonny @LynneMcc @pearsy321 @loubylou26 @juliepadfield @BailsFreak @rachaelhoss83
hargreaves_amy @MarkJamie1991 @iBerridge @tweetmecathy @NiktoriaM @16st5lb_wtf @RosieMayCope @L_Richardso
@DaBelRo @Rory_OB @SophieJaneWild @DanielleShreeve @BeachHouseRadio @peterstirley @aileenferg @DaleMeachen
HannahRuffin @Jeala_86 @goffy3105 @McHadden @amandan81 @r_campbell13 @LenaHart23 @penguinpiss @Loubielou0099
littlemissemmab @Lady_bakes @AaronTrousdale @andyjez @y1darney1979 @michaelspence89 @neilioF @roman_b_photo
noseycow33 @ben_cassidy_86 @waps999 @therealantonyb @jasonblood1 @redgillhall @roseyvilla @FltLtJRF @oldmanjames74
@genstainforth @Darrentunni @gmac269 @kelly_isaac1982 @kieranhouston1 @jabjaberico @Reefie2 @Jacksonmurray
downandoutin84 @EmFlanagan1 @AndyMiff46 @EdNorthridge @SambucaaMonkeyy @tezzaha @Colinmcintosh66 @henn1980
Blodgey1980 @Peterjepson @GrainneRita @3stars0103 @hasteele @HollyCParkerx @Linashbourne @curls59 @x55ssy @Arn
McArnis @MattcpK9 @Ruksarna @mosiejo @Joel_Boon @carolmckechnie @jaffalejaff @lisamarcusmatth @shaskins
mattgammarayz @Mr_Mike_1981 @jessieG81 @stuartL1986 @timmyhoyle @kieron_alp @DrewDanie @fordyforking
saratrimmings @real_fitzy87 @woundedcrow @coopswhufc @j0egoats @doted1512 @dan_bubb @mumsyalert @youngdannyt
@gemzy13 @DB_Kahuna @robbiesavage12 @NobbyBarnes1982 @lukeutd1 @JasonCreedLufc @RossyLaa @Gricypops
maudy77 @KierHS @evensam @AmyPeart @scooterderv @Merlyn_Jacobus @Missipam @LukeDwatson @sj_houghton1981
JoshuaPaterson1 @browneyedgirlx @Elissaf925 @Only1barnsey @chucky1105 @candycupcakes25 @coachwillgraham
michelleRMreid @JordanRS10 @LawranceCheong @WhatEvRadio @DabbsKebabs @DanEfc84 @rebeccaisbak @adamwalker1
@Jak2911 @Jodie_Jump @SteveKnightsDJ @jackwtanner @stokie_loz @philnelll49 @gavfinnis @mickheadxx @k4rlsm1th
Lingham1985 @emsicals1 @af210368 @russwagg89 @marialakin @SamPizTrewin @davewalker81 @chordle1 @kerriedur
@croftyleeds @Tiggatigerpus @Cactuscandy7 @SiBo66 @glowworm23 @missyclaire_87 @rosswarnes @p0w3ll18 @rj_sparks
marc_trowill14 @wyles101 @madisonhariett @richard_weare86 @falmai7 @SharyonTolbert @sarahjburscough @buckbyfan
@PrawnIdentity @leswilks977 @mindtheguyropes @Ginni_F @rosiearse @clairebusby1979 @kir714 @79sig @EmmaMcCorm
@30STM_Killjoy_ @sam_stephen @jayjaysmam @Jay_Tomkins @Thomas_Skerritt @michelajh @deb8805 @StokeDunc83
scottferguson8 @Davidminers @pault81178 @fi_miller1 @gooner_jay @gemboatkins @melanielowry1 @KaHLeL1701
PaulMcNally87 @salesboy77 @clairlou72 @lornacunneen @chimpy42 @Tia_7oaks @l1nders @tippex69 @DebbieLHo @Daverich
@pettsy77 @nimmyjewman @0151bluenose74 @scole7 @PRNewbie86 @fewy123 @SimonHobson1 @nigeltrainor @dawl

MY FAVOURITE RADIO MOMENTS

THE TIME I TOOK SIMON MAYO OFF THE AIR ...

This is a well-known story in media circles, concerning one of the greatest blunders of my career – which I got away with, I might add. In my very early days at Radio 1, around 1998/ 99, Simon Mayo was one of the most established DJs in the country and was playing his weekday morning slot, as usual.

It was about the same time as people were beginning to chat about using webcams in radio studios. The use of Internet and radio combined was a very new concept then. Somehow, I was seen as a person with a bit of technical know-how – I think it was something to with my recent Radio 1 job title of technical operative. Thankfully, I've managed to shed this misconception over the years. But back then I was regarded as someone who was remotely useful, so the website team enlisted me to help with their webcam project.

I was asked if I knew how to rewire the stereo feed from Simon Mayo's live studio onto the BBC website. I didn't know, but rather than admit it I, of course, said that I could and took an informed (or not, as it turned out) guess.

It seemed as if it should have been a simple process. There's a place called the racks room, which is like the main hub into which all the Radio 1 wires lead – it looks very much like an old-school telephone exchange. From what I could ascertain all I needed to do was unplug Simon Mayo's stereo feed and plug it into the online feed, which I did. And then a silence descended upon Radio 1.

Bedlam broke loose. People rushed, bumped and pushed their way around our fairly large offices trying to locate the problem. So I did what any sensible man would do. I ever-so-coolly left the building for a cuppa and a fag rather than get in the way.

When I returned about 20 minutes later, we were fortunately back on the air, as one of the engineers had spotted the problem and rectified it, returning Simon Mayo to his rightful position as one of the nation's best-loved broadcasters.

Chris looked bemused and leaned over to me. 'Where were you?'

'Nowhere, just popped out for a fag,' I squeaked in that high-pitched tone that yelps of guilt.

Mayo had been off the air for about 15 minutes, and to this day I still carry with me a certain amount of guilt, as I know I was ... well ... pretty much entirely responsible.

THE TIME WE CLIMBED MOUNT SHHHUSH

I've never been one for keeping things to myself. It's probably not the best trait when your job is to chat to eight million people every day. It's not that I'm a gossip or an intentional blabbermouth, it's just that I forget that some things aren't intended for public consumption.

On too many an occasion I've blurted out the line-up for upcoming One Big Weekends or inadvertently let slip when surprise guests are due to come on the show – to the extent that emails have circulated to the production department with the heading 'Don't tell Dave', which in fairness is probably for the best.

Some of you might remember that prior to Chris climbing Mount Kilimanjaro for Comic Relief, all of the team decided to take part in his extensive training by climbing a British peak with him.

We didn't want to let the public know where we were going – mainly to avoid the humiliation of people laughing at our lack of fitness and so that the paps didn't follow us up the mountain taking photos of us looking knackered, sweaty, rubbish, sweaty and a bit more knackered. For this reason, the location of the mountain we were scaling was to be kept secret when on the air.

Chris: 'Myself, Rachel, Comedy Dave, Aled and Dominic Byrne are off to climb a mountain. It's a bit of training for me and Rach and you guys will come in on Monday morning whingeing about how hard it is to scale mountains.'

> Rach: 'We're going to walk for four hours, and if you haven't done it for a while it's quite exhausting,'
>
> Chris: 'For a while, I don't think I've walked for four hours in my life!'
>
> Dave: 'I've been up Snowdon before but I think I was about twelve.'

Dave strikes again. For the rest of the show it became Mount Shhhush.

A similar situation occurred more recently when I accidentally announced that producer Sam was leaving, before it was common knowledge. Tina and I were organising a joint birthday party, to which the team were all invited and which, through coincidental timings, would also sort of double as Sam's leaving do. I mentioned this on-air one morning, not realising that Sam hadn't announced that she was leaving. The look of blank faces in the studio indicated to me that perhaps I had put my foot in it again!

> Me: 'Isn't that public knowledge? ... the fact that Sam's leaving??'
>
> Aled: 'Well it is now!'

Big mouth strikes again ... as The Smiths once said.

WRITING FOR GARY BARLOW

My favourite moments in my job always come when I get to see an idea or concept come to fruition. Quite often these great moments occur when I get to work with some of the many illustrious names that come through the door. Musically, down the years I've 'sort of' collaborated with McFly, Dave Grohl and Mark Ronson, to name a few, which is pretty cool.

But by far my favourite creative moment was when we worked with Gary Barlow on a song for Chris's birthday. I rewrote Take That's 'Greatest Day', making a subtle change in the chorus to 'Greatest DJ'.

On the off-chance that he was around, we got in contact with Gary to see if he could come in to record the song for us. Our producer at the time, Rachel, knew Gary from the pre-Kilimanjaro preparations which were taking place at the time, as Rachel was to climb the mountain along with Chris, Gary and all the gang. She sent him an email asking if he'd get involved and the following morning Rachel took me aside after the show.

'Gary could be in,' she whispered into my ear. 'He just wants to have a look at the lyrics you've written and then make sure he can move a few things round so he can come in this week.'

'Great ... um ... OK,' I stammered nervously.

Until this point in my song parody career, the only people I've ever had to have my lyrics approved by are Chris and Dom. Now one of the most successful songwriters of our time wanted approval over my bastardisation of his work before he would agree to collaborate on it. I'm still not sure why he agreed.

Gary couldn't have been a nicer guy – he came in and gave us a morning of his very precious time to record the song and shoot the video. It was a surreal moment as I was instructing Gary on various note and lyric changes in his song. He was a gent and utterly gracious throughout. I think he clearly recognised my raw talent and was as humbled as I was to be in that studio! Ha ha!

Some say he could be
The Greatest DJ in the world
He wakes us all up
Each boy and every girl

He talks me
He talks me
Everyday when I brush my teeth
He talks me
Some say he could be
The greatest of all the DJs
He brings happiness
And sunshine to all of our days

We all hear him
We all hear him every day
We all hear the show
And it's almost his birthday
(Sunday, Sunday)
(Is his birthday, birthday)
His birthday
(Sunday, Sunday)
(Is his birthday)

Ohh Dave spoke to me (On Monday)
Dave spoke to me
Said the show was a little light
We need a parody
Ohh ohh happy birthday
Happy birthday
For this would be cheaper than a card
On your special birthday

Some say he could be
The greatest DJ of all time
I could say some more
But I'm struggling to make this verse rhyme

Ohh, and the podcast is great
I download it for ma mates

Ohh the podcast is great
Ohh, ohh, woo ohh ohh

Dave spoke to me (On Monday)
Dave spoke to me
Said the show was a little light
We need a parody
Woo ohh happy birthday Chris
Happy birthday Chris
Alright
Happy birthday
Woo ohh ohh

WHEN EYJAFJALLAJÖKULL STRUCK

Like the rest of the world, at Radio 1 we're still at the mercy of Mother Nature. When Eyjafjallajökull covered Europe in ash and all flights were suspended, Chris got stuck in New York and Dom got stuck in Mallorca. The whole thing was a logistical nightmare involving Dom driving across Europe and Chris having to buy six new pairs of underpants.

At first, with Scott Mills covering, it looked like we might have the week off, but in New York Chris found a solution that would keep us on the air.

Using the American satellite radio station Sirius, which until very recently broadcast Radio 1 in the States, Chris was able to present the show from New York. It really was amazing. By setting up this studio in New York and with a satellite link, he was able to anchor the show from across the Atlantic. We stuck a laptop with a webcam on top of a box in our studio so we could see and chat to him and, bar a few minor details, he presented the show from another country. It was quite an achievement as the show sounded pretty perfect. Listeners would never have guessed there was an ocean dividing the host and the rest of the team if we hadn't said anything.

I think the success of that week had a lot to do with how long we'd been working together. I remember us all getting a big pat on the back from our big bosses at the end of it. It was a pretty impressive feat of technology and teamwork, if I'm honest.

REVERSE-A-WORD

It's always the simple games that are the best. This is one of my favourites and is easy to play in any situation. Give it a go at home. Despite Chris constantly ridiculing the game for being 'stupid', it actually made it all the way to television, appearing as one of the illustrious Challenge TV's pilots presented by Scott Mills.

RULES
Two players, plus one game host

The host spells out a word backwards. For example, 'mouse': the host says e-s-u etc. When one of the players thinks they know what the word is, they buzz in by shouting out his or her name. Each player only gets one guess per word. You start with short words, increasing the length of the word for each round. You get one point per letter of the word that's unrevealed at the point you correctly guess it. For example, if you guess the word is 'pigeon' after the first letter is revealed you get five points. If you wait till all but the first letter is revealed you get one point. If you wait till they've all been revealed then you're clearly an idiot and get no points. The person with the most points after the agreed amount of rounds is the Reverse-a-Word champion.

DOG OR PERSON?

I came up with this highly complex and intellectual game back in 2004. It never went on to reach the lofty successes of, say, Car Park Catchphrase, and many people phoned in to say that it was so bad that I should be sacked. Chris did actually throw me out the studio when I did a trial run-through, live on air, saying: 'Go outside and wait until someone calls you back in,' as a result of my awful yet highly intellectual game. It may have appeared rubbish, but I like to think of it as being avant-garde and ahead of its time, even though I'm not entirely sure what avant-garde means.

RULES

SECTION 1
The game host says a name, such as 'Lassie', for example, and the contestants have to guess if the name belongs to a dog or a person.

Here are some examples for you to use:

> Name: Freeway
> Ans: Dog (*Hart to Hart*)

> Name: Alfred
> Ans: Dog (*Heartbeat*)

> Name: Tyrone
> Ans: Person (*Corrie*)

> Name: Einstein
> Ans: Dog (*Back to the Future*)

Name: Ian
Ans: Person (*EastEnders*)

Name: Arnold
Ans: Person (*Diff'rent Strokes*)

Name: Roley
Ans: Dog (*EastEnders*)

Name: Wolf
Ans: Person (*Gladiators*)

SECTION 2 – THE NUMBERS ROUND

Like all great games, Dog or Person? isn't straightforward, no, sir. In the Numbers Round the contestant has to convert human years into dog years. As we all know, there are seven dog years to every human year, so if the host says 70 the answer is 10. You basically divide all numbers by 7. Simple, right? Now, for the scoring you get one point for small numbers (1–30), two for medium numbers (31–60) and three for big numbers (61 and above). The contestant can choose what size of number they would like. There are five turns each in the Numbers Round.

DAVE REVEALS ALL (SORT OF)

The thing with this book is that there isn't really a huge amount of structure to it all, which is good because it allows us to just randomly lob in stuff willy and indeed nilly. The fact that the set-up to this next section contains the words 'lob' and 'willy' is quite apt really, as it's the answers to a sex survey that appeared in a newspaper years ago. Short of material, Chris decided to do it on-air with me and Grey'ead one afternoon (as in he asked us the questions on-air. He didn't try and nob us.)

1) **What sex are you?**

   Will – Male
   Dave – Male

2) **When did you lose your virginity?**

   Will – 19–21
   Dave – I think 18 but it might have been 19

3) **Where did you meet your partner?**

   Will – At hospital radio
   Dave – At work. Well, I was *technically* working in that
      nightclub

4) **Have you ever started a relationship via the Internet?**

   Will – No
   Dave – I can't work the Internet – not even for porn!

5) **How many people that you have met via the Internet have you slept with?**

Will – None
Dave – None

6) **If you are currently in a sexual relationship, who is it with?**

Will – Girlfriend
Dave – (did not answer)

7) **How often do you say no to sex with your partner?**

Will – Never
Dave – (did not answer)

8) **What gets in the way of you having more sex?**

Will – *EastEnders*
Dave – The sideboard

9) **Are you happy with how often you have sex?**

Will – No, I'd like much more sex
Dave – I'm reasonably happy

10) **How long does sex usually last from first touch to completion?**

Will – More than two hours
Dave – More than two hours (I'm like Sting, I am. Well I'm semi-tantric.)

11) **Which TV programmes reduce your sex life?**

Will – Football
Dave – *How Clean Is Your House?*

12) Have you ever thrown a sicky from work to have sex?

Will – No

Dave – No

Chris – I've thrown a sicky from sex to go to work

13) Have you ever had sex at your workplace?

Will – No

Dave – No, I've heard that it's a sackable offence to have sex at work and not to have a TV licence!

14) Which of the following have you experienced ... threesome, partner-swapping, her dropping off?

Will – Her dropping off

Dave – (didn't answer)

15) Are you or your partner having an affair?

Will – Yes

Dave – Yes, obviously

16) Which of these men would you want as a lover ... Eminem, David Beckham, Jude Law or Justin Timberlake?

Will – None of the above

Dave – Not fussed about any of them, to be honest

Chris – I'd have Jude Law. I think he would be soft and quite tender

17) Who would you rather have as a one-night stand ... Jennifer Lopez, Kylie Minogue, Cat Deeley or Jodie Marsh?

Will – Jodie Marsh, she's mucky

Dave – Kylie Minogue

The alarm goes off in the morning...

TEDIOUS LINK

TEDIOUS LINK – PROPOSAL

Aim – An opportunity to play a recent classic song at the same time every day, and create a music-based feature for the Chris Moyles Show.

Mechanic – An agreed list of songs will be drawn up between ourselves and the music department under the guidance of Sarita. Each day a selected song will be played in the agreed time slot, and the tracks will link together from one day to the next as a result of a convoluted and rather tedious link. Each day we will refer back to the previous day's record, by way of a set-up to the featured track.

Music – The aim is to feature 'Radio 1 Anthems' from recent years. Huge records which people will look forward to listening to once again, as they sit in traffic or struggle through their homework in their bedroom. From Oasis to Orbital, from Blur to Basement Jaxx. There is no specific musical category, as long as it's good.

Possible Time Slot – It is proposed that this feature could occupy a slot towards the end of the show where the 'in-car' audience is at its peak. Possibly 5.30 p.m. or thereabouts.

Thank you – Dave

Without doubt, Tedious Link is certainly the longest-running feature. It first came about in 2002. Basically it's a piss-take of Jo Whiley's tenuous link. Jo would get callers to try and link one song to the next within a few steps. It was done as a straight feature, but to me it was just so ridiculous and random that it needed a bit of fun poking at it. So I jotted down a proposal.

I'm the first to admit that my Tedious Links are quite often not the most accurate elements of our show and over the years the team and listeners have picked up some howling mistakes. One of my worst was when we were broadcasting the show from Portugal during the 2004 European Championships. Linking the song 'American Pie' into Nirvana's 'Teen Spirit', I stated: '"American Pie" is a song by famous American singer Don McLean, who's sadly no longer with us, a bit like Kurt Cobain from Nirvana.' It would have been seamless if it weren't for the fact that Don McLean was and is still very much alive and kicking, and the night that I made said monumental gaff he was actually performing a concert in Glasgow. Whoops! I blamed it on human error and the fact that my Internet was down that morning, making fact-checking tricky, so I went with faith and instinct in my encyclopaedic knowledge of music. Sometimes, however, even music nerds have an off day. I tend to have about two a week on average.

GET A CHICKEN

It's a common scenario . . .

You wake up in the middle of the night, you go to the kitchen,
and you fancy a boiled egg. But hey, you're all out of eggs. That's right, you're
clucked… because you don't own a chicken.

You know, chickens actually make eggs…in their ass.
And it won't cost you a penny!

SO IF YOU WANT TO LIVE LIFE IN THE FAST LAYYYYYYYYN

GET YOURSELF A CHICKEN

AND GIVE YOUR FAMILY A PET… THAT PAYS ITS OWN WAY

From the people who brought you pigs, cows, ducks, lambs and rabbits

THE AFTERNOON SHOW

Our world changed monumentally in September 1998 when Chris received a huge promotion and moved to the afternoon show. Not only was it a massive step up professionally for both of us; it also meant we would be working normal civilised hours again – a big relief. We were very happy, to say the least. We would now be hosting the second biggest show (after breakfast) on the air.

It was the real arrival of Chris into the mainstream and an opportunity that we would both relish. Looking back now, I guess it wasn't always a given that I would move with Chris; but I'd like to think I'd made myself an integral part of his show by then. And Chris was very inclusive in the fact that it always appeared that I would move up the ladder with him.

It was a new world for both of us. We went from getting up at 2.30 a.m. to rising at 2.30 p.m. if we wanted to! We both felt as if all our Christmases had come at once. It was a golden era. We'd rock into the office around lunchtime, have a spot of pie and chips in the café, and then casually begin to prep our show, which ran from 4 to 5.45. We were back in the pub again by six. Cashback!

The ratings were great and all of a sudden we were a mainstream commodity. Well, when I say 'we', I mean Chris, really. It was his name above the door and with that he carried the pressures of the show being a success or a failure. All of a sudden he started popping up in tabloids and pretty rapidly he became a household name. Meanwhile, my voice became well known, rather than my face, and I was able to enjoy the vast degree of anonymity that radio offers. Something I've always valued.

While the show was, in essence, very similar to the Breakfast Show you hear today, when I listen back on tapes there's a cocksure boisterousness that I'd like to think we've since grown out of. One of the main differences was how much easier it was to react to the day's news events. I remember that the day the boys from S Club 7 got busted smoking marijuana, we spent a lot of the show poking fun at them with childish quips about their drug habit.

'Roach, Skins and Weed'

When you're in a clean-cut pop band
You have to behave, or they will slap your
    hands
We were out smoking gear in town
When the law came up and took all our names
    down

We didn't see the copper coming
No time for us to start running
Got taken to the local nick, cos ...
Smoking dope gets you arrested

```
Roach, skins and weed
We all smoke marijuana
Roach, skins and weed
In search of instant karma
The record company has thrown a fit
And said that we're all in deep shi ...
```

The ability to respond to the day's news is certainly one of the biggest differences between the afternoon and any of the morning shows. And, thinking about it now, I guess I do quite miss that element.

I always liked it when we got the top impressionist and long-term friend of ours Jon Culshaw in to do a feature relating to the day's news. One of my favourites was when we got him to play Frank Bruno and Lennox Lewis. We constructed this call where Bruno was repeatedly calling Lewis the night before his big fight. It was amazing how many people bought it, even newspapers! We were absolutely flooded with complaints. I mean it's not exactly feasible that Lennox Lewis would be taking calls on the night of his big fight. Another funny one was when we got him to call Michael Winner as Eric Cantona to ask for acting lessons. Michael Winner completely bought it and really wanted to help Eric, saying: 'You'd need a tape. I'd be willing to direct that and get the other actors in. I'd do that without charge, Eric my dear.'

WHERE WERE YOU WHEN . . .

Looking back over the past decade, and more, the day that probably stands out for most of us is 9/11. It was the day that changed the world and we can all pinpoint the moment where we were and what we were doing when those towers fell.

Don't worry, I'm not going to go off on a geo-political tangent and start ranting about the whys and wherefores of the various wars of the past decade. I only mention it because we were in the studio getting ready to go on-air when the attack took place.

Even today, when I look back on the news clips, I can't believe that it actually happened. When I see the footage that is still continuously played on TV, I find it so very hard to believe that it is real and isn't something from a Hollywood movie. I think it's the defining 'Where were you when it happened?' moment of our generation, just as JFK's assassination was for our parents.

On that fateful day, we were doing our usual in-studio prep before the afternoon show – checking emails, sifting through the papers for any material to use on the show. Mark and Lard were on-air when our producer at the time, Will Kinder, told us to flick on the television because a plane had crashed into one of the Twin Towers. In my mind, it was just a light aircraft and something relatively minor. Like everybody in the world our jaws dropped when we saw the reality of the situation.

Mark and Lard immediately cut to a news flash as the events unfolded. Of course they, like us, had to suspend any stupid and comedic features. I can vividly remember all of us from the afternoon show – Will, Lizzy, Chris and I – stood silently in the office smoking room watching the news through a glass window as the second tower got hit and the severity of the situation dawned upon the whole world.

For a while we weren't even sure we were going to go on air; I mean, Chris and I aren't the typical people to carry the BBC's flagship radio station during the world's biggest crisis in decades. Obviously we couldn't do our normal show as it was all a pretty sombre affair. We just tried to keep things tight and relevant, giving as many updates on the event as possible, while maintaining a professional manner about the show. It wasn't the time for our normal show style. I vividly remember Will and I scribbling down pages of relevant scripts for Chris to read out between music and news flashes as updates kept flooding in.

The show took a more poignant turn when we got hold of this regular listener who used to tune into our show in the States – Joe. He'd emailed us a few times and had been on the show a few times before whenever we were running a relevant segment. So we managed to get him on. He'd got out of Manhattan on his scooter and was looking out over the city from across the river in New Jersey. It made for some really relevant and on-the-mark radio as we were able to get genuine first-person information from an eyewitness on the ground.

It was the first time we'd ever done a fully serious no-nonsense show. I was really proud of us as a team and Chris as a broadcaster for being able to switch it up and deliver what was necessary for the occasion.

'The Cheese Song'

I like cheese because it's really nice
And it's also eaten by mice
Cheese is made from
Sort of off-milk stuff
Moo! Moo
I really like cheese
It is great on toast with ham

Cheese comes in all different shapes and sizes
And in all sorts of different flavours
You can have hard cheese and soft cheese
Like Edam, Gruyère and Cheddar cheese!

Take a look at my cheese
It's just a wedge of cheese
There's nothing left here to remind me
Just a small, hard wedge of cheese
Take a look at my cheese
It is just sitting there
Oh please won't you eat my cheese?

BATTLE NIPS

We ran with this game a few times before scrapping it. Despite being, literally, minutes of fun, we felt it didn't quite translate to radio.

RULES
The game is multi-player

You will require a copy of the *Sun/DailyStar/Sunday Sport* (any paper that shows boobs). One person draws a grid over the page, creating boxes 2cm x 2cm. Number the boxes down the side; letters across the bottom.

Each contestant then gets a go at trying to hit the lovely lady's nipple in Battleship-style hits. Each time a nipple is hit you call out 'Nip Nip Hooray!' The winner is the first contestant to hit both nipples. He/she can then lay claim to being Master of Battle Nips.

THE BREAKFAST SHOW

'We had the best hours in radio and we threw it all away!' – David Vitty, January 2004

I guess this is the part where I should harp on about the Radio 1 Breakfast Show being undoubtedly the biggest radio show in the land, if not the world. I should probably then go on to say how it's such a privilege and honour – how it was a realisation of a long and hard-earned dream for Chris and me. But on that first arctic morning in early January 2004, as we all shivered our way into work under the velvet-cloaked skies of midwinter London, I felt like we'd made a dreadful mistake. Bleary-eyed, we could only grunt at each other as we all but mainlined caffeine into

Dominic 'bubble head' Byrne

our veins. I had to share my reservations with the team – we worked the best hours in the world and we gave it all up for this!

Thankfully, that was an isolated low point. Once we got over the shock of swapping a 3 p.m. start for 6.30 a.m. it's been an easy ride – mostly.

The leap to doing the Breakfast Show was huge for all of us. For Chris it was the realisation of a childhood dream; for the rest of us it felt like a big pat on the back from the bosses. It was what we'd been striving for. One of the great benefits of doing the Breakfast Show was that we got to create a fixed team.

Of course the show has changed over the years. In those very early days we had such good intentions. I remember we planned on having a daily, pre-show meeting at 5.30 a.m. – a full hour before the show starts. Oh how things have digressed. Chris now gets in as the 6.30 a.m. news is being read, I'm upstairs frantically printing off Tedious Link and Car Park Catchphrase. Poor old Dom and Tina have to get in around 5 to prepare the news.

CAR PARK CATCHPHRASE

HOW TO INVENT A SILLY GAME FOR RADIO

One of my many ridiculous duties as Director of Comedy on the Breakfast Show is to come up with game ideas. Regular listeners will know that these games come in all shapes and sizes with varying degrees of success. Basically they're quite random – some are shit and some are *really* shit. But despite appearances there is a process that I go through to make up these silly games ...

STEP 1 – HOOK BEFORE CONCEPT

I usually come up with the game title first and the game afterwards. It's an arse-over-tit method but it's how I work, a bit like coming up with the punchline first, joke second. With Car Park Catchphrase, I remember going in one lunchtime and chatting with producer Will, as the first very raw incarnation of Car Park Catchphrase was actually born on the Afternoon Show.

'I want to do a game where we get people to use their car horns as a buzzer.'

'Let's incite road rage on the streets of Britain – I like it.'

STEP 2 – COME UP WITH THE RULES

Games ideas will come in many forms – for a long time, Will Kinder was my muse. Fire at Will was one of my all-time favourite games. Oddly, Will didn't like it so much, pulling rank and cancelling it after I clocked him in the temple with an AA battery and a can of Stella.

Will and I always got on very well creatively. So with Car Park Catchphrase, we initially went to work on coming up with a game based on car horns – it was a pretty wide spec. We basically racked our brains for any old game shows that we could rip off. Catchphrase was so simple that it translated onto radio beautifully.

STEP 3 – GET A JINGLE

It's amazing how even the flimsiest feature can sound high-spec and professional with a well-done jingle. Our jingle-maker, Sandy Beech (seriously), is the best. He adds his magic touch and even manages to dress up and polish my most turdy ideas.

STEP 4 – GET A CELEBRITY INVOLVED

When we started Car Park Catchphrase, Chris did the Roy Walker bit in his awful Irish accent – he sounded Dutch. The show didn't quite reach its brilliance until the real Roy came on board. We started off by getting Roy down to do one recording session with all the generic intros etc. It's now morphed organically into us getting him down eight times a year to reel off six weeks of daily scripts in advance – some people still think he comes in every day! I always try and pin the dialogue to an upcoming event, be it Glastonbury, Chris's birthday or, say, the World Cup – whatever makes it sound time-relevant. All in all, Car Park Catchphrase is probably the most labour-intensive part of the show!

ROY 'THE LEGEND' WALKER

I get quite star-struck whenever I meet Roy. Even though I write all his scripts and have fabricated this alter ego for him, I still find it disarming actually to work with him. He's a real old pro and is now very much a part of the show's extended family. While Roy has a thriving career hosting nights on cruise ships, I think his daily cameo on the show has been pretty good for him by thrusting him back into the mainstream. He now does quite a lot of student nights and has a bit of a cult following. He even hosted a live Car Park Catchphrase at Norwich University where they got two Lotus sports cars onto the stage.

Over the years I've kind of scripted Roy to be quite cutting and dark – which he isn't. I'm not sure how it came about but I've even alluded to the fact that Roy's character has a special friend

CIDER STREAM

THE FUTURE'S BRIGHT...THE FUTURE'S APPLES

DEBT CAN BE A HUGE PROBLEM...especially if you're a student.

Books, rent, rizlas and chocolate.... they all cost money. But now there's a way of cutting down your overheads, with the all-new **Cider Stream**.

Cider Stream is proven to reduce your offy expenses by up to 50%!

Apples go in... cider comes out... it's that simple!

You'll be amazed how much further your grant will go as you enjoy the luxury of cheap, strong cider...on tap.

So,reduce your student debt today... with the all-new **Cider Stream** – and see how much you can save!

CIDER STREAM

THE FUTURE'S BRIGHT...
THE FUTURE'S APPLES.

The makers of Cider Stream accept no responsibility for poor exam results linked to the use of this product and frankly anybody whose primary expense is cider and rizlas is a sponging loser who deserves to fuck up anyway.

CLAMS DIRECT

HAVE YOU BEEN INVOLVED IN AN ACCIDENT INVOLVING A CLAM OR ANY OTHER KIND OF SHELLFISH IN THE LAST SIX MONTHS?

Because if the answer is *YES* you could be entitled to cash compensation.

That's right…take Mr Flange: he slipped on a carelessly discarded clam while at work in Hartlepool and won…
TWENTY THOUSAND POUNDS!

Or Mrs Bartrum, who found a clam in her hot chocolate at work in Newton Abbot – and thanks to Clams Direct she won…
FIFTEEN THOUSAND POUNDS!

We can't change the past… **BUT WE COULD CHANGE YOUR FUTURE!**

Our representatives are standing by now… waiting to help you make a claim –

BECAUSE WHERE THERE'S A CLAM… THERE'S A SCAM

SO DON'T SUFFER IN SILENCE… WHEN YOU COULD SCREW YOUR EMPLOYERS FOR ALL THEY'RE WORTH!

SIMPLY CALL **0582 123 666** AND SPEAK TO CLAMS DIRECT TODAY

WE'RE WAITING FOR YOUR CALL

called Matthew. Recently Roy, Matthew and their 'pen friend' Juan all went to Download Festival – they could only get a two-man tent and it was all very cosy, apparently. Considering he's definitely part of the old school, he's a good sport and always has a laugh with us when we're doing the scripts, especially when we get him to sing. Roy Walker's reinterpretation of some of the Radio 1 playlist gems is one of my favourite things.

TWITTER

Twitter is an odd thing. There's no way of denying it, it's just odd. For ages I fiercely resisted the urge to broadcast the mundane and proudly stood up for my Luddite principles, until I was advised that it could be a good thing career-wise and reluctantly joined the ego warriors. It's something that I'm still not proud of. I've always considered myself to be quite opinionated (hopefully not in an obnoxious way) and felt that my private life should be private and was frankly none of anybody else's business. In contrast, Aled, Dom and Chris would be merrily posting about what they were having for their tea or what they were watching on the telly, and I was pleased not to be part of that. The problem with principles, though, is that they're seldom practical. Like communism and honesty, they sound good on paper but don't really work in practice, and I had to meekly climb down from my ivory tower and sign up with the Twitterati in order to self-promote for survival in this media jungle.

I think the reason that Twitter has been such a huge success is that it is perfectly suited to shallow self-obsessives like myself, who can compare themselves with their fellow cocks by the number of followers that they have on their Twitter account. I like to think that I'm not one of those people and that numbers aren't important to me, even though I currently have 275,207 people following my every move, which increased by approximately 75,000 during my stint *Dancing on Ice* (more about that later).

If I tweet about brushing my teeth, filling the car up or losing a sock in the wash, people will respond as if I've just said something life-changing and earth-shattering. I haven't of course, because nobody ever does. Everyone just electronically spouts irrelevance that thousands of people lap up on their laptops because said tweeter once appeared on the *X Factor* auditions or had a walk-on part in *Emmerdale*. In the same way that other people's crap seems more appealing and enticing than your own, people can ignore their own loved ones and everyday lives in favour of someone else's school run, Friday big shop or dark wash and in turn fuel the self-importance of these super-bores.

In many ways, much as it is a fantastic way of publicising oneself, in order to cynically cash in on the lucrative Christmas book market and pay for that holiday in Tenerife, it's still something that goes against so much that I hold dear. I still wish some days that I'd been able to stand strong and maintain my loyal Luddite ideals and valued prejudice, but the truth is that I didn't and succumbed like everybody else. For that, I'm clearly no better than the rest of those that tweet, and ultimately feel a little bit of a hypocrite and a lot of a twat.

While I'm extremely chuffed with my 275,000 followers, it's nothing compared to Chris with his army of 1.5 million! When Chris got stuck in New York last year during the ash cloud incident, he got pretty bored kicking his heels around the city on his own. One night he sent out a tweet saying 'I'm in this pub in the Lower East Side (or wherever it was), anybody who's around, come down for a pint.' Sure enough, after about 20 minutes people started trickling into the pub. Over the course of the night he managed to gather together a rag-tag posse of about a dozen Twitter followers to hang out with and have a few pints. Everyone had a lovely time, a few drinks and got to meet some new people. By all accounts it was a really amazing evening. I think in that context things like Twitter can be seen as a pretty cool thing.

@stevedewey57 @GemmaParkman @pen_clarke @SarahPaul7 @walishkris @1978deano @mick_wilson668 @LeZahLo0 @
KevPenfold1 @EIFIONF @jidsprice @alvin2030 @rubes077 @RGrocutt @brunge77 @DanialBrann @Dazzler136 @clarepear @
shindigt69 @nannie_rie @jerryjezzer @robfawsitt @Si_Lester7 @FoxyFraggle @bigalfraser @AstonMillward @Xemolindo @
MummaJak @toriatwinkletoe @mrsglendinning @neilcoyne @lisamckee43 @Grantking100 @ericdwaynegriff @Sadvillafan @
Eglese19 @snoopbod14 @suzannevirtue @andmck1981 @vandy1989 @leet2607 @OllieWalker85 @martynsevery @
SFROrdinaryBoy @Joner1983 @SmallHumanBean @barryd77 @littlewil1980 @Pic_South @tasands1 @BigNose_13 @
daveyboi294 @paul_crooks @JasonNorth3 @c_longworth @PaddyBreslin @liss_griff @Macauleyd @RachelMyers21 @lanzey25 @
chriswatki1974 @geordieharry @nettychawner @geordie_l @LittleTashiD @els1142 @HaywoodJoe @leearmo59 @M_I_C_K_Y_C_12
@kelleysheehan @dan_morris81 @SteveT14780 @Telebug1 @carpemter @abbyegg @dazzlerlight @NUJ_Cheshire @Kitchclothing
@LeilaRittey @LewisJones7 @flissgee @FergiHop @speries @marshproudfoot @tonypark3r @CharlieHarris98 @hayleyjlbaker @
Mimannee @orionbooks @Phlz @J_dog21 @BlakeCrane @NicMhathain @Jimbobjamess @ArticleseHub @Dannyboy19300 @
gingergeordie @patslimboyfat @soosiefandango @chris_topping @JimGellatly @EmmajaneDuggan1 @Steve_B1878
@Marcusknight91 @countrysideint @slimslaney1 @voicebanktech @gem_jo @jamie_vincent @nickhughes04 @milessutton @
kingAlexOfLuton @pauldalton1973 @Sweebee1977 @realsolaruk @ChrisAllen94 @dez_cooper @tel3611 @Scottmitch888
@ADKI968 @FionaFroggit @amyrebeccapage @SamWagner @quartermansh @pixie_penfold_x @gadgec @mark_jubb @drawe91
@MyEdoCoUk @jennywren1075 @Danielwhitwell @melhaji @mattybundy @cheeser83 @GarethWhitaker1 @wardel1972 @_
iazzjazz @Jezmunkeh @AgentXFootball @Ianlinforth @Georgegiraffee @Kizkins @Fraser9White @KikkyT @x666jox @dazmbooth
@Ludly @Wi11marino @ryanlukerussell @Chrisscougal @dannytATCC @Missamylindsay @Lukaz_25 @BrotherCharles @bryatk @
therealrabsie @aberry99 @Koicatbird @k_win8 @acampbell1985 @debilennox @LSRfm @dani_hunt @ajausten @stephenslade1
@nathwwfc @Abbss_84 @figwain @daniellakantor @yorkshiregemm @RoyRace9 @paul_Greenland @MARKWILL29 @Daniel_
eamer @mynameisSTACEYb @Milli1111 @FactorFiftyOne @jacquikellie @beth_vs @Bethanymills7 @jones799 @MrRickwood @
saudargaitex @craigspeakers @GordonBentham @berrycj @kirsty_lee89 @matty2stone @TracysTweeting @thelor83 @miles2687
@Rich83swan @andyatkinson73 @KrisJohno @Rudgeramma @smdunn1976 @butchyboyd @lythalla123 @laughdotcomedy @
liamcarberry93 @JoeHuggins23 @ne1menswear @grano69 @Mike_Gulliver84 @TheNottmJoker @dcguitargod @adracup1 @ian_
beale1968 @AdamWade2 @vipz_koa @sarahpeace26 @nikkiiii76 @ChrisSweepReed @RorieCowan @Holtom10 @JoannaStone93
@G21Rispin @jess_x18 @FutureproofPR @HazelB2112 @True4kinblue @LeeMilne88 @Me_Birch @AdamFill90 @mikesmart75 @
harphead @MilkNoSugarJack @ChrisJLonghurst @MissKane2011 @lozzaaxxxx @garyp10 @Alistair16 @aliedotcom @supersam27
@Keithw1966 @sbriggsey @manclandman @EmilyLangley98 @bobbytayls @EllsBells24 @kimmyyates @lauraandrews90 @lamkinr
@Maceyroyal @darb101 @tkerrster @RichVenner @GeorgiaRoseLee @thekdsauce @StarkidGleek252 @jules080670 @Bell27
@1CERCA @loulou_dodd @empen10 @lennoxniro10 @amywaters04 @RorySaggers @maggz_82 @Cookie2121 @jonknight1983
@paul_catlin @Mksp8 @Sassybing70 @Rikk1982 @DJ_Pikey @w00dall @heidi2211notts @skotferguson @10jackster @
Matthewbrunt @Tina_Fure_Hayes @tanyaroach @Worm_1980 @SallyBrader @Horrors218 @halller15 @staceymeak @KirstyADean
@MattTRose @sarahjayne_01 @nicholasgwright @moochthomas @Bu11man12 @Benquers @linny1010 @janevwallace @
conorisagooner @mudoff @lukeball91 @ChristophWhit @cheekylittlered @sara14366 @tvremoteking @ElliotMetcalfe @gilliano27
@MeeshaBennett84 @frankiebhoy1980 @joseba87 @kofhillboys @taylor_tash @camerkazi @tommoc84 @shirleysheds @Sharan23
@ColinHey @Jen216 @ellie_barnesy @RuthieCA40 @kimico99 @Rotum @Up_the_tweeter @JordyBrannan @Chrissie41 @
keeleycole @shanrh14 @RoryGallagher48 @loopylyndaloo @joel_thompson83 @Mortonstorm @ricoalexander85 @clogsie1
@missmearkat @ivegotabigone @pat571465 @cathrynp4 @stephenbarrett1 @kingswayking @Nptonbbobrfc @KatieBorley @
bobbystewart_1 @Jasonberry50 @CGlobe @isit_haveyou @BillyJGates @vickivicki90 @steven_mcp @sjshipp @garyreason
@napolean79 @SuperSonicMuzik @ben_2912 @bicklar @emma_ian @phillip1974 @Emma_W3 @krisc182 @ThePaulish @
DannyGreaves1 @gazhedges @Leejack1984 @grockall @edspruce @andymezz78 @Emily_Rees2 @Skies24 @mattyirons @
ShaneyboyRoss @Eldringo57 @SueJones74 @D_J_Morgz @jazbeech @Bluelungbutter @james_weare @Jamesm_Pearce @
racheljlw1 @Robghosthunter @alinapleskova @hanny_collier @peatock @brynjones73 @080592vicky @Michael_Vass7 @j_kim_carr
@19don89 @J_Mac92 @rjpedley @exoonline @johnson1988 @davetmassage @rachelwatson10 @laurenclaire119 @jjlivinglife @
EmilyCarter28 @CSefc1878 @HannahNaomi28 @FancyDressed @benteacher @EllieWhite__ @rubberb0b @JakeBalde @
shufflindotcom @DanLiptrott @louise71evans @lee_old @TaraHounslea @pinkeylolo @LukeShirley @lil_miss_willz @666rizlaz @
lisaspencer69 @MaeveHussey @mikesouthwell84 @Nikki9979 @darawlsmassive @JackNicholls3 @craig__manning @style_amy @
FrancescaByron @mandyp28 @Antm81 @kerryt108 @JamesSBowers @fionadsaints @Adamlett_14 @jacksilcocks @JingoJangoGirl
@dstrachan78 @glennday1 @VickyOdders @AdHolmes84 @dazaat66 @1nelly1 @staceayrobyn5 @dufferelli @Prawny44 @
Joshrgsport @JustPeteriffic @darrenladdoking @pauldino @CraigWilliamso3 @tirangaa786 @MarkLaw90 @RaineyMinx
@TREEZYB @whuyoof @BeccaGardenFarm @voodooloopy_lou @mattwit1973 @samjmoore87 @SpionkopDave @coyleisgod @
danvile81 @jser9992 @thewardinator @Jordan_D_Knight @mantle08 @David_Gods @djleethubron @lei_archer @SamanthaGioanna
@julesmaried @jonnyologist @Mickybreagan @themonkeytamer @qunburpo @lizburns35 @Jamesjimbo24 @hutchess80 @
BubuGoesDeep @mark_cam @ElbowBeer @Spud7154 @danchitty @VDribble @gareth1881 @craig595 @HandsomHarrison
@jimbobshag1 @dpnippy79 @dooheath @DavidMac1876 @Rossm84 @terry_hodges @jjswilson @Gillsfuture @nlmoulden @
ucyjane88 @stoddy27 @sphinx_p @benwhincup @Deano7112009 @kags42 @owen_beers @RobbieJ90 @A_Buzzer @murph294
@AC_55 @KarenJPickering @alex6bird @aeroycroft @Lisajo67 @Heroicab304 @kirtley1987 @lucynorth1 @Matt_walks77 @
Sprightlysarah @aarongsindle @EmiilyGraham @xxooLJooxx @moseleyp @brfc83 @RossTwentyOne @huxifer @BenjaminMarsden
@Matt_Flavell @SorchaC @beanychick81 @6_tinkerbell_9 @Trhino10 @daisyharriet91 @craig_fisher7 @fieldingsteve @stepool @
ElliotJenkinson @Jeniash @karlwallace @helbels1988 @xJenReidx @crayzeewhorse @Lakhan_Odedra @mikeyheadley85 @
SineadRenold @Kim2411 @chrisjones138 @mamakazzbar @Graham_bullock1 @howellpro @LaurieLazenby @tintin_official @
meganbrooks1989 @mcc_caoimhe @psomer76 @kahvebistro @Dominicnorton @SarahLKemp @kieranchadha @fozzy9675
@pretty_wowers @sainthope @sargeyboy1 @KellsBellsXxx @1980JCF @milenamedic @AliceBridger999 @Snakes44 @
dannyboygunner @danwinnals @httpxyz @Vertie_Moye @Bulman92 @WisnuSwat @christoppenney @MamaSalmon @Carolyne_
Bogema @Taz_Matin @Mw_87 @tomharries1995 @Swan_Robinson @carltunaturner @mummy2twobeauts @ls3112 @BrettSale
@Ac23686 @Dannilatarche @crogtheplumber @iamwhufc @tprwilliams @FountainJosh @dreemgirl_uk @Sloseph @whenmicecry @
DJBarry31 @Cllett @beermonsteruk09 @A_L_R_27 @AlanLemon @mjw1993 @SophiasBelle @mairikeir @nes2002 @djcj191 @
top_boiii @CpWalker9 @adriancoad @Kingy__77 @Binnsey24 @debs392 @gregharling @HelenJWhittaker @jakefbush
@laurarichards22 @cavendish52 @re_ple @samantha10903 @Mullan81 @LauraHoff1 @EleeshaPreston @BeccaWhitehead @
arichley84 @davlar99 @garethmcm30 @Davejb1989 @JillCraigs23 @SaraBowden1 @MrsKerriH @BenjyMorton @milolo66
@SaraBurns74 @bennybois83 @emcapper @mbradshaw007 @Fenel1aCS @AmandaCSuffolk @Corinthia76 @Bloxwwfc @real_
slick_rick @emma_louise29 @georgeFJ @RichardTollman @violetkccpickles @KRSCurtis @JMWilko @guylaine_roker @fishy189 @
sjbrookes2 @Lolsgurt @VikkiStanovitch @daniellieb16 @SammyO44 @ToneSloandog @alecboyd82 @studioremixes @Phila87
@martinturner86 @kimlouisedean @Solihull_BC @LiamOMalley2 @briggs_katie @lizp2711 @gkb82 @sj_allen92 @emmaderrick
@Yazlangley @Natalieledger @Feeble_beeble @kirsty_elder @Hals29 @JOHNKNOWLES6 @mcrcity @JoanneG79 @tereb27 @
mrfimcd @richiewarner @StaceyParry @scoobyroon @b3ef @DannyJones90 @ChrisRock39 @fifihelen @pigeonbasher @
lucyloulou82 @hil_walker @BigMarv1 @thesasman @swalesgirl @tgilch @Sheapdowg @vickysp83 @jedimasters001 @TheSMitchard
@RhysCrockett @becdiver @mattkilpatrick @MouseMagic1 @MissyRoud @geoffwaits @d_elworthy @KieranDowns1984 @
Joewhite987 @taylorclair @RebeccaPeryer @janegordon84 @buxton_nick @milliemcq @chriscjoy @Yarrow85 @sibby101 @hedheed
@BigDave2009Uk @MickRobbo1982 @drew_kenny @mikedunnie87 @underworldjam @linseymarie13 @samcj75 @ashwrabb
@3ting @lea_321 @robspongewilcoz @DontBe_aDingBaz @PropPenTyn @moore_tasha @nickoo_h @smarttaity @rachel_tayler

@mal020811 / AwS
What's the weirdest thing you have seen in London on your way into work?

Postman Pat and Jess.

@daisdrisc / Daisy Driscoll
Do you like olives?

No.

@CreakyPuppet / Creaky
What's your favourite Premier league ground other than Goodison Park?

St James' Park.

@steve_mitchel1 / Stephen Mitchell
What would be the best advice you could give to someone wanting a career in radio?

Do loads of work experience and never take no for an answer.

@PAPACALLSOP / Callum Allsop
As you are known for giving away secrets, what's the worst one you've ever given away? And how did it happen?

The entire line-up to Radio 1's Big Weekend. I'm not quite sure how it happened.

@LiloGreenhill / Lisa Greenhill

On a scale of 1-10, exactly how shiny is Dominic Byrne's bald head?

3.

@Grace_Says / Grace Findley

Where did you get your folkface outfit from?

Camden Market, North London.

@bigc1978 / Matthew Corke

If you can be over- and under-, can you just be 'whelmed'?

Probably.

@JBEngland08 / JB

Do you ever hear from David the photographer who was brilliant at the word game on the afternoon show?

Not for years, unfortunately.

@wallpaper_girl / Ellie Gibbs

How yellow do you like your bananas?

Very yellow.

@Fezelak / Faisal Akhtar

Dancing on Ice ... For the money or midlife crisis?

For the outfits.

@robynmurphy1995 / Robyn Murphy
What would you rather be, an elephant without a trunk or a duck without webbed feet?

Duck without webbed feet.

@susandevonshire / Susan Devonshire
Who was the best Dr Who?

I'm not sure.

@yeomanphill / Phill Sandford
Do you think Convoy should be remade? Maybe a GB version this time?

No.

@PAPACALLSOP / Callum Allsop
Who's the funniest person youve ever met and why?

Peter Kay.

@plumber_nick / Nick Sandy
What is the most memorable moment in your life?

This question, without a doubt.

@sherelyn79 / Sherelyn Pontremoli
Can you cook a nice omelette?

Can I? No, but I plan to learn.

@Gav_Kennedy1976 / Gavin Kennedy
Would you ever lie about your size. (eg feet, height or any other personal?).

No, I'm quite happy with what I've got.

@marcmfc / Marc Straub
Was your wedding ring really found?

Yes it was.

@NickLees / Nick Lees
What is the average life span of an angel fish?

4 years.

@NickLees / Nick Lees
How much wood would a wood chuck chuck if a woodchuck could chuck wood?

6 logs.

@DaJoBa / Daniel Bailey
How do we know if our question gets in your book?

You've just seen it, haven't you?!

@nealparry / Neal Parry
How do I turn on the washing machine?

It's the big button on the left.

@bfanciulli / Ben Fanciulli
Can you close your eyes and raise your eyebrows?

Yes.

@kevblyth / Kevin Blyth
When it comes to sauce, are you a red man or a brown man?

Red sauce.

@chalky337 / Dave White
Can you poo and wee at the same time?

Yes.

@croggers1 / Craig Austin
What's the best part of your life right now?

My daughter Nicole.

@mikelaupton / Mikela Upton
If you were going to be executed tomorrow, what would your last meal be?

It would be fish and chips and beans.

@miss_penni_x / Penni X
Do you ever see yourself getting married again?

Who knows.

@kellyfthetwit / Kelly Farrell
Would you rather be absolutely freezing or boiling hot?
And no you can't have a fan or a blanket!

 Would rather be cold than hot.

@crouchy221 / Craig Allington
What question do I need to ask to guarantee being in the
book? :P

 This one.

@David_Lloyd_ / David 'Lloydy' Lloyd
How did your first day at Radio 1 go?

 It was interesting. I had Nicky Campbell throw a minidisc
at my head. It was then I knew I was straight @ the deep
end. We've since made up and we laugh about it now.

@rachelmaltby / Rachel Maltby
If you weren't doing the amazing job that you are, what
do you think your life would be like?

 Not as good as it is now.

@ElliotBurns90 / Elliot Burns
If you could go for a pint with anyone ever, who would it
be and why?

 Gandhi.

@LozzaPattyPerry @diggydoh @bex_sun @elliey16 @roseheidi @wjplayford @stevie64murray @Naomi1405 @iklenik @charliehowee @BenM_x @donut0302 @spaceygiirl @jamie0nufc @Sezmum @polarii_parties @matthewperrett @Wightgoods @pikki1980 @incidentstu @mathos_guyos @Laura_Lu84 @beyondcolouring @AliceeDix @DanniFraylich @will_hanks @mtflowers8 @JonnyLaird @AaronStoker0 @kylemurphymufc @vikkilawman @LukeGawth @Lucyx_HVH @XxMissPhoebexX @tealcottage @slw0810 @Jedwiggiedavies @izzzysmitth @georgiespeller @a_carroll1989 @Hayden78 @stu_gough @hecklerboy75 @titaniaqueen @AmberArbuthnot @HannahPreston9 @chelseajenxo @baigsyboy @pcairey @VHorwell @NaomiB9 @Johnny_Cooke @chris_foxwell @jimbob1001 @Nicola_Anne95 @charrthomson @MichelleBaldeh @kimharbs @Benheane @ChampTravel @paul_yeandl @lollypop013 @LisaKearley @atd_design @Hitchy1998 @kllyc1 @mitchRYANwhite @gazbo144 @ishisnamejohn @suecounse @odonoghueclaire @therifkindpoint @KirstyLMcKinney @debshaugh @alway5introuble @GemsLL @sorutherford @jaxterj @richardhamburgh @evsbach2 @EmilyTabitha_ox @Street69 @SamHanna1 @THE_A_Plumb @Gallcock2 @NatashaGeraldo @tmtdigitalprint @JonathanGPayne @tuffmuff259 @RegPharmTech @phatlad46 @IWIDFSC @j23abbo @stavrosthegreek @dazhorrocks85 @fighting15s @jillterrycakes @JakeRodg24 @teasel35 @nateymatthews @Alexvilla1 @messyhancock @SparkyDaveW @Wickwarlowther @jintymc @M_Hodgkinson @thedanielreed @Staceylovecraig @abigailvz @chrissdouglas @Raci_gilmore @Tactilecazza @cortina44 @ididitagen @PUGHBOY76 @Dannycat90 @ElleP123 @HannahJadams88 @shaunmjones @koffee79 @adamhevs @kitemk @richthackray @mrspoisondwarf @Coreyronk @markbroughton79 @krisdowse @333frankli @ecirpeel @lordofthelodge @EJaaayyy @DanniellaD @garybealsey1985 @vickyogden1 @leebasil84 @keithandlucy @oliolioli84 @woodiewoodster @HarrietScarlet @Mandi1982 @naomibrennan @OiOichesterBoii @Gary_Nordstrom @JayRichards90 @Nuggie @swanny145 @hayleyrigler @EdWoodGolf @VanessaHunt1 @robin_pyke @wellman19 @Dave_Coull @ErnesiderLisa @johnyeoman92 @hayleylady84 @paulw23580 @michaela076 @Sazlberry78 @abbyw87 @Titw @brucecrisp @moaningmartyn @alisonmcud @garry_cheyne @Andrealake1984 @davexdanni @DangerMouseFC @chrislewis1991 @kt_hewitt @LCT_75 @Chlobo_AHill @sandraclambert @HelenLouiseMee @MattCollins_91 @Tamworth79 @Simon_Fawcett @ChrisBickley5 @ThePeoplesGroup @janeyb210 @rdavisongamlins @santuck17 @NatashaLees @Nick89Smith @ruffers50 @atifji75 @ando19730803 @1medders1 @RinataOnIce @Fiatbaby @scoobyswinney @frednell7 @lollylaus @Nicolamitford @CHuggins88 @SarahDeebs @manselway @Popz_LouiseXx @spartan99999 @ChrisCantillon @HellyHel @nathanb121 @IndieTheNinja @craighollowood @Averma_Insights @samsamY_16 @hickling_adam @stenav1969 @Karla_Will @andybowen71 @darrenjamesw @DanielTimmins1 @LouisaMaun @JamieMillar89 @mikehargreaves1 @danka17 @keeneyr @laheredera12 @caffyn321 @Loubs7 @rugbyball64 @isonhughes @gillielanelane @dylano8 @ashTamblyn @brendan_sheerin @skyblue1972 @GeorgiasMusicX @Wullie33 @Annie_Pannie86 @simon_marcs @NottyNic @simplejay1895 @LaurenLVKardash @lovelyloui2 @richygunny @Abby89 @tillyandtom @jenger17 @glassman123 @LukeMonaghan10 @DarrenMfc03 @seniormark @anton_ahmad90 @amygreenhalgh91 @bigkriss6678 @maxsamuelz @rigbyson @moffatt_claire @scottm1ddleton @michellemose @amymurray9 @brunost1170 @AmeliaGardner8 @Sianox @melemmett @lauraMnoble @gemboblyobs @KELLYLOVESMOYLE @jensothegreat @lwaitelittle @danarcher22 @mickylad45 @JRoberts89YNWA @shaneleeks @garald99 @gemlar1 @Ockyyy1996 @slforsy @daniel_seiles @paperartillery @theEdharris @JMcGennity @CanaryDan4 @emsbucks @nathanchaplin @Hayzhog @selinafogg @KevinArgent21 @wainewarren @StigsFatCousin @Nick100uk @dsmythe31 @OMeggie @aylalou @JFish01 @Magicmill76 @Richie76_1 @D7canton @jonash_87 @richpearson32 @SammiUnsworth @ann_boardman @gazzyonebomb @GinglesHammer @NELeighton @markgardiner40 @mpep @aimeejosiephine @markmongan @paulwatson1972 @debs_tickler @Kellyloves13 @8erKid @DavieRobertson8 @matt_j_bell123 @Notright @bearikins @tyson957 @GraemeAustin1 @louiseburton14 @sazzle1a @ajithkanayi @selbyshbk @james_moron @mellythrash @linzibrown7 @kellymrogers @cat_thumbs @Lorelei44 @manofsteel73 @kaAzZeR1 @guycleveland @goonerbaker8 @MeganWalkden @rpaskin1 @HannahR1988 @ekim1784 @siwall1982 @stevierout @ChloeBanks @YannahSchou @WishesandAngels @beckiejones52 @PawnstarTrav @clemo211283 @john23dodd @ritchiej19 @jeni_jen @mattstevens1993 @iain71 @Gibbons203 @joshrudge @sjbbb @robertsimmen @maphill66 @welshylfc @andyharper66 @mhastings1981 @shaolinfly @nalgeruk @creating_havoc @si_j_brown @MissB_84 @Reggie73 @rk2719 @JanetteHall1 @charlfaffer @Boardy8 @duggozinett @MarkCox10 @mattcarson69 @Sam_beale87 @J4jays @CherylRathbone @kellgraham7274 @CAJames321 @carloslufc86 @BexiLaw @BigBoyOli @SouthFrodfarmer @MisterSamwise @mart999999999 @paulmugs @neilno9 @mhooper76 @ScottMitchellUK @martingautrey @croydemansions @ktbaybee0101 @PalmerVicky @Holls246 @andypeacock @wombournematt @BrendanDKB @dave_wilson78 @kenithdogard @emmaredgar @IanWilky @andywallis74 @jenfie7 @RoyEFC @nerderer16 @Heavenly_7 @06taylorj1 @JamesDavies01 @layclerk @mike_p_7 @sammiejoholmes @AndreaCharley @kelbob @bray_lewis @leeusher22 @not_white_tom @Stuartlivesey82 @LAB_1988 @hayleyaowens @JohnInSwe @janey2702 @Ididot_Glen @mrsmcg1973 @clare_cooney @musicmantlk @R4CH33 @hbjfc @NikkiBaker9 @kmi25xx @Loid_san @Fritha80 @richardjones162 @btnholidayhomes @mucker001 @81_woody @Berniepaul15 @markyr29 @smilybeanbag1 @darrencmorgan @frowster @B3ccaNoble @Djtazza @jim_adamson @tking384 @lee22r @LisaGold82 @steeps14 @gailgg66 @carlsruh @littlespuggy @breenster83 @curlyshew @stevie_uts @breconlingerie @nataliedm86 @COLINJWP @RachelTostevin @stueymills18 @ronnieaz79 @zmm32 @andreaocc @Throbbos_05 @mrsnutterly @kirstylou4 @welshmilky @MattHardwick99 @jamesmaddison @Ellie_Mountford @traceyflack @lauramacvicar1 @mark_cavanagh @keelgm @andywilsonpe @toffequei @Gazwright3 @TheBEXmusic @katecarnaby @nrj_boy @josearle @johnlowe6744 @harryjamieson04 @jbc_5th170205 @littleemjane @RBuck3rs @Franklymint @BenPlayle @Togusa82 @littleyin @RebekahJohn @STAGECLAN @Gazzamobb5 @Marklen14 @Sirkirkes83 @clairecove @Paul_Stuart @shelley175 @clarebezza @BellaMai2 @jacyszyn @Andy_strickson @Iamsparkycus @Edinburghcentre @ElleshaT @morleyb @gazedwardsgaz @phill007uk @tallythandi @mudhuter @MelanieGrannell @jayelektrik @FinneyLucy @tomaz808 @puckty @alliarnold74 @slb452 @aj_south90 @tmukkaa @ladylauramcc @katiec1973 @pusharski1 @HanWordsworth @di_dray @jmcmullen1988 @Loneill96 @swyatt86 @Churchy10 @JustineColborne @Laloulla @Noyesboy1 @WARLORD383 @ValAnne888 @davidssscott79 @SteRedgate @leggi7 @jbugg64 @StephBeechener @HenryScott_ @Shaz2463 @nelface @jackthommo80 @laurabowbrick @urban_chick7 @jimmyfromleeds @GMan36500 @sharpystar @Rebecca_Carton @ianlyons7712 @jamiehillen6806 @lisapegwilson @ringman79 @InsideViewMusic @markcrowder6 @Stevetownsend2 @mr_rae @aliceevans_ @michaelwarner88 @MHanger68 @al_robc @MikeJackaman @Chaynes1811 @EloiseEvison @tweettwoo77 @Lauren_1499 @MichaelTarbuck @Lisa_Lisad @JenDarlington @LadyBoromir @Stroppysal @villyvilly1 @simon_fletch @SJM80 @sophiapoole24 @MrsRennz @Tommo26 @karlyhill121 @LiamJJJones @Geekogrande @Marketingregina @o0amynoos0o @watttwo @leanbean_87 @LukeBrentSavage @richsettle @1Danniella @williamsjon57 @boobooobahbahboo @xxsuperstarrxx @Mcclinker @AimeeJones84 @cosworth76 @Hoopey1991 @dickie_ted @dadisabaldyplum @DavidMelonHead @CraigGilly @X_FactorBingo @dobsmith11 @Madman899 @Tuxey @GerrydeBrun @Aggybizz @charlie_580 @McGinz @nozza_LUFC @alimcclune @AbiFowler @chalkie77 @robertforrester @xrayjacky @gmangobluejays @sectioned_dan @j0shd0yle @RuthBill1 @doughlicious @mattcollins141 @uglyadam2 @Meggy1236 @Wimpers1 @Speno06 @LiamCroninUK @official_jamesc @pcurtis135 @PenelopeD23 @AmandaJaneHomes @pondhia @DavidAxford1 @kmcg1982 @Trend17 @EllaCoakley @theboywonder3 @ZoeGodfrey1 @PaulLynch85 @LeeannMcDonald1 @Sally_RB @elainema34 @BrianCarter14 @hellorach @Kezza_Lou @Cathschof @darrenboyle1 @SerenaStanbury @EmmaJarrett @philiebbbb1402 @Marcmc1980 @Sam_Lenny @PIDJIOW @Lou0274 @swg1983 @PhilMarlow1978 @MahoneyHel @graeme_26 @mark_portsmouth @hayleyfieldwick @msraynerwrites @discoswift @iamdannybs @Chezzabarn @lukeburr77 @Cara_L_Murray @hartnell88 @Deanowb @alfie_1969 @janinejo @Tom_Rogan @alex_tottenham @mickfitz2011 @shabbarecords @laura5ft2 @rachelashmore76 @jaypay19 @SammRobinson97 @jeffner_ @c4stle @SianPritchard1 @LGM82 @StringerPaul @SarahJayneCole @weston1603 @staceynix7 @lynda2559 @Leon_albulena @adambruce11 @Daryl_is_Here @LINCOLNFAN92 @mrsnicb @joshuadunning @kidzonerb @JedNewton @Gavlar1981 @NMWealthall @stumac70 @cheesy_wardle @cablitt @abbie_chetland @clairehunter15 @willers87 @lulu7815 @LayneyTee @algarjames @Russkyhatton81 @lilllegsy @DanBrown5915 @DoyleyBoy1998 @brandyqueen72 @dcpltd @adgray13 @cpstoddy @paulmiller33 @Leonardotriper @TheTanyaRock @lukeyyyy_1996 @Jaymez76

THE LA TRIP

Sometimes my professional life feels a little bit like a holiday. A recent trip to LA saw us rubbing shoulders with all the Hollywood A-listers and the Village People, who happened to be staying in our hotel. We went and did the show from the States not so long ago – in September 2008, as I recall. Whilst in the City of Angels, our 'work schedule' involved interviewing America's biggest movers and shakers, such as J.J. Abrams (*Lost* creator, among other things), Dave Grohl and Pink, although it did afford us some downtime that we thought might be nice to use for lounging around our rooftop pool with a few beers. Sadly, though, we were there to work and work we did, as we received orders to go and be creative: 'Go and make some nice colour features for the show.'

'Well, we're in LA, so let's go and find some celebs,' I suggested. We'd done all the other touristy things so we wanted the see how the other half live in Tinsel Town. Dom, as ever, was more than happy to take part in some mindless titting around.

Fortunately, before we left London I'd printed off a list of Hollywood celebrity addresses that I had easily found on the Internet. I did wonder why this secret information was so easily available, and figured that there must have been some scope for out-of-date information and wrong addresses; but I decided to print the 20-page document nonetheless in case we needed it, and this felt like the ideal time to employ the fruits of my top investigative work

The one thing that we didn't want to do was look like tourists, so in order to pass for genuine Americans during our LA Star Search I bought a couple of LAPD baseball hats from Santa Monica pier for me and Dom, which I thought – together with the huge SUV that I'd hired – would make us look like bona fide locals.

The look we were going for was that of a couple of hired bounty hunters as we sat high up in our gargantuan SUV and cruised around the palatial streets of Beverly Hills and Hollywood hoping to get a sighting of a Hollywood A-lister – although in reality we probably looked a bit like Dappy's two dads.

We also found a larger-than-life lady on the corner of some street in Hollywood who was selling 'official maps' of the stars' homes. Realising that her map would most probably be more accurate and up-to-date than the one I'd printed off in the office before we left, I happily paid her the $20 that she was charging – something that Dom said made me appear to be a gullible idiot, and the sort of thing that exposed us as tourists, despite our massive vehicle and LAPD baseball hats.

Even with a total lack of actual success, we enjoyed our LA Star Search and it even inspired us to write a treatment for a (as yet uncommissioned) TV series. We know that we'd be brilliant at it, and that it would make amazing telly, so I would imagine the TV executives to whom we pitched the idea are just trying to work out the best time to schedule our Hollywood exploits, so as not to clash with their other big shows. Whilst on patrol in our sports utility vehicle, we ate foot-long subs and drank sodas while spying on the homes of Bruce Willis, Jackie Chan and Sly Stallone, to name but three. Suffice to say, it was a total disaster in terms of celeb-spotting, although at one point we did sing 'Hello' outside Lionel Richie's house, only to be told by a grumpy-looking security operative that 'Mr Richie hasn't lived here for nine years!'

The closest we got to actual celebrity contact was at Pierce Brosnan's house in Malibu. We had a conversation with his Mexican maid through the intercom, who politely informed us that 'Señor Brosnan had gone out for lunch.' Three hours of waiting outside his house failed to result in a sighting of James Bond ... although we were just chuffed that the address we had was still current. In a way that made me feel better about spending $20 on a map, although Dom still said I was a nob and that we got ripped off.

We'd have been better off staking out Broadcasting House back in London. Such was the failure of our celeb-spotting, we eventually resorted to tailing an official 'Star Tours' bus. You know the type, with the gaggle of shuffling socks-and-sandals, visor-wearing OAPs. They were being ferried around the celebrity homes of LA and appeared to be more organised in their star-stalking than us.

It didn't take long for their attention to turn to this elephantine SUV that was creepily following them. Soon their faces were pressed against the windows, trying to see who was muscling in on their tour. Rumbled, we skulked off back to the hotel to have a couple of beers round the pool, which we felt we deserved now that we'd put in a decent shift, and done a proper day's work!

DAVE'S AMERICA DIARY

The first time we went to the States to do the show back in 2002 was one of those pinch-yourself moments in my career. At the time, I kept a diary of the trip, which I found while leafing through notes to write this book. It's a nice little insight into how much fun we had (and it's an easy way of bumping up my daily word-count a little, which always helps).

DAY 1 – MONDAY, 29 APRIL 2002

I can't remember the last time I felt quite as tired as this. It's now midnight on Sunday and we're in the middle of the desert on the way back from the Coachella music festival. We're all due up in approximately five hours, and by my reckoning we're at least two hours away from seeing our pillows. The day seems to have gone on for ever, due to the combination of the distance we've travelled, and the fact that our bodies are rapidly trying to adjust to the time change, which has put us eight hours out of sync. Jet lag can be hugely disorientating, and all of us look and feel severely jaded after the events of the day. That said, in terms of what we wanted to achieve, it's been a very productive first outing.

The Coachella festival takes place in the middle of the desert about three hours' drive from LA, and this year it played host to the likes of the Foo Fighters, Pete Tong, The Prodigy, and Oasis as the headline act. Our aim for the day was to get some interviews with the acts concerned, see some of the bands and soak up the atmosphere in this bizarre but beautiful location. Oasis played superbly to what appeared to be a slightly weary and apathetic crowd. Perhaps the weekend had taken its toll on California's beautiful people, but nonetheless they sounded fantastic as we listened and rubbed shoulders with showbiz luminaries such as Robbie Williams, Drew Barrymore and Cameron Diaz. It has undoubtedly been a very surreal day, as we desperately try to come to terms with our surroundings. Any weariness that we've felt throughout the course of the day has been instantly nullified by the fixed grin that has lit up the face of our competition winner Paul Titley. I don't think he's stopped smiling since the moment he realised he was coming with us. During the course of his first day away he's met Pete Tong, Beck and Robbie Williams, with Robbie's parting words being 'Say goodbye to the lad from Cannock for me' as he disappeared into the distance complete with flat cap and customary minder. Paul is understandably chuffed, and his wide-eyed enthusiasm at all that is thrown at him makes him a pleasure to be around.

Tomorrow sees us do the Warner Brothers studio tour in the afternoon, where I apparently have a 'surprise' to look forward to. I always feel a bit apprehensive about surprises, but in this case I suppose I'm quite excited at the prospect of this mysterious treat that Will has apparently organised for me. Today has been long, bizarre, confusing and hugely enjoyable. I would love to describe it in more lucid detail, but I'm so tired that my faculties aren't working properly, and the dawning of day two is approaching a little sooner than I would care for. If tomorrow is anything like today, then it will be something to look forward to. Our competition winner Paul is looking forward to it already. I just hope he can wipe the smile off his face long enough to get a bit of kip. We shall see.

DAY 2 – TUESDAY, 30 APRIL 2002

Day two in California, and there's no let-up in the frenetic showbiz orgy that is the Chris Moyles Road Trip. Last night's late arrival back from Coachella allowed me the grand total of 90 minutes' sleep. However, this was a good hour more than Will and Lizzie, who were busy in their rooms editing our Noel Gallagher interview in time for our first show. The lack of sleep resulted in us awarding ourselves a lazy morning by the hotel pool in the company of Guy and Craig from Elbow. Caesar salads and sparkling water were consumed by the weary team, while Guy from the band was busy raving about his new-found love of strawberry daiquiris. Once again, it wasn't your average Monday morning, but it did provide a much-needed rest after the physical and mental exhaustion of the previous day's round trip to Coachella.

Having successfully completed the task of being Pete Tong's disciplined and dedicated desert deputy, it was time to allocate Paul his second challenge of the week. This time he had the task of arranging and undertaking an interview with a 'pop star' of his choosing, provided it wasn't Guy or Craig from Elbow, who were a little too accessible at the time. I thought that this would

result in Paul spending the day in his room, frantically
phoning around in the desperate search for some
D-list 'has been' who would grant him five minutes of
their precious time in order for him to complete his
second challenge. However, having seemingly sat by
the pool for a mere five minutes on his mobile, he had
managed to set up an interview with Christina Millian
at two o'clock at the headquarters for Def Jam records.
With phase one complete, Paul could relax for another
hour in the sun before donning his best clobber for his
meeting with the aforementioned Miss Millian. While
he headed off in search of celebrity gossip, we travelled
north to Burbank for our VIP tour of the Warner
Brothers studios.

On his recce for this trip a fortnight ago, Will did
the studio tour and returned to London excited at the
prospect of the 'surprise' he had arranged for me. I was
still feeling a little apprehensive, and spent the half-hour
journey to the studios trying to work out what it was they
had in store for me. My surprise arrived twenty minutes
into the tour as I was confronted by the entire set of
The Dukes of Hazzard, with the 'General Lee' parked on
the set gleaming in the afternoon sun. I got to sit in it
and have a pile of photos taken, which I believe is not
the norm on this particular tour. They had apparently
brought the car out of storage especially for me, and the
hospitality of our guides Dean and Catherine made a
very memorable day all that more special.

Tomorrow's agenda involves the potentially daunting
task of interviewing legendary Sex Pistols frontman
John Lydon in the afternoon, followed by a black-tie

party for the Gumball Rally at Hugh Hefner's Playboy
Mansion. I know I'm using the word 'surreal' a lot at
the moment, but with that sort of itinerary for a Tuesday
afternoon in LA, it's difficult to find a more appropriate
adjective for what lies ahead. The Lydon interview can
surely go either one of two ways. My fingers are crossed
for a trouble-free meeting of minds, although with the
evening's focus of attention being the hiring of tuxedos
for tomorrow night's party at the Playboy Mansion,
you get the impression that it's not John Lydon that is
foremost in people's thoughts for day three in LA.

The Chris Moyles
Show Team circa 2002.
Lizzy Buckingham,
Will Kinder, Chris and
me looking moody in
the desert somewhere
between LA and Las
Vegas

DAY 3 – WEDNESDAY, 1 MAY 2002

Having breezed through his Christina Millian interview,
Paul's hobnobbing with the LA showbiz set went from
strength to strength as he and Chris ended the day
boozing with Chris Evans, Vinnie Jones and half the
cabin crew from Monday's transatlantic Virgin Airways

flight. He looked as if he was suffering the effects of the day's exertions, as he crept into the studio this morning with his trademark grin, bedhead hair and pungent ale breath, but it took only one sausage and egg McMuffin to get him back up to full strength and ready for the next exciting chapter in the tale of Titley's travel tasks

This time he was set the challenge of getting the new Starbucks single by 'A' played on a US radio station, using only his new-found musical knowledge, blagger's bible and copious amounts of the customary Cannock charm. Whether he achieved his objective we are yet to find out, but in the meantime we set about preparing ourselves for our eagerly awaited and slightly daunting interview with legendary Sex Pistols mouthpiece, John Lydon.

I must admit that this interview worried me a little. I always felt that it had disaster written all over it, and that our scheduled hour-long 'chat' with the man formerly known as Johnny Rotten had all the potential of ending after about ten minutes or so, with Moyles and Rotten parting company due to differing opinions and mutual hatred. Fortunately I was wrong, and the interview proved to be both amusing and thought-provoking as Lydon lamented about his views on life, love, politics, the monarchy, religion, music, the class system, the welfare state, more politics, and a bit about the benefits of the Californian sunshine to his sense of mental happiness and psychological well-being. Chris actually handled it very well, and the two of them seemed to get on surprisingly well as they put the world to rights under the glare of the midday sun. With that out of the way and in the can, there was only one thing left for us to prepare for mentally, as we donned our tuxedos and set about getting ready for the evening's Gumball Rally party at Hugh Hefner's Playboy Bunny Mansion.

From what I can gather, the Gumball Rally is an annual opportunity for the créme of over-privileged public school hoorays to race their flash cars from A to B in a vulgar display of wealth, skill, good breeding and more wealth. They finished this year's 'Gumball' with a flash party and awards ceremony at the aforementioned Playboy Mansion high up in the Hollywood Hills. The setting was magnificent, and Emily, our PR contact and host for the evening, couldn't have been more helpful and welcoming; but in fairness we felt a bit like outsiders. It was a party for the competing Tarquins, and for the silicone-enhanced birds who wanted to sleep with Tarquins, and with us not fitting into either category we felt a bit like we'd gatecrashed someone else's do. That said, the evening did provide plenty of laughs and we didn't by any means have a bad night. I suppose we'd just built it up a little too much in our heads, and realistically it was never going to live up to the bikini-clad, champagne-filled-jacuzzi image we had all envisaged.

Next stop is Las Vegas for what promises to be a culture-fuelled orgy of the senses, once we've negotiated the six-hour drive through the desert from LA. Our current track record for getting lost on the roads in this country means that most of our journeys take twice as long as advised, so I'm hoping that we get it right this time otherwise we'll be lucky to get checked in before Thursday. Once again a long and surreal day is drawing to a close. I'm trying to think of a profound statement with which to round off today's log nicely, but to be honest I'm absolutely shattered and frankly can't be arsed.

Viva Las Vegas

Chow
X

DAY 4 – THURSDAY, 2 MAY 2002

The lack of sleep is starting to take its toll on me. Since we arrived on Saturday night, I still haven't amassed more than ten hours' sleep in four nights and my body is crying out for a rest. This may sound as if I'm moaning and I don't mean to be. It's been a truly amazing trip, with each day being a once-in-a-lifetime experience, but we're cramming so much into our days that there's little time to recuperate, and at the moment I'm feeling decidedly weary.

Today's adventure was the long-awaited roadtrip from Los Angeles to Las Vegas. It's about 250 miles through some of the most spectacular desert scenery you could ever wish to experience. There wasn't one disappointment throughout the whole day, and our decision to drive as opposed to fly was completely the right one. Eight of us travelled in a two-car convoy stopping periodically for food, photos and fag breaks along the way. With us are a journalist and photographer from *Maxim* magazine, recording the experience for posterity from our point of view, and financial necessity from theirs. We managed to get what I hope will be some fantastic photos to illustrate the article, which *Maxim* are due to run sometime towards the end of

June. It's actually been a very visual day, which is somewhat ironic, bearing in mind we work in radio. I can't possibly put into words how stunning today's drive was, and can only hope that the photos that accompany this instalment of the diary do justice to what we experienced today. It's now gone midnight, and tomorrow morning's call time has just been brought forward to 5.15, in order for us to make sure that everything is working properly in our Las Vegas studio set-up.

The only thing left to say is that we are staying in one of the grandest hotels I have ever set foot in. It's a huge sprawling five-star affair, and is, in fact, so big that I've only seen a mere fraction of what it has to offer. Once I've been for a nose tomorrow I'll be able to give you a better picture of what the whole Las Vegas experience is all about, but for the time being I'm off for some kip in the biggest bed I've ever seen, in the most flamboyant and ostentatious town on earth.

Viva Las Vegas

DAY 5 – FRIDAY, 3 MAY 2002

Las Vegas is a bizarre place. No sooner do you think you've got your head around it and it surprises you again. It's a town totally devoid of taste, and as soon as you think you've seen the most disgusting and crass display the Western world has to offer, another one pops up to pale your previous thoughts into insignificance. Having done the show and dispatched Titley off to area 51 for a spot of alien-hunting, we were scheduled to be in the Luxor Hotel for a lesson in the noble art of gambling.

We arrived en masse to be taught some croupier skills, when I suddenly realised I was going rapidly downhill with my newly acquired flu symptoms, and was going to have to retire to bed. I'd been bunged up all morning, and as we stood in the middle of the casino waiting for our tutor to arrive, my head started pounding, and the combined effect of the lights and the incessant drone of the slot machines made it feel like I was experiencing Satan's symphony first-hand. My duvet was calling, and after a couple of aspirin and an hour or so sleep I was feeling better, although, to be honest, still nowhere near right.

We received an email a few weeks ago from a couple of listeners who said they were getting married in Vegas while we were here. They requested that we might be their witnesses, so with the potential for entertainment and the show in mind, we headed off to the 'Little Chapel of the Flowers' to be part of their special day. Despite the drive-thru Burger King opposite, and the sign above the chapel advertising Firestone tyres, it was a truly pleasant affair. Mark the groom compared his pre-wedding jitters to the sense of nervousness he got before getting his tattoos, saying 'It's a bit nervy beforehand, but once you're in you're okay'. To be fair he did look better after the event as he lit up a Lambert and Butler and seemed reasonably relaxed as he contemplated the life-changing experience he'd just undertaken. They were nice people who had travelled from the far-off shores of Basingstoke to make their lasting commitment and, having seen them later on in the hotel bar, they looked every bit the honeymooning couple, albeit a bit jarred.

It's been a truly extraordinary week. We've had too many great times to mention, and the reactions and enthusiasm of our winner Paul Titley have made the whole thing thoroughly worthwhile. He's been an absolute star and a pleasure to be around, and is currently trying to mentally prepare himself for the homecoming shock he's about to receive as he instantly joins the Cannock showbiz set. I'm confident he'll be able to handle the pressure and feel that he could actually make a killing in the world of after-dinner speaking with his Vegas anecdotes and Beverly Hills blatherings. He's a top lad and I wish him all the best, although if I'm honest, I don't think this is the last we're going to see of the Titmeister.

Outside broadcast trips such as this take an enormous amount of planning and co-ordination, and while there are far too many people to thank for the week we've had, special mentions must go to Will, Lizzie, Jude, Mick and our engineer Steve Richards, whose endless hours of endeavour enabled this idea to become a reality. In addition, the Chris Moyles minisite has covered and supported so much of this trip behind the scenes, and it's the efforts of our favourite Whitley Bay web monkey Scott Cawley that have produced a site which I believe is as good as anything I've ever seen. We set out to do a week away and deliver five cracking shows from the States as part of Radio 1's 'One Life' campaign. I hope that we came somewhere close to achieving that, and that the shows were as good to listen to back home as they were for us out here. It's been a week that I believe none of us will forget. For those of you that made it happen – Thank You.

Just two weeks after this, my Dad lost his battle with cancer aged 63. I mention it here as the trip to LA and Vegas, more than any other time in my life, was probably the biggest challenge for me – in terms of trying to balance my job commitments and living a very privileged existence workwise, with real family heartache and struggle back home. To be fair, I had been doing this for a while, ever since my Dad was diagnosed with bowel cancer in 1998. It changed everything and had a profound effect on me, and the rest of the family.

His new-found philosophy of 'life's too short' was my primary motivation for leaving the security of the BBC and taking the tricky route of going freelance, which so far (touch wood) has paid off. It was a huge decision to make and I couldn't have done it without my Dad's blessing, as I sought his advice on most things. For the next four years, at times, it was a case of 'putting on the mask' when it came to doing the show with Chris and the team. I had to try to balance all the fun and frivolity that comes with titting around for a living, by ending the show to leg it over to visit Dad in hospital, or get on the phone to Mum to get the day's news. I had to try to separate all the heartache of what my Dad and Mum were going through in order to carry on. I would just go into 'show mode' to get through it and there was therefore, a very real chance that I wouldn't be able to go with Chris and the team to the States in 2002.

My Dad's cancer was now at an advanced stage and there was nothing further that could be done for him. Work knew that I might not be able to leave my family, and if I did go then I was on standby to fly back at any point. Having discussed it all with Mum and Uncle Dave, Dad's brother (who was an amazing support for the whole family throughout Dad's illness), it was decided that I should go and they would let me know if the situation were to change. So there I was hanging out in the Playboy Mansion, or sitting around the pool in our Beverley Hills Hotel seemingly living the life of Riley, but what people didn't know was that behind the scenes I was spending a lot of time in my hotel room on the phone to Mum or my sister back home, with all of us in tears and going through the hardest thing that anybody has to go through.

It was a really tough balancing act, but I got through it and managed to get home to see Dad for those last two weeks. I feel fortunate that I got to spend every one of those days with him at his bedside before he passed away on the morning of the 17th May 2002. It was the hardest thing I've ever experienced and there's not a day that goes by when I don't miss him.

Dad

REALITY TV

I haven't done much in the way of telly, reality or otherwise, but that which I have done normally involves me dressing up in some kind of ridiculous outfit and making a tit of myself. I really don't mind, as I think you go along with the whole panto aspect of said situations and opportunities and either throw yourself in, which in some cases I have done quite literally, or you don't do it all. I'm always genuinely quite chuffed to be asked to do reality telly, because I never consider myself to be a famous person, and certainly would never describe myself as a 'celebrity'. Maybe I should be more showbiz and discerning about what I choose to do, although I can honestly say that in terms of what I've done in my very brief list of reality TV appearances, I've thoroughly enjoyed myself and had such a laugh in such a surreal environment that I don't really see any downside. I think it's the fact that I find it weird being on telly shows that I watch! I'll sort of zone out halfway through the filming of these shows and see the set as if I'm watching it from the comfort of my sofa at home, and then think ... what the fuck am I doing here? ... I'm inside the telly!! Which is weird.

One of my first such experiences was on the BBC's remarkably highbrow game show, *Hole in the Wall*. For those unaware of this sophisticated show, it involves contestants standing on the edge of an ice-cold pool while a wall with a hole of varying size and shape comes at them. The contestant has to make it through the hole without being pushed into the water to get points for their team. If that isn't ridiculous enough, all the contestants have to wear crash helmets, elbow- and kneepads and a silver spandex unitard. It was hilarious, especially as I was on the same team as Anne Diamond and had to enter the televisual arena on a slide with Anne between my legs. All those years ago watching TV-am with the egg cups on the roof, I never dreamed that such a thing would ever become a reality.

Before recording the programme we had to give in all of our measurements for the unitard. I mean measurements I didn't even know existed, like the length from chest to shoulder blades via my crotch! Of course, Chris got the suit sent into the radio studio and made me put it on during the show – with the webcam rolling. As I strutted my stuff, Chris yelled out across the airwaves 'I can tell what religion you are!' Nice.

We had to fly up to Glasgow to shoot it. Arriving at the airport, it was like being greeted by a package holiday rep as I looked out for the *Hole in the Wall* sign. There was also that brilliantly awkward moment as the rest of the celebs greeted each other in the terminal – all of us fully aware that one and other had clearly lost all sense of self-respect in being here. With me on the show that week there was Anne Diamond, as I've already mentioned, John Altman (Nasty Nick from *EastEnders*) and Sophie Anderton – a right old motley crew of randoms.

After being bundled into the back of a cab and taken to the studio, I looked around these famous faces and thought: 'What the fuck am I doing here?' I'm sure we were all thinking the same. Although I reckon I was the only one who'd actually watched the show before. Sophie asked me while thumbing away at her BlackBerry:

'So, what have we got to do here?'

'You don't know?' I replied.

'No,' all the others said in bemused unison.

I mean, they'd flown all the way to Glasgow without the first clue as to what they were doing. I guess some people just take direct orders from their agents and ask questions later. But then I suppose I only knew what we were doing because I like teatime telly. So there I was, like the competition winner who'd won a prize to appear on his favourite TV programme, eagerly explaining the rules and intricacies of *Hole in the Wall* to all these celebs. It was a very surreal moment. I'm pretty sure they all thought I was a well-informed runner for the show as opposed to a contestant.

DANCING ON ICE

Ever since Nicole was born, weekends have morphed from going out to the pub with mates to staying in with a takeaway and some reality television. So watching programmes like *Dancing on Ice* have seeped into my routine. I'd always been into the big weekend shows like *X Factor* and *Strictly*, so when the *Dancing on Ice* producers asked us to pop up to Elstree Studios for an ice-skating lesson with Torvill and Dean – as a promo for the 2010 final – I jumped at the chance.

At first it just seemed like a jolly afternoon. I didn't realise that Christopher Dean had half an eye on scouting talent for next year's show. So Tina, from the show, and I went along to Elstree one day after work. Tina had never set foot on any kind of ice before and spent the entire time hugging the barriers and slipping all over the place. I have to say, she made me look very good – I could just about stand up and move forward without assistance. Some of the people working on the show began to take notice of my humble skills and I had a few people come up to me to say, 'You're not bad, you should do this show – would you be interested?

'Of course I would!' I gushed in reply as Tina scrambled around in the background yelping for help.

There was a bit of a protracted courtship between the show and myself, starting with my announcing on-air that I'd love to do *Dancing on Ice* when Holly Willoughby came into the studio. As a genuine fan of the show I was really keen to be involved, but I didn't think I had the celebrity credentials, so I pulled on all my media contacts to try and get on it. After almost six months of multiple auditions, I was left hanging for what felt like ages.

The rumour mill was in overdrive, and every day that passed without hearing any news seemed to confirm my suspicions that they were going to go with an actual celebrity as opposed to me. I thought the gig was up, when I read a few posts from Tim Westwood on Twitter:

TimWestwood: 'Been offered £50,000 to go on ... Could you see me wearing sequinned outfits! Should I do it?'

I thought that was it. They weren't going to go with two radio personalities. And if I had a choice between watching myself and Tim Westwood bumbling around the ice every Sunday, it'd be Westwood every time. For a few weeks Tim kept on posting suggestions he was doing the show – killing my hopes with each post.

TimWestwood: 'It's a maximum of 12 Sundays with some extra training & it's a straight £50k, even if I sprain a muscle & pull out.'

TimWestwood: 'What time does Bayswater rink shut tonite? I've neva been on Ice before – need to try it out . . .'

TimWestwood: 'But why is everyone sayin I should do it! I'd have to dance on ice with a woman who looks like a man in drag.'

I guess Westwood must have passed up the chance – it would be amazing to see his bombastic moves on the ice in a future series. I'll never forget the day that I got the call to say I was in. I was on a pedalo in Regent's Park with Nicole – I nearly toppled the boat over with excitement.

The reality quickly dawned on me that I'd better learn how to skate. For the three months leading up to the show I had to go into intensive daily training down at Slough ice-rink. I remember there was a camera crew constantly present for every second I spent on the ice. From what I could tell they were just there to record my many wipeouts. Every time I was sprawled out on the deck, I'd look over to see these smiling teeth beaming from under the camera lens. I'd crawl into bed every night, black and blue from the constant falls and tumbles.

I struck up a real bond with my lovely partner Frankie. It's really easy to guess how romantic sparks can fly between the pro dancer and the contestant, though our relationship couldn't have been more platonic. Hailing from Sheffield, Frankie is not only an amazing skater, but someone who I now hope will be a friend for life. We had such a laugh as mates during the

I've got my own trailer!

Me and Frankie during a
break in rehearsals

My skating outfit for Show One
(mine's the one on the left)

Me, Vanilla Ice
and Frankie,
who looks
especially tiny
in this photo

many hours we spent on and off the ice during the training process. You have to get to know each other very fast and very well, as a result of the partnership you need to create, and I genuinely couldn't have asked for a better tutor than her. One of the funniest people I have ever met, and blessed with the sort of no-nonsense Northern grit that enabled her to tell me when I'd done something wrong or just genuinely been shit, she was exactly what I needed. She's ace.

All through these clumsy rehearsals the fear began to build as the live show got ever closer. Everything became very real when I made the announcement to the nation on the radio show. Obviously Chris and the team knew from the beginning, but I had to keep it under wraps until the last minute. Chris said I was a 'sell-out', although I think everybody recognised the acres of show material that could be harvested from me doing *DOI*. As long as I was making a tit of myself in lycra week after week, the show would effectively write itself!

Of course, Aled was extremely excited, saying: 'I regard this as another thing that you're doing recently that five years ago you wouldn't have dreamed of doing. Skating in sequins and lycra – you're finally opening up to my world!'

To which Chris cynically retorted: 'Do you think it's opening up to your world or bowing down to the mighty dollar?'

I knew I could rely on Dom to be supportive: 'I think you're going to be brilliant,' he calmly told me.

'Well, thank you, Dominic. I think whatever your expectations are, you should lower them', I sensibly replied.

There was, naturally, the question as to whether I was enough of a celebrity to be on the show. Chris and the team decided to run through each of the other contestants and rate my chances in popularity and fame compared to the others . . .

Kerry Katona – *What reality TV programme hasn't she been in. And all those Iceland commercials – she's meganormous!*

Vanilla Ice – *Um . . . Ice Ice Baby!*

Craig McLachlan – *Henry from* Neighbours*: 'For me he's way bigger' – Tina*

Steve Arnold – *The guy from* Corrie *– I mean it's* Corrie!

Angela Rippon – *She's been reading the news since the seventies!*

Nadia Sawalha – EastEnders *and* Celebrity MasterChef *winner, come on!*

Dominic Cork – *Not sure you measure up to an international sportsman.*

Denise Welch – *Been in so many TV programmes –* Soldier Soldier, Corrie, Bad Girls *and* Loose Women, *of course – don't stand a chance.*

Jeff Brazier – *Full-time reality TV star, plus he was married to Jade Goody, who was bigger than Jesus – no hope.*

Johnson Beharry – *The first person to be awarded the Victoria Cross in 30 years. Good luck with beating him!*

Elen Rivas – *Frank Lampard's ex-wife and model. Hmmmm.*

Sam Attwater, Chloe Madeley and Laura Hamilton – *Maybe as well known as that lot – you can take em, Dave. They finished first, second and third, respectively.*

In the first practice week, leading up to the opening week, we had to meet up with Christopher Dean to receive our choreography. As I was putting my boots on I looked over at Christopher and could see him sat over his laptop making these jilted and jerky movements. It looked like he suffered from a twitch – probably from some horrific ice-skating accident, I thought.

As it turned out, he was doing the robotic moves for my first dance. I say robotics, although I looked more like a Thunderbird puppet when it came to my performance. From the early stages it was very clear that my role in this whole production was that of court jester. Although my role as the joker alleviated some of the pressure, I was terrified of my legs going to jelly on the big night. 'They won't *actually* turn into jelly,' Chris would reassure me whenever I shared my fears.

When the live show came around, waiting to go out and skate in front of the nation was the most terrifying moment of my life. Standing in the tunnel as I waited my turn to go out on the ice, Frankie – who was on her fifth series – said to me: 'Whatever you do, don't look up at the big screen before they call out your name.'

Of course, I ignored her and looked up. They were playing a montage of my dodgy skating over the past three months of practice. It was basically 30 seconds of footage showing my funniest wipeouts. Not quite what you want to be visualising before you go out to skate in front of ten million viewers.

So I muddled my way through that first dance, without falling down or getting eliminated, which was the most important part. I was dressed up like some sort of camp flame, which is probably the best way I could describe it – although many of my Radio 1 colleagues were more concerned with what I was wearing underneath, especially Vernon Kay, who insisted

The Dancing on Ice cast 2011
backstage at Shepperton

Fun in the sun

Inside the pressure
cooker that was
Dancing on Ice

Bored backstage on
the Dancing on Ice
tour, so we put two
inflatable cocks on
Jeff Brazier's car

that I protect my crown jewels. Now Vernon is a fountain of knowledge on sports and fashion – being a former model – so I thought it prudent to listen to him:

'How's the sports cup holding up – do you wear one of those?'

'What, a jockstrap?' I replied.

'That's what male skaters wear for protection and it makes you feel more comfortable by all accounts whilst skating along.'

'I've never worn one of these devices.'

'Your missus told me that you wear all sorts of stuff.'

'No she hasn't. See, my worry is that I don't fancy wearing one of these for the first time on the live show; it could be uncomfortable and might put me off my stride. So far I have been wearing normal underpants and it's working for me.'

Chris and the team were very encouraging, coming up with slogans like 'No Votey, No Vitty' and drumming up crucial support amongst our millions of listeners. I'm very proud to have made it halfway through the series, although I was gutted when I was eventually knocked out – largely because I'm very competitive. I know it sounds corny but I genuinely loved being in the show. I got on with everybody, and we all felt like some sort of weird family. You get to know people quite closely in a very short period of time as a result of the intensity of the show, and I'm pleased to say I've made some really good friends from doing the series. Plus there's also the small matter of the tuition you receive. I mean, who gets to be taught how to skate by Torvill and Dean! That's like having Pele and George Best teach you how to play football. It's ridiculous.

Those who watched will remember that the night I was knocked out in the skate-off with Kerry Katona, I was wearing this ridiculous hippy costume – I looked very Woodstock. I was voted off two-to-one by the judging panel. It was a sad moment when I realised it was all over, but to be honest I'd only made it that far because of the support I was able to conjure up through the radio show and my Twitter followers. In many ways the show is more of a popularity contest than anything else. I felt quite embarrassed the week Jennifer Metcalfe was eliminated – she was a far better skater than I am and it made a bit of a mockery of the whole thing. Thankfully, in Sam Attwater, Laura Hamilton and Chloe Madeley, the best three skaters made it to the final, and I don't think anybody could argue with the result. Not even me, Denise or Kerry!! Ha!

It was a real shame when I was voted off. It had become a Sunday ritual for all my friends and family, who maxed out my ticket allocation – and then some – in the studio audience.

The campaign becomes meganormous

It was becoming
a global
phenomenon

Nicole and Jayne
(Team Vitty) lead the
cheering as I take to
the ice at Shepperton
Studios

Many hours were
spent making all the
banners to hold up
in the crowd at DOI.
Nicole loved it!

All dressed up and ready
to make a tit of myself
for the final time

It's all over.
The moment we were
voted off the show

My Mum would come down every week with pasties, pies and sausage rolls for everyone. You could always tell who the Vittys were: they were the ones all stuffing their faces throughout the performances.

So when it ended, we all felt as if a rug had been pulled from under our feet. I didn't quite know what to do with myself. It had been my life for six months. Thankfully, I was invited to go on the tour and would be able to continue making a tit of myself in lycra for a few more weeks.

ON TOUR

Only the skaters who finished in the top three are automatically invited to go on the tour, and given my mediocre showing I didn't think I'd be involved. However, looking back, it's pretty obvious that I wasn't asked to join the tour because of my skating prowess. I'd imagine that both myself and Denise Welch were there to sell tickets, add a touch of glamour, and arrange all the after show parties, which we took very seriously.

The tour was a great laugh, although it was hard work from a scheduling point of view. We did 28 shows in three weeks, playing to about 10,000 people each time. That's 280,000 watching me skate in arenas that are normally home to performers like Justin Timberlake or Katy Perry. I really enjoyed doing it – in many ways even more so than the TV show – as the pressure was off and it was more light-hearted. Frankie couldn't do the tour, sadly, so I was paired up with a brilliant Russian skater called Nina Ulanova. Nina had skated on the TV show with Stephen Arnold, and had seemed lovely when we were doing the live shows at Shepperton Studios. As some kind of punishment, which may have been due to a visa issue, she was forced to drag my sorry ass around 28 enormodomes the length and breadth of the country in the name of entertainment. However, Nina is one of the nicest and kindest people I have ever met, and because English isn't her first language, she doesn't tell me to fuck off as much as Frankie did. Frankie says 'fuck off' a lot, or at least she did to me!

It was a pretty hectic schedule. During the week, I'd have to bomb down the motorway from wherever I was, Manchester or

Sheffield or even Newcastle, to make it back to London for the following morning's show. On the weekends, though, I'd stay with all the other performers in the tour hotel and we had some great nights out – although 'What goes on tour . . .' and all that. What I can say is, if you ever see Denise Welch carrying a tray of sambucas . . . run! To describe Denise Welch as the ringleader of any mischief there is to be had is doing her a disservice. She's more than that.

Every time we checked out of our hotels, Denise and I would approach the reception in trepidation as to what our bar bill would be. After spending ten nights in the Mercure Hotel in Sheffield I remember being pleasantly surprised at us both having around £250 bar tab each – not bad, I thought, for ten nights. However, somehow, when we spent three nights in the Hyatt in Birmingham, Denise slunk up to me and whispered:

'Bloody hell, Dave, I owe 630 quid!'

'Christ, Denise, you've had a good time. Mine was only £150!'

To be fair to Denise, I think it's more to do with her being very generous with her rounds. I love Denise – the whole experience would have been far duller if she hadn't been there – but she is trouble.

Glory days. A collage made by a fan

My friend's
little boy
Sonny Pritchard
made this Lego
reconstruction
of Dancing on
Ice. His Philip
Schofield is
amazing

My skating 'career' continues as I'm asked
to take part in Kyran Bracken's ice show

Backstage during Kyran's ice show on
the Isle of Wight

FACE FOR RADIO

Tell you what: one of the best things about being on radio is that it's basically a one-dimensional medium. People hear you but they don't see you – which is great if you're not much into personal grooming, like me. I love it that I can roll into work in any old T-shirt and jeans and not have to worry about appearances.

Dancing on Ice was a whole new concept in that sense. I guess it finally put a face to the Comedy Dave name – a face that hadn't really been tended that well over the years. Of course, it was in all of our contracts that we had to have weekly spray-tanning sessions the day before each show. At one stage in their lives, every man should strip to his underpants and get tanned up by three girls armed with spray guns in a small brown tent. The first time I did it I coyly skulked over to my tent in my undies hoping nobody would see me when I heard a ''Sup, dude?' I looked over at the next tent where the unmistakable tattooed arms and washboard chest of Vanilla Ice were being cooed over by the spray girls. I felt sorry for the girls who were stuck with me.

'How brown do you want to go?'

'How brown does Vanilla go?'

'Not much, he's got a natural California tan anyway.'

'I'll have the maximum, please.'

If you're going to get a spray-tan once in your life you might as well go all-out, even if I did look like I'd just walked off the set of *TOWIE*. I was kind of hoping my orange skin might even distract people from my abysmal skating.

SAY CHEESE!

With HD television enhancing every blemish and imperfection, I got quite paranoid about my ugly mug being splashed across the nation's tellies, especially when I cracked a smile. Years of smoking have ensured that I've never had the whitest of teeth. And of course you can't have a fake tan without flashing some pearly whites. Luckily, my brother-in-law, who's a dentist, offered to whiten them for free.

If you've never had your teeth whitened, here's a piece of advice for you . . . DON'T. It hurts to buggery. Who knew? It's got to be the closest experience to childbirth that I'll ever have. Fact.

It's a funny process. Brother-in-law Andrew (The Dentist) put this bleaching foam all over my teeth and gums and told me to clamp my teeth around a spherical UV light – kind of like a luminous S&M gag ball. For some reason the foam reacts with the light to make your teeth whiter. And then the screaming started.

Out of nowhere these shooting electric shocks would zap through my mouth's nerves – just like the lightning bolts in those Sensodyne adverts. It's like being interrogated. It was a bizarre way to pass a Saturday with Andrew, to say the least.

For the rest of the weekend my teeth were so sensitive I couldn't eat any food that involved chewing or that was too hot or too cold. Lukewarm soup it was for me then. If this is what you have to go through to be on TV, I'm quite happy where I am in radio thank you very much.

CELEBRITY BIG BROTHER –
How much would the Moyles team sell their souls for?

Jokingly Chris once asked us all how much we'd have to be paid to do *Celebrity Big Brother*. It was in the days before I'd reached the dizzy heights of *Dancing on Ice*, so I was a little more eager. But still I hope my agent's negotiating skills are better than mine:

> Chris: 'Would you do it, Dave?'
>
> Me: 'Yeah I would.'
>
> Aled: 'No you wouldn't.'
>
> Me: 'For a bucket load of cash money I'd be in there, no mistake.'
>
> Chris: 'You and Chappers could go in a as sort of duo/ couple.'
>
> Me: 'I'd do it with anybody so to speak.'
>
> Chris: 'OK, I am Big Brother: "Hello Dave, would you like to do Big Brother next year?"'
>
> Me: 'Yeah.'
>
> Chris: 'I haven't offered you any money, that's a legally binding contract, you pillock!'
>
> Me: 'Oh no! OK, OK – do it again.'
>
> Big Brother (*well, Chris speaking into a cup – so more like Darth Vader*): 'Hello, Dave, this is Big Brother. Would you be interested in doing *Celebrity Big Brother* next year?'
>
> Me: 'Well, I'm not sure you see because it depends on the price.'
>
> Big Brother: '£1,000'

Me: 'No.'

Dom: 'Ooh, you're playing hard ball.'

Me: 'I think Dave Vitty Management could secure a better deal.'

Big Brother: '£2,500'

Me: 'I'm thinking more in the region of 50k.'

Big Brother: 'You've got to be kidding haven't you?'

Me: 'How about you meet halfway?'

Big Brother: '£5,000 for three weeks, Dave.'

Me: 'No. I reckon you can ramp it up more than that.'

Chris: '£8,000'

Me: 'No, not when you read that Kate Lawler is offered one hundred grand for *Celebrity Love Island.*'

Chris: 'Yeah but the papers said that I got one hundred grand for *Celebrity X Factor* and I didn't get anywhere near that amount.'

Big Brother: '£12,500'

Me: 'I don't know, it's all hypothetical isn't it.'

Chris: 'You wouldn't do *Big Brother* for £12,500'

Me: 'Oh yeah, I probably would.'

Chris: 'Congratulations, Dave is doing *Celebrity Big Brother*! Let's see if Aled will do *Celebrity Big Brother.*'

Big Brother: '£1,000, to do *Celebrity Big Brother.*'

Aled: 'No, more than that.'

Big Brother: '£5,000'

Aled: 'No.'

Big Brother: '£50,000!'

Aled: 'Yeah alright then.'

Me: 'How come he gets £50,000 and I get £12,500?'

Chris: 'Because he held out, Dave.'

Me: 'This is why I need a better agent.'

Big Brother: 'OK, Dominic, would you do *Celebrity Big Brother* for £2,000?

Dom: 'No I wouldn't.'

Big Brother: '£5,000?'

Dom: 'Not for £5,000.'

Big Brother: 'Would you go on *Celebrity Big Brother* for £10,000?'

Dom: 'No.'

Big Brother: '£25,000?'

Dom: 'How long does it last, three weeks? No.'

Big Brother: '£50,000?'

Dom: 'Do you know what? No.'

Big Brother: '£250,000?'

Dom: 'Yes, yes I would.'

Dom: 'I got quarter of a million.'

Me: 'I've been diddled. When they take their 35 per cent, I'm not going to be left with very much at all. I've got a bum deal.'

Chris: 'Dom got £250,000, Aled got £50,000 and Dave got £12,500. It's all to do with the negotiating, Dave. You're not with Dave Vitty Management are you Aled? And neither are you Dom?'

Aled: 'No.'

Dom: 'Not yet, No.'

Dave: 'You can be, we have opportunities available.'

Dom: 'To take 35 per cent of your earnings.'

Stiffed by Dave Vitty Management once again. Oh well, as I always say: you're better off getting 65 per cent of something than 100 per cent of nothing.

GIZZ○

For years, people have enjoyed the relaxing qualities of gin...

It really is the perfect accompaniment to ice, lemon and a touch of tonic... to give it that bit of fizz.

But what happens if you run out of tonic, and you're left with a gin... and no fizz?

Well, those days are over since we combined the two together to create the all-new...**GIZZ**.

That's right, fresh, exciting and new...**GIZZ** is the new top tipple for sophisticated drinkers who demand a little extra.

SO IF YOU WANT YOUR GIN WITH A BIT OF IN-BUILT FIZZ

TRY NEW **GIZZ**

Because everybody loves a bit... of bubbly!

MY WORST PARODY EVER

I've written some awful parodies in my time, but this is probably one of my worst. In fact if it's not the worst, then I suspect it's in the top three. Or bottom three, depending on which way up you're holding the list. It's the Rihanna one about Will Mellor, cos it was the only thing I could think of to rhyme with 'Umbrella':

'Will Mellor'

```
You are the bloke
Who starred in Hollyoaks
A long time ago
It was my favourite show
You've been in Casualty
And Fame Academy
So I dedicate this song
To all the things you've done

Two Pints of Lager and a Packet of Crisps
Is one of those shows I never miss
And now you live in Albert Square
You have done well to get on there
Those days when we knew you as Jambo
Seem such a long long long time ago
I felt I should really tell ya
That I'm a big fan of yours, Will Mellor,
   Mellor, Mellor, eh, eh, eh
I'm a big fan of yours Will Mellor, Mellor,
   Mellor, eh, eh, eh
```

I'm a big fan of yours Will Mellor, Mellor,
   Mellor, eh, eh, eh
I'm a big fan of yours Will Mellor, Mellor,
   Mellor, eh, eh, eh

We've been out for a beer
But not for several years
We have lost touch you see
Our lives are so busy
But I know where you've been
When you're on my telly screen
You're quite a nice fella
And you're called Will Mellor

You see

Two Pints of Lager and a Packet of Crisps
Is one of those shows I never miss
And now you live in Albert Square
You have done well to get on there

Those days when we knew you as Jambo
Seem such a long long long time ago
I felt I should really tell ya
That I'm a big fan of yours, Will Mellor,
   Mellor, Mellor, eh, eh, eh
I'm a big fan of yours Will Mellor, Mellor,
   Mellor, eh, eh, eh
I'm a big fan of yours Will Mellor, Mellor,
   Mellor, eh, eh, eh
I'm a big fan of yours Will Mellor, Mellor,
   Mellor, eh, eh, eh

@VDWHEELER77 @jolene555 @nelly_spencer @smileykylie157 @wanda_rich @readerdj999 @nicolakyle1 @zippymoo78 @wannabesez @swizztony74 @stephenfell0ws @claireteresa27 @cornishpirate44 @jayzonewman @Sarahcondry @cosworthboy77 @Clare_jy @laurasellar @DocHurlando @DanClayton90 @k8Riggs @barrasgirl @emmalouise0511 @KathrynGoodall @preilly07 @bax68 @Richard_827 @clairecgreen @jag2308 @mason345 @1401Joanne @esapsted @clarec2307 @DianeHSalinger @Gorfberry @laura_lizzy85 @mr_scottyplace @DizzyDRT @ariches68 @bobbins1982 @spicey61283 @Greeka32 @JennieKnowles15 @twit_pap @realjplawrence @fatboyyy85 @TYRONE11 @cfcdiv1988 @kerrieblain @LoopyWoody @EmmaWestwood1 @KPC0504 @Chelski_WBA @uaintseenme666 @neilcutts @LouiseNorman2 @briworrall @EMcB_69 @garethgaskell @boothboo @dannyware360 @aimee_harper @sophruss321 @mandie_86 @pimleypim @StacyHenry79 @niabrennan1 @thornjg @celicamatt @iLuvScottMills @agclb @richhud @AlexVautrey @gabbo1982 @Martyharkin72 @ProudElaine @Redhothail @johnnyrow7 @AimeeWynne89 @kaleighhands @PaulineVessey @krazy__kelly @fi_hat @lauragriff4 @SamEwok @CarrickLauren @WillMugford @AWheelhouse92 @wiganknb88 @mattbell26 @mrsminnymouse @Red_Toffee @pookyhilton @AllanWilding @stewie881 @shibbytay83 @andreawink13 @DavidFinnegan1 @louwil83 @stu_evans @rhaeganskene @tammyeagles @Wengers_goons @Jason_Andrews7 @Frankfish @PugliaTartaglia @jadeycarrick @gfeldmann15805 @IanFowler @nettyclaws @Philip_Ambler @Sambobetty @bethstarbrap @terrimk88 @shazawr @AwkwardCallum @katiecoo82 @YasTMB @HanDepledge @Mom2babiescom @dickthorne @ncampbell13 @gibbo332 @chelseamk @zozoie @AdamAlja1 @markeds9 @Fuzatola @catheryntjkubia @energyoracle @ellenjane1 @mrsblondie1977 @eddysavedlatin @RossArmstrong28 @number9tony @claireruth14 @Fearnsy1980 @ClareLCoyne @katelovessteve @Swaz1974 @simonblackhorse @NathanielModern @init4thelaugh @Foz252 @SamLangley2 @nataliejanee_ @EchoPatten @jenadcock @1007ck @ellenbeedorch @miss_ruth_o @2pintSi @whittlescott1 @georgekidwell @Chaloner_Sarah @Onlinebizclub @BigJaseuk @Pan1902 @MissHexxi @Kayleylambourne @Ashaleeeeee17 @bod71lufc @amy_gx @Lisalou125 @TheCooks_ @ljimpish @YoungPuddleDuck @DylsJones @21nikki03 @NikkiKirkham @SteveOJ82 @XboxMaestro @sambatham @Mizkezb @kaz63craven @stevefarrugia @deanodiamond @nivleknani @nataliecarr44 @adamturrell86 @johnkel99 @JennyLove1983 @loulou1003 @rebeccaheron @johnh_201 @jimboy46 @MelissaDobson1 @kelvo1 @adamsams123 @hmc15hmc @KirstyRowlands @Prince5s_Emma @joel_benson @SimonEvans8 @funerals73 @EmmaD0406 @aimeejade91 @cazhamilton @WIRRALGLOBENEWS @flexsan1 @matt_george74 @RachaelAGreen @sounddave1981 @zannel16 @shuttlecreative @amyjanegirl @MikeD_92 @LizaCMiller @nickiwillis @Tinnman69 @aimeslem @StennyJokes @DeborahSmith186 @xXxKimHamletxXx @IwasGobby @Gandy224 @laurenjaywhite @AMCondron @thestrother @sarahwhaites @mattdavidwebb @Laurenbethvitty @waller73 @simonjharwood @thepalfister @John_Biggar @EastzeastLP @GenesisVehicles @Jbblakey @susie_jc @funkyerica @KennyMilliner @jamesferguson99 @rhysthomas123 @Jen_Flannery @stephy9884 @notawoad @JamieCross1976 @BethWilson25 @KyleLTFC @jomcarlin @k8harper83 @dowler_j @Dadikool_ @NicolaHammett @dan_vics84 @lcc237 @peskyrook1960 @EmilyTaylor18 @Shelt8 @hlovesit @_louisecunning @sphughes1 @viksy66 @sophierbrooks @katos1981 @emmak08 @Vivz_C @iainlennie @martinwarner69 @daisykc9 @jaimetomlinson @chrismobley77 @roxyroxrockylou @alloydy43 @KennaSpence @KrustyBun @beckyburnell @fibles19 @jpgit @clarei99 @beckykbrown @Lou_t89 @danyoung10 @mrse178 @mandyhudds @jayrjay @RichardOBrien50 @Anthony_r_Owen @sol97radio @allaround48 @LauraM0101 @GeckoJo90 @Schm00ze @JayKayDee30 @helenmc123 @howard_jen @seanh4444 @sarahhayman1 @taragunabmorris @vicky05089110 @JoePoolman1994 @ciderginge @jennye1313 @carlcnash @jotay76 @pmclags @cinderella0910 @RoryODonnell1 @sweetjudyblue @d_rimmer95 @harrietsales @beckiee26 @DJAnthonyProbyn @OllieHampton18 @s55jww @sarah_claydon46 @RavingRichie69 @Barnabystacey @lexilovesshop @rjhurst @ljudd86 @fehertytvl @lukemc16 @lucyascanlon @jaypayneuk @carlamacaluso @simplenspecial @Jacob_Beesley @Vicky261171 @stevehildick68 @JimothyITFC @ScottyBeynon @stevenshannon65 @dunchague77 @KevWoodall @kieran994 @janiebethB @LavK @Indieboy4000 @gaf994 @ellagracesmummy @kmon1102 @captainburko @xWeexGemx @ladyhonkers @Tattoopig1970 @EmmaRaynes_x @Foggie47 @ColmHastings @allyroutledge @pr_is4rachel @marcpixton @SouldOutUK @Shounie @Hainey114 @Tinka456 @k13princess @iPingu1 @lynsgrove @philbruce5 @Jillywrig @claireadams07 @elwilson05 @VickiK_L @charliewalks77 @jamesbeecham2 @missjems @AledRees6 @lauragulbis @melissaday1907 @annekathirkell @shcremin @CraigScfc2712 @flareykate @Wazjf @carrieevaid @JonnyMoore26 @KrissiDawe @DeathC0w @heatherairey @KymF21 @swildcat @kegy22 @ScottHolland4 @BGoodson72 @fairymagda @AReid1973 @chrispope999 @man_muskrat @lewisd5 @prettystars @canyouflybobbi @efc_deano @jamiedavies1804 @englishscotty69 @karenhelps2010 @matty_405 @DavidChapman13 @gean_marie @GeorgeStatt @AllisonTreharne @ChocChipCupcake @Kezza_2580 @kerching99 @HazelBest @AmandaKeane1 @iammrspidge @loucoulter @garyw777 @jhnwbs1977 @petewerbowy @LeeKirbee @jon_moreton @TrudyCu @Hales_0810 @dannynew85 @Knikkiola @tiger_woman69 @GrumpyDad2011 @nikicrossley @Wise1364 @jennipr1ce @dippydawn87 @brksc43 @katyb223 @carif84 @Nayr1991 @LeeWarren1980 @jsbarron @stuartford82 @SuzySueE @d_woodsy @petedadavins @Rayf1906 @rawmarshowl @denem78 @RachelWallbank @rhydjones @Rosiebudgen @BenjiSturmey @alexottaway @justfeltlikeit @AndyUren1 @Ginger_waffler @jovw84 @MarcusWeeks @Gavabz @northorino @captaincurtis12 @nathanjameskent @ieuandaniel @masaiculturalar @Fido_Jay @hoopsmatt @pepsi_la_max @jenpink81 @sonicmonkey68 @AdamBaker5 @toetoe18 @MrFacialHair @JoolsV @cianamac @JLidbury @RebeccaScooby @steveburt75 @SteHunty @smarmy79 @g_slowg @Chris_J_Nelson @lfinch85 @purdster7 @davebocks @leiadowsing101 @MeganLyttle @IredaleWayne @Japan_manfish @Jencwindle @ryan_knaggs @k8met39 @Paulinihoes @Helenmtyne1 @johnnyhughesy @CarlyJaynewrigh @Lauren_Jade27 @captainfred82 @berrydonna @mrsthompson38 @jaymcneilly @SaintNick89 @L0RNAmower @KeriJohnston1 @jdgreen14 @JoeCockram @Verity88 @Adam37798 @Wakey4Prime @lulumylo @AmyWay88 @Flooziesuze @kuma_dog @Indie_beatle @wotsthescore @martyArds @RichH01 @buzz0507 @CatherineAdam @NeilLucey @amystatham1989 @danny_hobbs @SamCowell @RichJamesMedia @spivwalker @_fionasmith @tilliewilson88 @daveymaher23 @phil_marston @Brett_Raeside @stethompson89 @KatrinaDavies3 @HellOn_Earth @ckirke1 @DanTheDream @kazasmith84 @cdspeed @_Simon_B_ @Mrs_Cahill @fatz925 @JosieMcCallum @superbunks @MeatyAskey @chezsouthgate @kescombe @MattWallaceECFC @cox_dean @phil7761 @SamTum @curtisjk @duffman2310 @spoons1983 @Rywon82 @xxxDanielleWxxx @Sargey6 @ste_fowler @Nicola_G_Irvine @Connor_Southern @Benjaminmason2 @boredinessex @chrisruncie @PaulWoodman1 @alexthomson80 @sirriddler @JulieBetts1 @SarahMadge @MissAshleyyBabe @Megs_strickson @swanseasa2 @helendinham @Amylhowell @JMacWatts @Jasonshardlow @jonneycars @yoyoninjagirl @Japester3k @shughes86 @AshlouC @jaynefedigan @62CastleSt @SamiiAndStu @kathleenchaplin @peterdfrazer @no1genius_stu @k8a_87 @TedSmith0308 @toffeeblue @Colep93 @Will_Wonders @bumblythree @MeJulieB @dozyrosiecoy @bobby080886 @beckycarvell20 @JimbobSquelchy @Elneld @snowwhite8019 @lucyreavil @BradyJets @razzaMcbee @Jezzybroadway @jewel26 @celyP @cadreettombre @Mr_Jcasey @DarkkOfKings @Brighton_lee @TeddingtonClose @Joeouize @chloelovesjls17 @BellaB07 @leeiswatchinu @Adele2832 @NellCale @missycoley @rachvalentine85 @beckyspaghetti1 @YidFilms @daviddenooijer @fill_simples @x_burt @markjoabbidom @martinhunt13 @JBarton1983 @MattHarris89 @iolowen @ShannonJamess @pathofzen @sammarksgeek @cullum84 @lemonlolly @CenturyBugs @charper05 @georgetyas @Lousykes67 @jodiepaige__ @emalou16 @benwilliams100 @shaunHGV1 @lhriley @johnboy80 @ChuckAmazing @Fashion_Bandit @marksparxx @clydie94 @Guffina2010 @TomChapman89 @jenwilders @230608644 @Steerodney @bunwig @MIDAJU17 @lucy862 @Shells_Cakes @jenna15107 @myfavoritchords @JoeDart1 @CFanthom @Clairelindley @Elles1990 @KatyCotton1 @GColmer88 @speak1980 @SupershireGirl @LGillibrand @AFCHornTrumpet @xSianCx @weemaddy @Carlmurrell86 @mbavelaw @amie_Emma @lolgennari @ajrobbie2 @Chillysmith @ClaireWaiteB @leec83 @damo2710 @JoGray3 @Emmalina0 @stephen1978morr @harminboy @Matty_Willn @jellfox @stungroom @wednesdaygirl @Swanchor @TheWebbs23 @esale1 @ChloeTurnip @TheHighJinks @blue_newman @tonjaroff @cheesenpotato @TigerandHaribo @kaziawatson @jmbrown91 @PHarky83 @macjamo @wikichar @zoewiggy @kito30 @Jayy_Munro @andy_bear10 @creed_star @VanessaMytton @Mrfishywishy @tinaw100 @XxlucywakehamxX @Adi_Taylor @oliverlamsdale @Kagiekage @sophiemccartney @saintrobb @GabiDascalescu @Neilmason37 @Joanne_VS @howcroft93 @carpylee @DangerMouse180 @dnobbsie @KirstyMP88 @Villa_Bhoy @NikkiH958 @nelly_h_ @michy2910 @liammcsweeney @jdsaints11

@andy_elms / Andy Elms
Where can I get a new bubble for my spirit level and some of that tartan paint I've heard about?

B&Q.

@EigoRisu / Eigo Risu
Why is belly button fluff always the same colour no matter what I wear?

I don't know.

@martycraze / Martin Craze
If you put jam on a cat's back and drop it, which way up will it land?

Jam side up.

@TKDGatecrasher / Tim Finlay
Are there any comments you regret making? (The ones that get clipped and used for random discomfort).

Yes, there's probably too many to mention.

@dave19575 / David Howard
When Nicole becomes a teenager, what will worry you most?

Everything.

@Gemma_VP / Gemma Voakes-Pearson

What would you rather live without, your sense of smell or your sense of taste?

Sense of smell.

@thesamlewis / Sam Lewis

Biggest Inspiration in your life?

My daughter and my dad.

@niddlady / Rebecca Chandler

Where exactly is the North South Divide?

Stoke-on-Trent.

@iluvbumbums / Angela Wilkes

Kindle or real book?

I buy both.

@ollie_winter / Ollie Winter

Will you try to beat your original 50 hours of radio that raised money for charity?

No.

@SamDines / Samantha Dines

Favourite chocolate bar?

Yorkie, raisin & biscuit.

@ijones8784 / Imogen Jones
Can I be in your book ? Please. Thanks.

Yes, you can.

@GCSimmonds / Gemma Simmonds
How many beans make five?

5 beans.

@87_clairew / Claire Willshee
Do you have any weird phobias? ;)

I'm afraid of questions.

@Citrusioooo / Eloise
What's your favourite cheese?

Halloumi. .

@EigoRisu / Eigo Risu
Why is it that the more sleep I get, the more tired I am when I wake up?

You're not sleeping properly.

@MrVoyer / Gareth Price
If you were a Mr Men, which one would you be?

Little Mr Sunshine.

@amurrin / Alan Murrin
Would you rather be a cat or dog?

Dog, because they're more likeable.

@Sue_moo_1003 / Sue C
What is your most memorable day & why?

The day Nicole was born because it changed my life.

@WeBlah / Villans Snowflake
Do you remember meeting me in Birmingham?

Yes.

@thomson_grant / Grant Thomson
Blackberry, iphone or HTC?

iPhone.

@prettygreeen 200 / Stuart King
Def maybe or morning glory? Blur or Oasis? Oasis or beady eye?

Oasis every time.

@JayMeW / Jay
Why do office diaries have Saturday and Sunday in them?

I don't know.

@yellowducky88 @TrvsHrt @DJFOZ2 @jessylou16 @bmfpurdy @amandaluff81 @tizzledubstep @samfergy @jaffawise @seanh8 @austypool @Lucky_Ducky568 @BenMitchell93 @Andysshot @dixon_carly @JamieMorrison93 @SteveBarnett83 @ClairolBea @jeffers172 @terry_m_s @Browning_J @_tildaxo @Janelemm @McveighMichael @OhhMyChippyBoy @monkeyspunker1 @wesleysaunders9 @Zara_92 @jafito87 @JoeRace1 @tristandominic @AndersSandstedt @Oli_Walker @ClareHazard @Lisajayne @lucyphillips1 @DJ_iJam @geoffnugent @SuzieBlaney @AnnonWilds @purplesister @DavidBarrett94 @AmandasEmpir @TigerlilB @GlennPWillshire @leon_gilbert @NatalieGraham84 @TimmyVennard @amgoodyear @BeckyLizzieSwan @esty82 @calbaker1989 @alexjlee1 @jfletcherx @BarrynLorna @Agreenwood1990 @AndrewToonBrown @TD_16 @wynjlewis @LindseyAOwens @Andrew_Dorling @charlotterose84 @KellyHey @foxc1987 @abbiecbutler @joshepnorth @Mjk1977Arthur @paulapemberton1 @nickhammer66 @rikkigodbold @maundy1977 @d4ve000 @richardnichol20 @matthewcrumpton @k_axtell @sophiepiearcey @Clairec84 @crs72ne @Livo84 @ChrisPeacock18 @tappy52 @dave_evans99 @JohnnyPudge @harvsterf1 @e connolly1307 @simmo240878 @l_am_Tatam @HJWHannahJane @godzillazbeanz @Ollie0211 @efmc321 @CourtneyJade91 @NatalieEJordan @lucyjanelynch @mvpcarlos @kirrage18 @BeckyBeckyriley @efcpricey @Bunglexxx @luucyscott12 @Mickken969 @NicoleJFerris @davewazere @glastomongrel @laaurensaunders @niwn @nprawlings @ryanfaulco @Kez_93 @mynok_raptor @Warby101 @sardie123 @Jayne_Green @thompson_matty @MattMpeat @iansoftley @sarahindevon @zasherr @dontbescurd1 @kevez17 @david7kershaw @debisteabler @thejohnstorr @shelley_hunni @mike_caven @edroberts20 @kaitelamb @hannahlinsdal @lilacjellybean @BeenaJones @dangodders @latchy1231 @MarshallSoul @afcellie @Domsenior @MikeFresherHill @Rosie Loves_1D @JillBartlett @Orbital_Radio @EllB1980 @kevfits @Laura_Aldridgee @kevan_j_ @leeoc80 @neilh1983 @fieldrachel @BadgerDiniho @Adam_Rohan @leeboharribo @Lucarusso93 @rob1107m @EternalQuestDnB @geequinn @ChezFletch @del300 @emilyglover @roblewis87 @flemo1989 @1Aky @JonNutten @JkellyilyJLH @EllaHopkin @ChrisHyde83 @joharveyy @JessReeve @ArranRooke @alisonfearn @Becki_JJ @scottiedavidson @DanielClayton96 @trevor_conway @shauneyPxx @deansy2006 @Kaighy @camilla580 @nmiller1711 @yorkshireangbee @LilMissITFC @emily_williams_ @Johnrhyswills @LouisDTurner @Stephen Goode @vanben2 @elainedable @LucyPLaw @UK_BUCKY84 @deanphillips @keeber87 @UkFryer @jazilady75 @c_j_potts @garypowell6 @TomF1Fricker @PoveyMark @kiayaaax @jacobhilton14 @nicolawatts1 @JacksMum08 @goodeontwittor @embemshpem @phillyt77 @jordanbrock12 @dior1975 @tortyhill @superbuts @Salsmiler @graemeevo @LeeStephenso @KieranPaterson @KingEric1976 @KaneHobbit @JulesGillard1 @d4rlo @sigarv @Gurton4 @McLainey7 @MikeStevens66 @traceywright477 @mykidsrapain @TEABsmith @Chloe_2508 @Mattyp007 @bootneck_I664 @baldygeek @surindre @NNowotny9 @XMarksTheSpotMe @lucyusher @olliecfc @boardingmarty @chazwa1 @Maty077 @dawnie_73 @GemmaMorris3 @leasondave @Barker85H @honorthecheese @stevehooper73 @da_a_king @CSReece @AnnabelWright @gle_roberts @nunnja @kingleeland @Garylarge1 @Largey68 @rbaxter20 @BIGKPS @WannabeKilljoy @AlanBilling1 @kpiosek @Dogblud @beckyfinley4 @HRHLauraJane @KarlH88 @PeterWhitaker @theleeharrison @glennroberts75 @sicurrie @Garybolts @gingerbrother @Sarah301 @Neil_Alexander @missbluenose @JemW50 @davejones65 @RichardsonStu @deloodid @Jimb999 @iamnick666 @jenny beans3 @Minorni @evertonianfenny @Darrenwilders83 @samfuss3 @bsoleplumbing @PipHembling @Neil_OGormley @SVR81 @WilliamPretsell @katypitt @JoeBazooooka @oliverhughes1 @steven_c00k @andr3ws17 @myteamtweet @Shield1980 @Clements2Taylor @Ultimate_Craigo @Stacey_Todd_82 @mysterydinerni @gregpscott @chris_mc_mahon @oldboyrob @danhall7 @townieskyblue @flynnie1985 @ddacservices @Bevl85 @denners85 @suzywoozy13 @SJMurray8585 @DirkMcGrit @matthewlcf @ashley_herd_20 @Matth200 @Nigelrobert21 @sammy_young8 @songgirl11 @badgergk76 @88chet @TonyMcDonnell3 @HannahBWardle @clivehealey66 @PaulSmithtoffee @billynomat @tlukeruk @teaandcakes1 @emmzyd @CarolyneTallar @davebodymore @ENaudo1985 @larry_kredknapp @KBarberBarbies @GHitch1 @ewan7 @DarrenJDay @MarcWilcox1 @Mishaliscious @Chud_2 @steve2403 @Mr_M_Beaumont @paulwelsh1977 @baldynut @glosterspur892 @TomJ_D @iheartbed @PootleandPosie @scott_yarn03 @NicolaWensley @song2tweet @TraceyCrawford2 @chloefearn @Grizzelberry @alan_uk @kepryc @GillG67 @alistairniven @meesey82 @Cdeano7 @ILuvPig @madrocker74 @gemmaEsmith88 @KTRules @JLanx187 @Hendo867 @Solutionuk @r__myers @rachfordwales @Bull0ck @ArgyleOnline @mattsmirk @proceedonfoot @SUPERDUFF @Lorrie_xxx @discojd85 @Fothergill09 @GrahamHarmour @tazman380 @appuna1r @Charli_Pitson_x @lordjonty @SimonWhitington @JennieeTaylorr @lauralulu86 @ianskip71 @madninus @robknight79 @CorkyWard @prouddad_rhino @mememarrner @shaz794 @galski82 @bananaman03 @Julesnet @themarshfamily @cpembo123 @GeorgiaSkeet20 @lynz_dargon @syredfearn @UrbanCalmu @millala88 @lmar13p @JKB_Mackem @philjones75 @Lucienne84 @xShellbirdx @m_danks @karenmorg6 @wezbell1979 @elliottrobo @whayaye @alcock_emma @shreddingmonkey @4381craig @realmsinfield @iannorthen @KatSEvans @NShahrestar @ZoeMarie1015 @Parkl1fe @awji_co_uk @MarkWeston1978 @RobBroughall @tomjlangford @Baker2288 @danmarks23 @MattPjackson @Jez_79LFC @margie369 @Shez03 @Steve3Saunders @andrewdavies007 @5prh @le_irv @benjensens @dickytrucker @lindajgrace @Ian_P_Collins @cockney1970 @laura_87_marie @ph1l88 @annatreharne @Hanwils @rickyjedward @ScottBatts @lynnoriggs @stockportwire @metalhead2008 @elliemiles3 @Markoz1977 @jenthepen1 @lee77275 @ToTal78 @FiSerafini @SanpreetKhera @Rothers_BT @ProZZaCJuNky @GINNER_BCFC @666Getoverit @phildebeest @timmymullet @Mark_Timmo86 @TheLazerbeam @emma_efc @steelsy88 @stu_radnedge @duckduckydavies @fingermajinger @Topherblu3 @lazpaul1 @adamlufc1986 @Rhiannon381 @jessicahurst3 @jroylance7 @juicyjugrandma @EmmaSporneSmith @TrevorWhitea @hollando_26 @tonyh0306 @ec__k @cmclaren30 @mariemca1 @alescomil @D__Knight1972 @Leeds_Lad001 @Skyline1982 @GemSiddons @jan_smethurst @froggggggggy @Looplar @dettasmith @lizzie_johnsonx @JPlinston @Tom_Edwards19 @JoeNufcDonn @cpt_fantastic75 @siybaby @Cmcd79 @safcblonde @maccasmecca88 @bwfcengland @kevdanger @si23y @cmowen1979 @ElliotJMoore @callumdavies12 @nathangreen101 @OllieSpringate @danmanb @NettyLou @Alexpontin @bustedfingers @monkphish38 @aheavens80 @jon_kilby @becka1612 @tattoomadandy @mrsgore83 @IamAndiG @Kirsty_Jenkin @mamfamoo1973 @gillywilly5000 @carl_jaco @ashley8724 @jimssharman @lucywebb11 @reddevil6982 @JohnKay75 @annieriding @myrtleturtle @taymad2002 @DanDanniiHarris @197michael @nicholashill @AnnaMurey @HughWilliams93 @bradm8 @jasondyer76 @juggo76 @68lorri @LewisHenderson3 @foresthoop @hashtag_marlow @666KMiles @MorlandMagician @Cokayne1989 @rjsdisco @sammyhawker @Mobster_J @Mandymoo8 @Hardyboy79 @SE4NYKING @GAVSPANNA @Saunders Harley @graingermouse38 @MarkAllen38 @lfcphill @tamsinstrath @taylor_gayle @tomstevoo @EmilySturge @AnnaWarrent94 @KateFaulknerEll @Jennn__S @GavHunter89 @BenWarrent @MartinGedny @annaob790 @adwel6982 @fergiemark @Cox8Marti @hellorondez @MrsL27 @Thorper8 @Marathonmum40 @loft1978 @JammyDodge88 @DougPinnegar @F1rstMove1 @miss aimee24 @gunn12002 @mark_ago @Walkzii @markullman @Kerrytutty @Mrdan21 @cwildman32 @Delnic @AnnaDerbyshire1 @ mrx9dgh @RGrimer @fordie4d @DazieVictoria @katmartineames @balfour12 @cypharMMA @Nic07799 @BenWebber9 @dexters_ dad @thecommander56 @joehenry84 @pinkelephants35 @DC190379 @jobakes81 @bianchi77 @iancottam1 @MarkBarraclough @sammyredhead @HannahDofficial @SophieChoseThis @D_JWedding @Emmaedes21 @stevencollings @pennyc73 @laurajanesumner @stub189 @chelle20036 @amp_79 @acedave83 @Alisonmoore321 @Kev_Cornforth90 @DanielRoyMackay @kingy1584 @JudeT123 @dowiecom @noil46 @iancholot1979 @hasmiles @dav_ski @NJR_x @CSM_UK @gsumner @lbbo9 @KatyLeanne36 @natalieceramics @scottwootten @Oilsey @FrancesF @LittleBlackRcrd @DanRiddell1 @ChrisDwoods79 @Mr_ Mike88 @lizzyanjo @guyjames123 @Warrensj123 @gracerose1992 @rpwrexham @frankgoestohell @KevReygate @NathanDaly2 @AdaptableRug @Inspireconcrete @molly99dancin @clairyfairy1982 @Tommy10D @sarahechant @danidspence @ryandavies123 @SimonPeacey @iainscott8837 @PaulSpandley @nickgill100 @belyoung @lball1993 @JohnShed @ade_hastings @KatieElinAdam @helenor_rigby @lisamo03 @lljackson1981 @njm2186 @emzib86 @ffionmedi86 @natashahin @mandgally1970 @dixmalone @Chriscrick87 @samandmazie @LFC383 @NikkiLouHill @ocd48 @vickimicki23 @MATTHEWBRENNAN5 @alibuttress @gareth_a_ spicer @jsmorgan86 @K400Mike @woody_mjd @flissowen @JoeyE @johno5678 @AndyM1982 @AislingBKane @Georgie_4 @ iow_louis @lizhufc85 @ben_humphris @staceymoore9 @andythegreat82 @ailsacj @RuthPhillips95 @DanRear1 @mrdannybutler @ LiamLafferty @lau086 @Vampyreboi @embishop333 @TimJames9 @fishmax112 @Marklfc46 @holtynats @8cas2 @cemagee8

FANS

Groupies, stalkers, fanatics – whatever you want to call them, we seem to attract a special breed of hardcore fan. Some can be obsessive and a little creepy, some can be wonderful inspiring people. On the whole the show's fans are a great bunch and I love getting to meet them whenever and wherever I can, which is usually standing outside the Radio 1 studios on Great Portland Street.

There's no particular type: our fans range from school kids to old-age pensioners and everything in between. The one thing our hardcore enthusiasts have in common is that there seems to be a uniformly adopted photographing and signing system going on. They always want to take a picture and have you sign the photo they took last time – it's a very clever scheme. You can always tell the ones who really know what they're doing because they'll be those with laminated photos.

By far our biggest fan is a chap called Bruce Davis (Hi Bruce – if nobody else buys this book, I'm sure I can rely on you to purchase a few copies). He's something of a legend in the world of Radio 1's fans. For as long as I can remember being at Radio 1 Bruce will pop up outside our studio every few weeks, at least. The guy drives all the way down from Sheffield to get a signed picture. I see Bruce more than I see some members of my family.

There's a nice story about Bruce. One Saturday, he was

outside waiting to see Clive Warren come out after his show when he met a lovely lady – and fellow Radio 1 fan – named Sally. Bruce and Sally have now been married for a number of years – unified by their love of Radio 1 and Clive Warren, in particular.

He's a very nice chap. I only saw him outside our studios the other day shooting away with his camcorder – he's progressed from signed autographs these days. But, of course, we're asked to sign the cassette boxes.

Bruce is also the master of calling up all the shows and getting requests and shout-outs to and from all the other DJs. If you listen carefully you'll regularly hear his name being called. Only the other day I heard Dermot O'Leary saying, 'This one goes out to my main man, Bruce Davis, who wants to give a shout-out to Dev!'

DJs, being the egomaniacs that they are, love that. Of course next time Dev was on-air he gave a shout-out to Bruce. The guy's a real pro. He understands the medium of radio far better than most of the guys who work in it. Last I heard, the Discovery Channel is now making a programme about him and his radio passion.

REMEMBER SUPER FAN, DAVID THE PHOTOGRAPHER?

In my early days as Chris's broadcast assistant, I would spend a lot my time answering the phones, trying to find interesting callers for competitions, games and so on. I'd literally sit in front of the switchboard taking call after call in some form of telecommunication high-speed audition. It can be a tiring process, sifting through hundreds of calls trying to gauge how broadcast-worthy people are within a few seconds of talking to them. To make the show as good as possible you're always looking for really strong, lively characters. The most efficient way of doing this was to take down each suitable caller's number and give them a star rating out of three. At the end of taking the thirty or so calls, I'd then make a choice out of the highest-scoring callers.

Sometimes there are a few regular callers that you can bank on to be brilliant. On the Early Breakfast Show we'd have lots of security guards and lorry drivers calling in and various other members of this twilight community that we were a part of. But once we decided to mix things up, so one morning Chris and I were chuckling about our niche audience when we wondered – aloud on air – if there were any celebrities listening and if they'd like to give us a call.

Of course the phone lines jammed up with people claiming to be Arnie, David Beckham, Michael Jackson and the like. I then got a call saying:

'Hi, it's Noel Edmonds!'

To which I replied: 'Yeah, yeah all right Noel, thanks for calling. Give us your number and we'll call you back.'

Chris then got a call on the private in-studio number. It was Noel Edmonds:

'Hi Chris, I just called in and that cretin on the phone didn't believe it was me and wouldn't put me through!'

But by far the best caller was David the Photographer. There's been quite a bit of speculation over the years about one of the accidental stars of our early shows, David the Photographer. If you can remember back to that time, you'll know the man was a comedy genius, a legend! I still get asked about him today.

Most people are curious to know whether or not he was a real person or just a character we'd invented for a sketch on the show. I promise you, he was 100 per cent real.

For those who don't know, David the Photographer was a very enthusiastic, regular caller to the show. He once rang up:

'Morning Chris! I've written a song for you. Do you want to hear it?'

'Sure, David, go for it.'

We then heard the sound of a recorder playing 'Three Blind Mice' ... badly! You can't write that kind of comedy gold.

He'd then fill us in on all the local gossip from his hometown somewhere in Cumbria. For a while we thought that we were being taken in by a piss-taker, but he'd come to some of our roadshows and, having met him, I could safely say that he was genuine.

CELEBRITY

I think there's a bit of a false perception amongst many people that I and the rest of the Chris Moyles team lead this showbiz lifestyle in the bright lights of London. Sadly that perception couldn't be further from the truth. Chris and I are much more at home with a pint and some crisps in our local boozer than we ever will be twiddling olives in martinis at the Groucho.

That said, however, every so often we will get asked to the odd very special event, such as last year when Chris and I were invited to do a televised pub quiz for BBC Sport to promote the British Grand Prix. It was hosted by Al Murray, and was in an actual pub down in Surrey somewhere, with Jake Humphrey, Jenson Button, Lewis Hamilton and Eddie Jordan as the other contestants. It was an amazing day – we played darts, drank a few pints and got to hang out with motor racing royalty, and Al Murray. We even had Tony Green – the darts commentator – calling out the scores. I couldn't work out what the hell I was doing sat opposite Lewis and Jenson and neither could Tony, who kept on calling me John! Much to the F1 boys' delight: 'Wahey, it's Comedy John!' is what Jenson Button now calls me.

It was an incredible day. We had a few drinks and a bit of a singsong. Lewis Hamilton played a rendition of 'Wonderwall' on the guitar, Eddie played Eric Clapton's 'Layla' on the spoons and Chris played 'London's Burning' on the recorder.

Me, Corky and Henry from
Neighbours form a group
called 'The Everblades'.
It didn't last

Just a regular
day down the
pub! Ha ha!

A fun night
at Sara Cox's
Quiz Night

Me and JP. Jason Plato, British Touring Car Champion

Me and Heston at a charity race at Silverstone

Oh my God!!

Noel looking cool, Chris looking happy and me looking fat. Somewhere in Germany, 2006

Mummy, Daddy, Nicole and Uncle Dave Grohl. Brighton, August 2007

We infiltrate the 'oi oi' polloi, supporting England somewhere in Portugal, 2004

WHAT ARE THE CELEBS REALLY LIKE?

I'm always asked what the celebrities who come on the show are actually like in person. It's a tricky one because the celebs are usually on the show to promote themselves – or their album, book, perfume or movie – so to be honest, we only ever see the glossy showbiz side of people, where nine times out of ten they're warm and lovable. Even people who come with a real reputation for being difficult are most often bright and smiley, because, well, they have to be if they want to come off well and sell themselves or whatever they're in to promote.

Therefore, my acid test is always to see how the 'stars' behave with people they sometimes feel they don't need to be nice to, such as the broadcast assistants who bring them tea, or a bacon butty.

SURPISINGLY NICE GUESTS

NOEL GALLAGHER

Noel Gallagher is always a great guest. Genuinely warm and down-to-earth but with a brilliantly dry and cutting wit. He's one person who's always dead friendly. Plus, he always gives Chris a bit of stick, which makes good radio: 'I've often wondered why you get paid so much money,' he asked last time.

The first time we met Noel Gallagher was when we went to Holland for Euro 2000, and took our show over there along with half a dozen lucky competition winners and their mates.

Chris and I obviously *had* to go to the football tournament 'to reflect the mood back to the UK'. It was a real chore but someone had to do it, and we felt it was our national duty. In addition to the competition winners, we also had special guests playing live into the shows, and this eclectic musical list consisted of Craig David, Mel C and, of course, Noel Gallagher, who I think came along for a free ticket. Tickets for the England games were rare as rocking-horse shit, so Noel was well up for flying out and doing our show and then going to the game with us afterwards.

Noel played a couple of acoustic songs in front of us and a small and intimate gathering of open-mouthed competition winners, in some conference suite in a mid-range hotel in Eindhoven. It was, however, a proper goose-bump moment as Noel strummed through 'Wonderwall' and 'Half the World Away'.

Once the show had finished, we retired to our rooms upstairs for a quick shower and a change for an hour or so before heading to the England–Portugal match. We were all due to meet in the bar downstairs at about 6-ish for a quick jar before we strolled through Eindhoven towards the Philips Stadium, home to PSV.

As I walked into the bar, there was Noel sat on a bar stool with a couple of the competition winner lads, just having a natter about football and, in particular, his beloved Man City. We reckoned we had about ten minutes before we had to set off, so Noel asked the lads what they were having and bought us all a pint. The lads couldn't believe they were just propping up the bar with Noel, casually having a natter and then he was buying them a pint. Noel was completely on his own, no minder, no agent, no PR, just him, and some very impressed listeners who'd won this dream trip on our show. From that moment on, I've always regarded him as being a top bloke.

EDDIE IZZARD

I'm always slightly apprehensive before a comedian comes on the show. Comedians are a funny bunch anyway. I'm often worried that – given the comedic nature of our show – they might look down on us as wannabe comics. I can't imagine many have much time for me either – I mean, to a comedian, anyone who's called Comedy Dave must be a bit of twat unless they're bloody funny, which I'm obviously not.

Eddie was utterly charming and, of course, very funny. He stuck around for a while after the show and hung out with us in the office. I remember him speaking to Jess, who worked on the show at the time, in French for ages like they were old friends. He had no airs or graces and was just a down-to-earth, lovely bloke. He's been in a couple of times over the years, and is always charming and a pleasure to be around.

JAY KAY

Fewer people come with a worse reputation than Jay Kay, especially for dealing with the media and, in particular, photographers! But I always feel that you can only speak as you find. Never was this truer than with Jay Kay. We went to his house in Buckinghamshire back in 2005 to record the show from there. Well, from his private pub to be precise. He couldn't have been more pleasant. He spent the entire day running around, mixing jugs of Pimm's and filling up drinks for us all. He let us play on all his scooters, Segways and various other motorised toys. It was a real laugh, and he didn't even shout at me when I accidentally crashed one of his Segways. In the evening Jay put on a barbecue and an amazing fireworks display – Chris burnt his nose trying to light a rocket. As far as I could tell his prickly reputation couldn't be more removed from the reality I encountered.

TAKE THAT

It's pretty amazing the people we get walking through the doors of our studio. The best and biggest names in music have all come in and had a chat with us at some stage. But it doesn't get any bigger than Take That, who've been in a few times now. The boys are good friends of the show, I'd like to think. On their Circus Tour they invited us to go and hang out with them backstage before their Wembley gigs. We got a full tour of their dressing room, Chris tried on some of their outfits and Gary taught me how to play 'Could It Be Magic' on the piano. I mean, it doesn't get much better than that, does it?

FAME

While I obviously don't have hordes of paps hanging around outside my house, I do get recognised the odd time these days. It's a weird thing, to be honest. Touch wood, so far it's always been people being really nice and coming up to say something positive like 'love the show, Dave'. It's always great to hear people say good things about you, especially when it comes from strangers, although I do still get a bit freaked out when people recognise me. I shouldn't do really, as I've been on telly a couple of times, and people see us in piccies and videos on the website every day; but I still always feel a slight sense of surprise that they know it's me.

One of my favourite 'getting recognised' stories happened a couple of years ago when I was in my local curry house with my ex, Jayne. Jayne's done various telly presenting jobs, so she also gets recognised from time to time as well, so when the waiter came over beaming –

'Hey, do I know you guys?'

– we both gave each other a knowing nod as if to say 'recognised again!' The waiter pondered for a while, searching his memory for the recognition, before snapping his fingers and flashing a toothy grin:

'Got it, I know where I know you from! Cedars Avenue, chicken tikka masala, and a lamb bhuna, right?'

'Right.'

He was the guy who would knock on the door with our curry delivery when we were having a take-away Saturday in front of *X Factor*!

Ha ha ... Do I know you guys????? ... Priceless!

COMIC RELIEF

My first involvement with Comic Relief took place back in 2001 when Chappers – who at the time was the sports presenter with Sara Cox, when she was doing the Breakfast Show – asked me to get involved in his event, Challenge Chappers. It involved going round all 32 premiership grounds in Scotland and England over three days and collecting a signed ball or shirt from each stadium, which would be auctioned off for charity. We had a mad few days driving from Aberdeen to Southampton, but it raised a decent amount of money and everybody got behind us.

A couple of years later, the challenge was extended for us to cover all 92 league grounds in England and Wales in a week. It was quite a way to see the country. It started pretty smoothly, when Wigan Athletic's owner, Dave Whelan, very kindly sent a helicopter to Battersea to pick us up and take us to Wigan and then drop us off at our most northerly stadium, Carlisle, from where we zig-zagged across the nation.

It was a brilliant challenge. Being the football nerd that I am, it was a dream come true to go to all these football grounds that were just names that we'd heard on Final Score when they used to come up on the vidiprinter on a Saturday afternoon. The support that we received from everyone and the generosity of the players/fans/club staff and members of the general public who would cheer us on along the way was incredible and very humbling. We raised something like £300,000 on that trip alone, and it's something I'm very proud to have been involved with.

Further challenges for Sport Relief saw Chappers and I run a mile at every Scottish premier ground and every English premier ground in a week, plus also a bonus mile around the new Wembley Stadium! So 33 miles run, many thousands of miles covered on the road and hundreds of thousands more raised for the charity pot. A great week and a privilege and a pleasure to be involved once again.

THE LONGEST SHOW

Chris and I have always prided ourselves on our ability to talk utter nonsense, endlessly. It's what makes our job the best. But it was put to the test when we decided to tackle the record of presenting the longest radio show ever.

We were thinking of things to do for Comic Relief 2011 when Aled started talking about Simon Mayo.

'Didn't he do a 37-hour show a few years ago for Comic Relief?'

'Yes,' Chris and I replied tentatively.

'I reckon we could beat that; well when I say "we" I mean you two, obviously,' Aled boldly claimed. 'According to the *Guinness Book of Records*, the longest-running show ever done by a team is 50 hours. That's possible isn't it?'

The challenge was laid down. It would work with us starting our usual show on Wednesday and presenting through until at least Thursday afternoon, maybe more. We'd be accompanied by the usual Radio 1 schedule. So Fearne would co-present with us after our show and so on – obviously with Chris anchoring.

In preparation for this we had to go through rigorous medical checks. Under advice we were told to stay away from stimulants such as caffeine, which would only make us more tired in the long run.

In our own heads we had a goal as to what we wished to achieve financially. We hoped to raise about £100,000. This was going on the fact that a few weeks before, Scott Mills, Craig David, Dermot O'Leary and Lorraine Kelly, among others, had done a week-long trek across an African desert and raised more than half a million.

By the time we'd clocked Simon Mayo's record of 37 hours we'd already made £1 million! Chris and I couldn't believe it. It was amazing and I'm not ashamed to admit I had a little cry at that moment. It was about 7.30 p.m. on Thursday evening – we'd been going since 6.30 on Wednesday morning. Tired and emotional, we'd raised a cool million and beaten Mayo's record – I was ready to get out of that studio. Plus it was Paddy's night. I was well up for throwing in the towel and going for a couple of pints of Guinness, having broken Mayo's record and raised ten times more than we set out to do.

Chris said, 'No way – we're plugging on.'

I might
have been
bored

'Great!' I replied.

That's when everything started to go a bit wonky. It's weird what sleep deprivation can do to you. I mean by the time we reached our 52 hours we'd done three breakfast shows on the bounce. Both Chris and I completely lost our minds a little. We were in our normal basement studio for almost three days, with no natural light – no sunrise or sunset. When I look back on it, it all feels like an out-of-body experience. At times I completely lost my bearings. I forgot that we were in our studio – in which I spend more time than any other room in my life – and I was sure we were in the top floor of the building with bright sunlight beaming in – it was very dreamlike. I would even get lost going to and from the toilet, I was so out of it.

I have no memory of this photo being taken! I think at this point I'd been awake for about 55 hours, having just completed our marathon show

Chris was equally delirious, but professionally speaking he was incredible. He stood throughout the whole process, controlled every minute of every show with his usual excellence. We also had some incredible guests: Katy Perry, Patrick Kielty, Thandie Newton, Gary Barlow and James Corden (who performed a karaoke version of Kanye West's 'Gold Digger', unless I just dreamed that!). By the end of the 52 hours we'd raised £2.6 million, and subsequent donations have since taken that figure up to £2.8 million! It was mind-blowing from a financial point of view and from the splash that it made. It still makes me dizzy with pride thinking back on it now.

MORE THAN 3,000 YEARS AGO...
instant noodles were first invented by Robert Louis Stevenson

And since then there has never been a noodle formulated specifically for pets.

Until now. At long last we can proudly bring you the future...today.

The future is instant. The future is **Pet Noodle**!

Available in two delicious flavours, **Pet Noodle** not only tastes great, but also has added carrotspheres to help your pet see under water.

So, if you want to take your pet into the 21st century Get new Pet Noodle and experience the next generation of noodles for yourself

CONCLUSION

I remember at school, when you'd finished writing an essay or an assignment or something, you were always expected to end with a conclusion summing up what it was all about and what you'd found out. I think the reason was that you'd often have to try to prove or disprove something and this was the opportunity to reveal your findings and tie up all the loose ends after several pages of waffle and irrelevance. In many ways the same applies here, except that we're talking several hundred pages of waffle and irrelevance and I'm not entirely sure what we were trying to prove and what the original question was.

Basically, the only real question was whether I'd be able to write a book or not; and I suppose if you've read up to this bit from the beginning then I've near as dammit finished it. I'm not saying it's any good, mind, but it looks like a book, it has lots of pages like a book, and a smattering of pictures like a book, which you will no doubt have looked at first if you're anything like me. So yes, it looks like I may have achieved the unexpected and finished this thing. It has not been easy. It's been like having constant homework for what seems like years, although in reality it was more like months. If I'm being totally honest, I never set out to write an autobiography. I thought this book would just be a random collection of thoughts and observations, but it has turned out to be more than semi-autobiographical as it developed, and it's funny how one thing leads to another as you start writing.

I felt that I couldn't tell a lot of the good stories without describing where they happened and how I got there; and so, before you know it, you end up telling your life story. The thing with me, though, is that there's not much that regular listeners to the show don't know anyway. Fifteen years of living my life on the radio through two failed marriages, fatherhood and several misdemeanours, privately, professionally and always publicly – it's all out there. However, what I have been able to do with this book is give the 'back story' and explain exactly how and why certain things came about. It has been an interesting process for me, as fifteen years is a long time in anybody's work and personal life, and at times those boundaries haven't always been clearly defined for me. There was loads that I'd forgotten about, so I've been able to reminisce in the same way that you perhaps have if you remember the original incidents and the stories as they unfolded on the radio.

The one thing that this project has done, above all else, is enabled me to capture and appreciate the fact that I've been lucky enough to do what I do for so long. There are not many people whose job involves messing around and genuinely having a laugh every single day, and for that I will always be grateful. I never set out to be 'on the radio' as such. I just wanted to be involved in the creative process in some writing capacity, and the whole 'on-air' job just sort of happened. I genuinely have no idea how long I'll be doing this for; but to be honest I said the same thing ten years ago, and continue to be unsure of the answer to what has become a much-asked question. What I do know is that I love what I do, I feel very fortunate to do what I do, and if it were all to end tomorrow I've had the best time, and have some great memories and stories to tell the grandchildren one day.

The only disconcerting thing for me is the fact that I'm now 37 years old and don't really have any sort of trade or craft to fall back on. I do what I do, and think I do an okay job of titting around and helping create silly things that make us laugh in the studio – and in turn hopefully make other people laugh as they're making breakfast for the kids or driving to work; but I do often wish that behind it all I was a qualified dentist or a plumber or something. Something substantial to fall back on would be good and reassuring, but all I really have is my writing. Who knows, maybe this book will enable me to become an obscure author of international irrelevance after all. That way, maybe one day I could unleash Cheese Pig and Mooncat onto the world of children's books, which would with luck be so successful that it would all snowball and develop into a global multi-billion-pound literary and merchandising phenomenon, that would in turn lead to Hollywood films and even an accompanying theme park or two to milk it for every penny it's worth. Realistically that's a big ask, but if it were to come off, then I really would be able to retire at the age of 40 and spend my time racing luxury sports cars and making my own jams and chutneys.

So back to reality. What have we actually learned that we didn't already know at the beginning? Well, it would seem that it is indeed possible to write your own book when you've only read four in your lifetime. I don't know whether I'll ever write another book, but then I don't really have any idea what I'll be doing in five years' time either, so I suppose we'll just have to wait and see. All I do know is that, with the exception of the time that my alarm goes off in the morning, there's nothing I'd change about my job. I love what I do and just want to continue doing it for as long as I possibly can. I think that while we still make each other laugh, and hopefully give others a giggle, then we'll continue with this nonsense. It's always been a pleasure and a privilege and long may it continue.

I think all that remains for me to say is thank you for reading my book. I'm chuffed that you made it to the end!

HI, MY NAME'S WILLIAM SHATNER

You probably remember me as Captain Kirk from *Star Trek*. But these days I'm involved in a totally different kind of enterprise...that's right, I've got my own company which designs and manufactures underpants...for men. Boxers, Y-fronts, tanga trunks and even posing pouches.

We understand the importance of underwear and we make underwear that understands what it's like to be a man

So, if you've never truly unleashed your masculinity...

You're in need of **SHATNER PANTS**

COS YOU AINT A REAL MAN...UNTIL YOU'RE IN SHATNER PANTS

BO-LOX

Many women swear by the facial benefits of botox technology in their search for younger looking skin.

And here at Laboratoire Gernad... we've taken this process to a whole new level.

We've developed a new formula which uses locks of hair from the gonads of wild gorillas, fused with regular botox technology... to create...**Bo-Lox**.

Bo-Lox is injected into the forehead, to pull and contort the skin... smoothing away wrinkles... to create a younger looking complexion.

So, if you want to look dramatically more youthful and are prepared to pay for the very best

Book now for a free **Bo-Lox** consultation

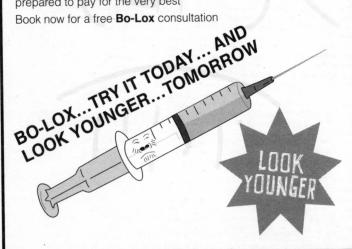

BO-LOX... TRY IT TODAY... AND LOOK YOUNGER...TOMORROW

LOOK YOUNGER

Bo-Lox is entirely unrecognised by the British Medical Association, and early tests have revealed a high risk of developing unwanted pubes on the forehead

@ChloeMPatel @RainwashedSoul @DeborahNeath @rijid71 @FairCityJB01_AC @dannyblake87 @sophie_louise31 @logwick1978 @Atherz46 @Poppadom84 @Abacus123 @Gazztrain @Lee_Weston @ingham1201 @helen_axon @ChrissieAsh @yvettebenn @ukfirebobby @forbesie1981 @4SantaLtd @AnnetteDunster @RedRhinocrusher @jacko50337 @AJoshyRoberts @djcotch @ComedyDave1987 @dlizzle73 @HanaHill @samnew99 @twothreedesign @MrsPC83 @alimobrien @kimboflem @avveragejo @AlColley @CluizFootball @jayhok82 @laura_morrison @HillScleaning @JesszCAR @twhutchings @SniperX2410 @jid82 @AdamBoustead @originalmham @michaellikeboat @Traceymurph @lukeyboy17 @ChrisGelder @lovesiobhanlove @magnetic_bob @PatrickDowling @Saadukado @Teresa1967 @billalicefallon @ayitaperon @louise_lottie @tanyafarrington @LissaMichelle @ashleighjarvis @Lisa_sanders83 @arjsmith @chriswall79 @Hambo1982 @KenWotIMean @luv_1D_alwaysxx @clungetastic @LGMparties @rossgriffiths86 @connDaly43 @1Dliam @simonrottie @kieranhepworth @vwdubpaul @gemsnorton @dirtystopout @sticks0710 @imynes24 @LauraMayPax @Michael_Ginge @willis_sarah @jperry999 @jamesuren1981 @cassie5mc @chrisalex9 @andylee1977 @stevesmelt @jamesmgurner @CareanGordon @Sophie_Oggy @GemB078 @deelee1122 @danairwaves @tonksblackbird @danmills646 @kjevans22 @tazman1980 @sallyann1984 @ChrisShaanDay @Nikki2000ad @doogiej7 @coops0151 @NeilCammo @UglyBetsie @MerlynStegeman @blommers95 @ThePriceIsWight @rosycheeks80 @davidpilditch @karlosayton @jaimee3875 @snakey1987 @tonigibbs80 @DaveRobins83 @bollypopdance @icecreamsar99 @pheeona @AdsGooner82 @Phil_Hughes9 @Duraay97 @shedboylinz @Foreign_beggar_ @ManusWheeler @LaurencePitt @emmafallon14 @bunjip35 @lauraboydy @fig24 @dobbindanny @clancybeth84 @Chris_Dav0 @zakparadise @tirj @lowry0209 @shaunmanning1 @gemmapink1 @trevorthomas74 @Robertadream @db_rhtt @officialAdzZz @mickey_thompson @TimothyDCook @wattmillis @wills324 @RichyPurcell @nanasusan54 @katiee_roo @beccacoombes21 @amybanks24 @themate70 @amandaeckley @lanamercer @RomeoJamie @mikadnarimik @Si_Rye @jboovy @mjamcphee87 @yickchick @hazeljacquline @Sallystarfish14 @inspectermills @adamfrater1 @xCarmenxAnnx @FinestHourMovie @NadineHendy97 @Lucyemboi1984 @courtneyyybbz @PaulaCam @Melly_Jayne_Mac @michbeaz80 @LordSward @samluke99 @ChattieBoy @DANHOCKINGS1985 @eaw287 @Pistal_18 @Dan_Crome @elainem1982 @specialfavours @jonnynoods @watto135 @danielw7 @Kellyklf @charliesimpkiss @Owenbarry1 @wattsy71980 @rayraysoutham @nickwarrilow @Hardo55 @helenni23 @955561976 @katie_somers @camdw22 @CRF_UK @GazWilliams1984 @LouisKowalski @christinegwilli @ChrisLindsay7 @Keli_Bee @af_davey @RowenaC @wallisrich @Matthay5 @lyndparsons @ItsPearson @susieh41 @dnt112000 @mattarmstrong74 @GlennCoachTrip @Ceriwynjones @richardsb007 @deanbanner05 @fivekayes @ruth_bond @Real_Banahna @laceyWylde @ClaireBradley @Kempie2008 @danbrooks151 @Paul25Robbo @treacle5 @tomsunley @julie4x4 @BenRobinson22 @AnnaHufton @PhillipWicks @nursecazza @jj1409 @avfcjona @karenrosemaryh @Thevoyne @dskene17 @lindyloohughes @joshgmoore @kdc127 @KellyAdamson1 @jaffastoat @jenx01 @georgefdavies @abslillington @HealeyEmily @TeddyK46 @IAmLukasJ @magiggs @Richardmxbrown @Helen_R_Harris @HonestBecky34 @Home_PT @pinkgemrubyloui @Ktcandrews2 @m4rcthomson @jbizzle_1985 @hayleym144 @Craigstothart @Jennmoo @sambocoro @lumpee69 @nffccobby @GemmellJ @BoomSykes @terrymoaner @Paulabrahams1 @raquels66 @MeganTheWhovian @kevhump1409 @carltongarratt @redmanliz @natalierichard5 @cgoodwin73 @DancingDawley @he11boy3012 @jamescook23 @leecjones03 @LBakCLO @spaine123 @SALLYGROSSMITH @GashMcC @Chrisrovers1 @clemcleminson @Craighopson1234 @stuart_bru @KimClitter @xFionaArmstrong @ncollins484 @ZuluTrucker @anthonymcc81 @BigTim1973 @pipavfc @coreyhorton @arctic_cat @L_Mac86 @JMyersdjmad @escobaraloplopp @GertieF @andy_p_ladd @vixsimpson72 @MrMarkAdamson @Beazer90 @rach_balfour @AzzaF7 @DazzaRolfe @Nicolaarmer @EmB1105 @fionatrafford @berrytopping @SarahWentworth1 @stephmemmory @plevans @jenuwin85 @N_L_10 @spencer_sara @bevdavies18 @Helly_welly73 @EmMoose @CallumXoXo @cooke8460 @claire_bear1 @AstonServices @paulcelias @nassondasilva @JPWharram @lesleywilford12 @_staceyp_ @lukesulli @wildlime1 @BekkaTS @burkess17 @Mattythekool @AllenStu @sarahmolloy27 @cazzycupcake @megsterrr_21 @Blower_88 @dannynosocks @knockedbean @mattyherrett @sjmeredith20 @craigholloway3 @ianjh77 @buckrodgers2 @Lewmeg @MPresto87 @JDHolt97 @ben_hamp @teddyrichards87 @choppymst @jetmond @bellyrob1980 @welshdix @MandyWild1 @shaunafinlay1 @lukiluke_90 @rossboy11 @dbeddis @dancerdudejay @dannyjsaxton @BennettSoph @emmandave22 @gembojo @JessicaBethanie @neil_roebuck @lilacflowers55 @JoshT_96 @KezChez1 @Legobrothers19 @NathanHall_10 @nledwards @Kevin_keep @tats0071 @seanySean0412 @Melowd32 @LibbyHadfield @ScudBROTHER @hollypendulum @Becca20120 @JonCardy1984 @Loganlocker82 @gazgraham1 @madamitzy @mcgrath1981 @holly_gav @helen_pickford @minx0201 @darrenjensen2 @1Travisimo @Emilylg09 @VNewbon @JodieFarrell1 @Laulaurz @ReannaParkinson @BillyRCloude @Sam_Ruddar @lauri2887 @jamescann89 @Jennifer21_x @emmies57 @Victoria_Booth @wilk32 @JimmySpices @JohnBoyBroon @dleck @daniellehulme @wayne2336 @Cdawg8reid @nixiebran @silverwulfx @cotswoldVilla @megsco45 @mikeh147 @scottyfix @RichardWiffen @Erekrose @michellepm45 @Kerrramba @adamnewman @Legand1980 @baltipies @geggysi @billy_baby12 @RhiannonParisse @CourtMariie @alexvlf @mickeyplumx @MattressMan92 @SophieCBennett @steveuk9799 @DaveG969 @mckenziepandax @TomKing16 @s4dev @Sarah_Jayne1986 @WDownes @EmPenguin91 @Daniel_Exley @Tasha_Taylor86 @sarahwatt3 @cockyhammer @Smudgie76 @stuartaustin69 @becpauldavis @AllisonFalder @SoDitzy @GemWalsh @2dl_dr @ankurssaali @Joeyorton12 @emmawimpenny @melyoungsy @Eleanor_Barlow @ad328isport @koliver6 @antellis81 @JuliaVBrewer @AlexakaGunzel @DSSlatter @paulmiddle @dibbleywmh69 @kirkaoglesby @HarryTowle1 @Gemma_Marsh94 @jackson_soutter @jad_bake @Shells_Belles @Emma1980xx @Katototheworld @lucycward @meeeeee96 @Helenjt87xx @chrisbrowell @Matt_williamss @vegasbaby06 @nicola1968dave @reddersUK @tillycoe @ruthwhittle23 @LouiseChilds @Lauraclwyd1 @ItsOnlyThatGirl @RemyFlare @RachelC1012 @WhatsChrisSayin @amwil15 @abigailworthing @JenB1209 @Qprfan1966 @Daniel_Allen455 @TheRealDRG @tonyclamb @tonythesheep @bazzam09 @katieraisback @joeldipple @brum006 @jharper210882 @allibob3 @Chapalar @BigCol6969 @jeffsy1981 @_LifeFoundation @gibby_83 @greg_cooper9 @piper_ann @Sallycounsell @millie_shaw @Spencey03 @leanneworth @georgiabieberr_ @EmmaDavis71 @simehowe1970 @SarK77 @MrsMoleski @Legend_DaveK @chrisbeel @thetrobadour @willf13pie @headchode @laurarob84 @macca2708 @olimac337 @Foxxinio @brookemf1 @zulumufc @askwilson @Lulufifi75 @detty3663 @ellie_dragon @unes_bop @PaulHCottam @BeadleAbout69 @jackdavis1998 @CrazyLeopard123 @Jozsefr32 @Hammers87 @eugeniaodonnell @jaykel46 @JAllsopp81 @Harrysmum63 @hadyn27 @djtrotty @Megs_x_x @AmyLHadfield @adamrigby1977 @ningmoss @SteWardale @JackSibbz @VerySmileyFaces @RuthieMcCartney @MsZoeyDee @johntwilly @SamanthaBrant1 @Hollycarty @wendy_66 @Lesley83 @SamanthaMellor1 @rutfid @lucyfrost1990 @megga_mark @alludoistalk @rd008 @richardbarber63 @Lyndseyritchie @ScottCGroom @hunti25 @LukeCarpenter15 @DaisyDudeLilley @booth_carol @rachie31hunt @LJ4N3H @edwardhopwood @DeanTasker @mike_p_photo @aptwilde @BieberlsKingJB @daveyboy73 @MissAimiBaker @F1squash @jonoilyk @Als_C @fairyheary @ratinthecity18 @JimSatchwell @ekuL_droF @ITweetTheNews @Aled_Miles @EllenJFletcher @Rwood1983 @gavnshell @Gfairb @princess_nicnic @LawrenceJones @nathancraig90 @shaundays23 @vixhaylings1 @littlemoomin85 @robbigears @megan_winfield @liannewoodhouse @TomAVFCHyslop @rick_d_moore @keej44 @Lee_Tunnicliffe @PrincetownFC @vicks333 @Dean77Smith @nushlh @lexylou_@craigb134 @AmyHession @bigmikesmith @JackieB1066 @Mattybee49 @TomDesmond87 @qwertarian @Kaye_Girl @podgecaz @Bensoiree @AllaboutMusic79 @LazzaBhoy @kings1275 @who_are_you__ @leebraddo @linzid83 @ChloeJade6789 @AmyE1993 @CraigHughes86 @CrapperwesT @Henrylee82 @chris_grovesy @kev3000gt @burtron79 @LizFrenchie @kielryan @Therealdannouk @tknox12 @blakeydavid @djwall78 @GemGingeButler @obutty @R0nB0 @MrPayabyab @Lorna_Mosley @robinbrucelee @sayerk23 @fleurtn @thepelicanlover @stinkychris @NadiaGreuner @john_telling @k_chalmers @karenbevan1963 @juliette230665 @_Stephens28 @samuelmorton @_J_Mack @alex_clibery @lucy500 @desisbored @scroy0901 @Jasonleesinger @CityPartyAngel @neilgilmartin @sifarrell1 @HazelBB @EmilyJChandler @farmerdarce @muckypupz123 @hollyprobert1 @RhianMoore @KrisMoondogs @hammymate @mattyhodgkinson @joematthewsIV @chrissyeng @GriffinNeil @mwoollaston @azzygy82 @Candierella34 @dancetillidie_x @SarahMcMenamin @TeacherEm1 @scottat2012 @Gnaughton2 @LeighKDonald @stubert30 @RyanLyden87 @NickMorley2 @jamie_o82 @squirrel_1975 @Gluey2011 @tim_skelton1976 @EllieDesmond

@dpreece1985 @TomBeardy @paul_strelow @iamthejayjay @piggington7 @GemmaBo23 @LouiseMacrory @EdNicdao @shoey_ Lyndlou2 @samcrook86 @nadz1976 @ports79 @Mywellbeing_11 @Scottbroadbridg @giggles_ruby @anthonytay1981 @cha @mattcobblers @jamanjidavidson @aminewell85 @deanosWithBeer @micknewlde @chriswheeler84 @zclees @Papa_Tont @Pap deere_hunter @jayneyd83 @beccilb @NicholaTuer @TomLongB @SuperRubes @Joeowl78 @tahughes1980 @OptimashPrim @MargaretDavies4 @jackbrewin89 @bigseanyF1986 @a1d3n2002 @Truly36 @dianaeclark @VickiOsbornMrsO @KatAtomicEP @ crutty1975 @TVickers20 @filteegroup @smalley1805 @lucydaisyhall11 @mikeharrin1 @jeanhamilton66 @Dawsy87 @bigcolin emmawilliams79 @Hayley_Finch @philharv @Mrjonsy78 @Shep_sambo @abbicockers @Megan8686 @jackt1993 @JadeAB @donnabailey @Vicwaaar @Drgilham @Dr_BatezHVFC @MrsEmmaHall @djohnson85 @Smallnort @Croftee @NBMBLU @Katiec @DarrenMCook @Mave_la_Rave @anorto38 @effy1987 @SimonSmith1988 @Quincyusha @Katew100 @NatCoops10 @bigm sexyevie72 @robpricephoto @rllew @TessaKing @Mandzzzz @becwiley @shakthehat @sini666 @serena_1977 @martinrkuhn @S reenie @OnlyInTheTaiwan @sianrodway @alicehope87 @idodrums @pcarter81 @VinnieV03 @Stringbop @twitfail88 @jamvanc HannahLouise60 @Amy_Ritter @nickjamesv @Lighthammer34 @camfuzed @helencartwrig @daveyj8619 @sophieolivia2 @pad beckhamslove @mademoisellis @craigtimblin @Helen_ed11 @jellykev @kirstieboyd @samkay51 @spudstickle @swerdychief @ shell_milne @dsenior86 @BARKELOS @LuceBlayney @Matt_Mac25 @crocmunch @DarrenP1983 @CharlotteBlain @Nick__Ba StephanieRoss24 @joe_lawless @gaz_davies31 @xLauraLou @tammihargest @westie721 @mandymoo106 @SammyGoph @L paul_J1986 @si_1979 @vickimcwoteva @AaronBernard @carlyjane29 @Joe_Henderson91 @craigfountain @Ryanke @bradvine @KayPyneMUA @tweedboy6578 @jonnywignall @AnnakathrynL @Willsabooby @benpykett @rhian300784 @MelanieSGraham @ YEAwards @dean290370 @Simonsmith373 @spang63 @murrayw17 @sallydunkley @andreaskuemmert @Fran_wich @farmanc tom_shawm @mdc1986 @marknic1980 @davidpalin @margread @OStubbsy @hjayc1978 @steveaylin @10kdgroup @bex SamWilliams9189 @rcl99 @wayneplummer @corky2706 @Nopholopholis @kelldubu @damianbulmer @zoomdriving @some dancingshark33 @antbenton7 @CharlotteOllers @Mattgall1983 @Marmite13 @tome2585 @TrickySi @johnfraser2324 @j_curbishl @YorkCityCentre @Gemma_doc @ste0smith @Kelly_Gipson @CathrineBarnett @penny_xxx @tomdt450 @Danilson1hutt @Da thelastfakers @simonpgu @jomaishman @SChester84 @DuncanRandall1 @SuperCatley @kelleecav @MCoxall82 @sunnivasko @SammybabyPink @leejellis80 @Shep_JollyBoy @maegst @HollyThompson87 @AwesomeDawson79 @CommunityFocusL @me jammjammyjammy @Dougal_71 @whittepk @AntsMcDowall @Pratty1983 @DJHellyer @CharleeyyN @JoBamforth @Seb220 SneakyGaming @Leachy1977 @HenryManson1 @Crossaayy @VickiHill2 @dcgermain1985 @physio_josh @CarlsB55 @Badger_B @awatters @maxineevans1978 @harrischopper @WillOwenJones @HelenRoberton @colacop1 @EmmaMcNamee2 @MrMadCycli @sarahjobo @KateD24 @padhark @dr_tomm @KarenCollinge @Kmozza81 @Aramblingtwit @KingstonDJay @manda365 @danr mjaynewalker @lanpmaloney @leese_peese @LadyP1983 @GillyM1 @Matt_Adams_ @Roojonnie @Plmt85 @Rich_vic @ryannnni @Alexbigmacjones @Sarah_VooDoo @mattboyce85 @nedge88 @Wi11sh @kooliej @Bexward @AnaaCarter @Brayf101 @anniebe @Marcusgibbons @IanJohnstone4 @Weemanmac @Karenmoooo @PhilipFarnes @JulesD1980 @SuzSwin @sowenuk @fiona377 @ @MelH150982 @clairetracy @xHachx @ChrisWhite999 @BalloonsbyNicci @Zazzy_Mac @seanpage11 @kingofbury @Ahamer' Susan_hinki @AishaBooo @joanieraw @kirstylv @Matt_mjs14 @Jezwhitedwr @hbowl @bigtmark @pctellie @ewells999 @na smartonetomany @CaseyMariee_ @ErinShankss @DawnLiddle @jojogogo16 @DanJMicallef @AntonyWarr @vickykilmister @KS StuartChadwick @tictactical @Gemmaaaar @michybrightside @chloeraymond5 @TeddyJones123 @HalesPixieWife @oscarmarsh4 @nick_fulford @johnstonleemark @hattymob @TheBarkingHand @westlaketim @racwhite1 @ChrisKirk16 @LeighBron @TonyJ3 INUENDO @calolsen @BIGALmr35 @pound72 @emskiwebber @EmilyWatts4 @stevefoster82 @liambatchelor15 @this_is_emm @Jbbarron @ezza1086 @Melissa_Foulis @louguest09 @dansam43 @MarsBarGirl97 @LouiseLePage77 @oac9211 @j_kharbanc kimberleysway @HollyGib689 @billys364 @LucheColeman @Sam_Davis_CER @27trevster27 @richiec86 @ChrisNorthwood claudiabromley @saycey1985 @AJPlumplum @ChristiMac @Danielwhite1986 @SamBlackburn84 @gh2512 @nessanogs @harr Teacher @Andrewkelham @alliepark1976 @cufc15 @MaireadHeavey @theonlyjoebrown @benn_hall @Allgood10 @supersally12 @ AnnaSanders8 @marmite__lover @matthammond83 @KarlStedman @GiddyElfin1230 @CStanley06 @KatieeLeahNS_TW @Qui Grace_Machin @MissBuzyBee @katherine_kitti @louakalewis @SamMarson @stephencliffe @Hugh_Fran @jemmyjemjems @m_ @xdaveclaire @jcarter10 @pricey13rtb @emily13_94 @EmilyPurds90 @irishgaz @e_jays @espilogs @Toppers_58 @colinR32 paulsharples78 @AFidd_08 @shagadooby @rsnabel @jckgreen88 @dboydaniel1983 @FizeeRascal @Ali_Hoskins @Flomaisie @ @johnsutty @_josiemccreton @simplykyle2011 @TomBennett1988 @SrBelinda @OliviaBennett92 @mcoopero @GaryDanielLynch Richieknighter6 @leah_lloyd @gowermonkey @claire2781 @jaystag1979 @dickiekent @Theshanks1 @daniel_wit14 @owenjt85 @ @PreshyDoog @tpclayton @AJHolyoak @elliotholman @KittyorKate @gemh138 @sarraagghh @JamiePover @k_mor12 @kerry craigblackmore1 @pinklilymusic @Zummerset_boy @donnambrown73 @dbonham82 @katyb45 @costelloshelley @PippaTwigg @ @WannoDoEverest @charlottekelsal @AndyT416 @kywall_mitchell @gdshipley @LeeShearman1 @ColinsFitBody @HeleneBarr @carldarley @Bullseye_ @allyvik @AEIJEM @CTweet46 @roylongley @craigp7777 @MyGameDevil @flipperclaire @sammorley_ RossiterLtd @Scottmmassie @seanandhelen @edfishclark @oscarknebel @saltshaker321 @jh2809 @jennifershaw47 @mrssa RaceDriversInc @hm_mae @redhud28 @dannyjones77 @jenramsden @bangerfingers @DafsCorsa @aaaahbooo @barramarra AL_81 @LufbraEnts @Steveevoblack @EmilyyWoods @pabsbailey @mross620 @paulftucker @tommyhadler @davewoll70 @billy Micky_Keen @LottieD @rach_richards @AlettaOcean1987 @cymro2477 @Aaaaamyfensome @leemward @clarkieg63 @chrwhi @ @willolner @rgoddard78 @AngelaRowsthorn @gembells21 @mccluskeyandrew @EmelyeFerguson @boocindy08 @EdKirkman @S @katiehighdown @mouler1980 @leigh7888 @libertine1 @pauliedesantos @poutygaz @jamiesimcoe @jsmcgann @stoxy1978 @SI @HelenWatts1 @ezraa123 @layla1904 @monk192 @Spanna120 @katiehobbins @Millieizzy @ksk26p @mrssjc2011 @KTM08087 @Paul_I_Bruce @jostokes1 @bryanminns @alwaysajolly @lauracampbellox @MissEMSawyer @NeatMoore @kateward100 @dut7 John_Floyd @kathashdown @LucyWinspear @kjdownes @julierady @hollymcdonough @TheGalleryAtBQH @LampyChris @What' helenearth73 @1871Danny @CaptainRanger @bolsachboy @stu_tagg1 @Lukelauren07 @gaz_cordery @ojapps @dawn22gale @ connieceeee @BekkiSimpson @angelfire59 @KrisSmith25 @chrisparker2001 @LucyBabes92 @McRurt @MacqueenK @PaulRea Fuller @WillBa1 @Droidy72 @barrymorris1975 @White_Mouse96 @cleopatrab123 @LucyyBakerr @sian13 @Katrinafinnerty @michaelhenda @scotty118 @NicolaRedhead @kirstie_thorley @LaurenMccabe2 @sophiabridge @ClaireTroup @SaraOMahony MitchellClegg10 @EmilyCliffe @GRussell1989 @chillobrown @Trindersaurus @JimmyEatWorld84 @Chris_Sandland @jstyring @ @maggiej53 @SarahCLynGreen @GailMaryMacd @hayleyp2468 @MickBeckett @aldis1993 @jamespell30 @LiamLBrown @Shotl chloejonesjones @djw_1972 @kimclark2311 @MrsNotSoAverage @attwit @babby_beale @leeann_brunton @gav0985 @jai @emmavaleriow @theresabrowne @cm_buchan @mollytimmons @KDCreative1 @nikkievepaige @rhiannon_r123 @pipermicha DB1876 @AndyClown19 @simo1973 @KerriQuinn96 @Vassclass87 @ChristmasQueenB @Shrub_Beanie @Hazel_Munro @redhe @theprodigalson_ @lewis_clarke88 @cogan_chris @LostGirlAmanda @AndyDrummer87 @saffronfidgett @HammerCampbell @ BradSCronin @rosie17692 @vickylouroberts @RhianWoolley @trotty72 @katie_leeder @Emfarla @Debb_OBree @DI5CO78 @92s mazlarge @Emily_Harrold @ConwayTwidder @subarusi @abimiles @CarlaJ1992 @Clareprin6 @ChelleHemmings @jaynelasley @ @Hayhoe1 @Malschnee @2e1bts @nnniixx @spreston89 @gemgem84 @MI55NCJ @Barry74 @skye99999 @Jenny_mcadam_15 Skelton87 @alice_hodson @DanielleThearle @seatbeltson @mja_atk @r0ebuck @fotheringham84 @gtreacy @MsNataliex @pom watkin @sparkeylowe @theemmap @Stef_J_Straw @CPimbley @AliceUrie @helmolotov @leannedons @ele_07 @guineapig75 @s vedderleeds @rudihq @28kittycat @freydais @cheezak @Lainie03 @Weasiewoo @Mgmvegasgirl @Emrich80 @Seresz @jorm @Graham_widaglos @Ptandetinaigloo @AbiiiNYC97 @captainhappy101 @alexday3 @Stevedean69 @SophieCowan1 @usman_ @kamakazi137 @PippaPage1 @missstelbel @ChildminderCaz @fionabarge1 @AmbiSud @jamesbakes @MattyDalton96 @amylon ElaineUpton @splitty_66 @GreatsLovesTG @julieseashore @kyle1705 @mirkys @bobb1ns_ @marsh_bear @ashwitcomb @linds_ aKerby01 @CoRnIsH_DaWn @LyndaBarrow1 @perreh27 @IamTheReal_Mr_T @adamncasey @sparkymartMUFC @smharley19 @RebRedd @SugarPlum_Cakes @Jasminaberz @pjm1990 @smarodgers @jcpmgray @scottyboy36 @cnharrin @onlyone